Islam, Judaism, and the Political Role
of Religions in the Middle East

Copyright 2004 by John Bunzl. This work is licensed under a modified Creative Commons Attribution-Noncommercial-No Derivative Works 3.0 Unported License. To view a copy of this license, visit *http://creativecommons.org/licenses/by-nc-nd/3.0/*. You are free to electronically copy, distribute, and transmit this work if you attribute authorship. *However, all printing rights are reserved by the University Press of Florida (http://www.upf.com). Please contact UPF for information about how to obtain copies of the work for print distribution.* You must attribute the work in the manner specified by the author or licensor (but not in any way that suggests that they endorse you or your use of the work). For any reuse or distribution, you must make clear to others the license terms of this work. Any of the above conditions can be waived if you get permission from the University Press of Florida. Nothing in this license impairs or restricts the author's moral rights.

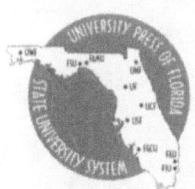

Florida A&M University, Tallahassee
Florida Atlantic University, Boca Raton
Florida Gulf Coast University, Ft. Myers
Florida International University, Miami
Florida State University, Tallahassee
University of Central Florida, Orlando
University of Florida, Gainesville
University of North Florida, Jacksonville
University of South Florida, Tampa
University of West Florida, Pensacola

Islam, Judaism, and the Political Role of Religions in the Middle East

edited by John Bunzl

University Press of Florida
Gainesville · Tallahassee · Tampa · Boca Raton
Pensacola · Orlando · Miami · Jacksonville · Ft. Myers

Copyright 2004 by John Bunzl

09 08 07 06 05 04   6 5 4 3 2 1

Library of Congress Cataloging-in-Publication Data
Islam, Judaism, and the political role of religions in the Middle East /
edited by John Bunzl.
   p. cm.
Includes bibliographical references and index.

ISBN: 978-1-61610-108-4

1. Religion and politics—Middle East. 2. Middle East—Politics
and government—20th century. 3. Islam and politics—Middle East.
4. Middle East—Religion. 5. Arab-Israeli conflict. I. Bunzl, John,
1945–
DS44.I78 2004
320.5'5'0956—dc222003057912

The University Press of Florida is the scholarly publishing agency
for the State University System of Florida, comprising Florida A&M
University, Florida Atlantic University, Florida Gulf Coast University,
Florida International University, Florida State University, University of
Central Florida, University of Florida, University of North Florida,
University of South Florida, and University of West Florida.

University Press of Florida
15 Northwest 15th Street
Gainesville, FL 32611-2079
http://www.upf.com

Contents

Foreword: Adrift in Similarity   vii
   Edward Said
Acknowledgments   xiii
Introduction   1

I. On Islam and Judaism, Muslims and Jews

1. A Religion's Self-Conception of "Religion": The Case of Judaism and Islam   19
Hans-Michael Haussig
2. Islam and Judaism: Cultural Relations and Interaction through the Ages   28
Nissim Rejwan

II. Negotiating Religions and Identities

3. National Identity and the Role of the "Other" in Existential Conflicts: The Israeli-Palestinian Case   61
Herbert C. Kelman
4. The Politicization of Muslim-Christian Relations in the Palestinian National Movement   75
Helga Baumgarten

III. Progressive Potentials within Religious Traditions

5. Democracy without Secularism? Reflections on the Idea of Islamic Democracy   99
Raja Bahlul
6. Religious Roots of Tolerance with Special Reference to Judaism and Islam   118
Adam B. Seligman

IV. On the Use of Religion in Contemporary Middle Eastern Politics

7. Imposed Normalization and Cultural Transgression: Cultural Politics in Egypt and Israel since the 1979 Peace Treaty   137
Joel Beinin

8. Islamic Themes in Palestinian Political Thought 156
   Alexander Flores
9. Israel, Religion, and Peace 166
   Avishai Ehrlich

Contributors 191
Index 195

Foreword
Adrift in Similarity

Samuel Huntington's article "The Clash of Civilizations?" appeared in the spring 1993 issue of *Foreign Affairs,* where it immediately attracted a surprising amount of attention and reaction. Because the article was intended to supply Americans with an original thesis about "the new phase" in world politics after the end of the cold war, Huntington's terms of argument seemed compellingly large, bold, even visionary. He very clearly had his eye on rivals in the policy-making ranks, theorists such as Francis Fukuyama and his end-of-history ideas, as well as the legions who had celebrated the onset of globalism, tribalism, and the dissipation of the state. But they, he allowed, had understood only some aspects of this new period. He was about to announce the "crucial, indeed a central aspect" of what "global politics is likely to be in the coming years." Unhesitatingly he pressed on: "It is my hypothesis that the fundamental source of conflict in this new world will not be primarily ideological or primarily economic. The great divisions among humankind and the dominating source of conflict will be cultural. Nation states will remain the most powerful actors in world affairs, but the principal conflicts of global politics will occur between nations and groups of different civilizations. The clash of civilizations will dominate world politics. The fault lines between civilizations will be the battle lines of the future" (p. 22).

Most of the argument in the pages that followed relied on a vague notion of something Huntington called "civilization identity" and "the interactions among seven or eight [sic] major civilizations," of which the conflict between two of them, Islam and the West, gets the lion's share of his attention. In this belligerent kind of thought, he relies heavily on a 1990 article by the veteran Orientalist Bernard Lewis, whose ideological colors are manifest in the title, "The Roots of Muslim Rage." In both articles, the personification of enormous entities called "the West" and "Islam" is recklessly affirmed, as if hugely complicated matters like identity and culture existed in a cartoon-like world where Popeye and Pluto bash each other mercilessly, with one always more virtuous pugilist getting the upper hand over his adversary. Certainly neither Huntington nor Lewis has much time to spare for the internal dynamics and plurality of every civilization, or for the fact that the major contest in most modern cultures concerns the definition or interpretation of each culture, or for the unattractive possibility that a great deal of demagogy and downright ignorance is involved in presuming to speak for a whole religion or civilization. No, the West is the West, and Islam Islam. The challenge for Western policymakers, says Huntington, is to make sure that the West gets stronger and fends off all the others, Islam in particular.

More troubling is Huntington's assumption that his perspective, which is to survey the entire world from a perch outside all ordinary attachments and hidden loyalties, is the correct one, as if everyone else was scurrying around looking for the answers that he has already found. In fact, Huntington is an ideologist, someone who wants to make "civilizations" and "identities" into what they are not, shut-down, sealed-off entities that have been purged of the myriad currents and countercurrents that animate human history, and over centuries have made it possible for that history not only to contain wars of religion and imperial conquest but also to be one of exchange, cross-fertilization, and sharing. This far less visible history is ignored in the rush to highlight the ludicrously compressed and constricted warfare that "the Clash of Civilization" argues is the reality. When he published his book by the same title in 1996, Huntington tried to give his argument a little more subtlety and many, many more footnotes; all he did, however, was to confuse himself, demonstrating what a clumsy writer and inelegant thinker he is. The basic paradigm of West versus the rest (the cold war opposition reformulated) remained untouched, and this is what has persisted, often insidiously and implicitly, in discussion since the terrible events of September 11.

The carefully planned mass slaughter and horrendous, pathologically motivated suicide bombing by a small group of deranged militants has been turned into proof of Huntington's thesis. Instead of seeing it for what it is, the capture of big ideas (I use the word loosely) by a tiny band of crazed fanatics for criminal purposes, international luminaries, from former Pakistani prime minister Benazir Bhutto to Italian prime minister Silvio Berlusconi, have pontificated about Islam's troubles, and in Berlusconi's case used Huntington to rant on about the West's superiority, how "we" have Mozart and Michelangelo and they don't. (He has since made a half-hearted apology for his insult to "Islam.")

But why not instead see parallels, admittedly less spectacular in their destructiveness, for Osama Bin Laden and his followers in cults like the Branch Davidians or the disciples of Reverend Jim Jones at Guyana or the Japanese Aum Shinrikyo. Even the normally sober British weekly *The Economist,* in its issue of 22–28 September 2001, couldn't resist reaching for the vast generalization and praised Huntington extravagantly for his "cruel and sweeping, but nonetheless acute" observations about Islam. "Today," the journal said with unseemly solemnity, Huntington writes that "the world's billion or so Muslims are 'convinced of the superiority of their culture, and obsessed with the inferiority of their power.'" Did he canvas 100 Indonesians, 200 Moroccans, 500 Egyptians, 50 Bosnians? Even if he did, what sort of sample is that?

Uncountable are the editorials in every American and European newspaper and magazine of note adding to this vocabulary of gigantism and apocalypse, each use of which is plainly designed not to edify but to inflame the reader's indignant passion as a member of the "West," and what we need to do. Churchillian rhetoric is used inappropriately by self-appointed combatants in the West's, and especially America's, war against its haters, despoilers, and destroyers, with scant attention to complex histories that defy such reductiveness and have seeped from one territory into another, in the process overriding the boundaries that are supposed to separate us all into divided armed camps.

This is the problem with unedifying labels like Islam and the West: they mislead and confuse the mind that is trying to make sense of a disorderly reality that won't be pigeonholed or strapped down as easily as all that. I remember interrupting a man who rose from the audience after a lecture I gave at a West Bank university in 1994. He started to attack my ideas as "Western," as opposed to the strict Islamic ones he espoused. "Why are you wearing a suit and tie?" was the first simpleminded retort that came to mind; "they're Western too." He sat down with an embarrassed smile on his face, but I recalled the incident when information on the 11 September terrorists started to come in, how they had mastered all the technical details required to do their homicidal evil on the World Trade Center, the Pentagon, and the aircraft they had commandeered. Where does one draw the line between "Western" technology and, as Berlusconi declared, "Islam's" inability to be a part of "modernity"?

One cannot easily do so, of course, but how finally inadequate are the labels, generalizations, and cultural assertions. At some level, for instance, primitive passions and sophisticated know-how converge in ways that give the lie to a fortified boundary not only between "West" and "Islam" but also between past and present, us and them, to say nothing of the very concepts of identity and nationality about which there is literally unending disagreement and debate. A unilateral decision made to draw lines in the sand, to undertake crusades, to oppose their evil with our good, to extirpate terrorism, and, in Paul Wolfowitz's nihilist vocabulary, to end nations entirely, doesn't make the supposed entities any easier to see; rather, it speaks to how much simpler it is to make bellicose statements for the purposes of mobilizing collective passions than to reflect, examine, sort out what it is we are dealing with in reality, the interconnectedness of innumerable lives, "ours" as well as "theirs."

In a remarkable series of three articles published between January and March 1999 in *Dawn,* Pakistan's most respected weekly, the late Eqbal Ahmad, writing for a Muslim audience, analyzed what he called the roots of the religious right, coming down very harshly on the mutilations of Islam by absolutists and fanatical tyrants whose obsession with regulating personal behavior promotes "an Islamic order reduced to a penal code, stripped of its humanism, aesthetics, intellectual quests, and spiritual devotion." And this "entails an absolute assertion of one, generally de-contextualised, aspect of religion and a total disregard of another. The phenomenon distorts religion, debases tradition, and twists the political process wherever it unfolds." As a timely instance of this debasement, Ahmad proceeds first to present the rich, complex, pluralist meaning of the word jihad, and then goes on to show that, in the word's current confinement to indiscriminate war against presumed enemies, it is impossible "to recognize . . . Islamic religion, society, culture, history or politics as lived and experienced by Muslims through the ages." The modern Islamists, Ahmad concludes, are "concerned with power not with the soul, with the mobilization of people for political purposes rather than with sharing and alleviating their sufferings and aspirations. Theirs is a very limited and time bound agenda." What has made matters worse is that similar distortions and zealotry occur in the "Jewish" and "Christian" universes of discourse.

It was Conrad, more powerfully than any of his readers at the end of the nineteenth century could have imagined, who understood that the distinctions between civilized London and "the heart of darkness" quickly collapse in extreme situations and that the heights of European civilization could instantaneously reverse into the most barbarous practices without preparation or transition. And it was Conrad also, in *The Secret Agent* (1907), who described terrorism's affinity for abstractions like "pure science" (and by extension for "Islam" or "the West"), as well as the terrorist's ultimate moral degradation.

For there are closer ties between apparently warring civilizations than most of us would like to believe, and as both Freud and Nietzsche showed, the traffic across carefully maintained, even policed boundaries moves with often terrifying ease. But then such fluid ideas, full of ambiguity and skepticism about notions that we hold on to, scarcely furnish us with suitable, practical guidelines for situations such as the one we face now, and hence the altogether more reassuring battle orders (a crusade, good versus evil, freedom against fear, and so on) drawn out of Huntington's opposition between

Islam and the West from which in the first days official discourse drew its vocabulary. There has since been a noticeable de-escalation in that discourse, but to judge from the steady amount of hate speech and actions, plus reports of law enforcement efforts, directed against Arabs, Muslims, and Indians all over the country, the paradigm stays on.

One further reason for its persistence is the disturbing presence of Muslims all over Europe and the United States. Think of the populations today of France, Italy, Germany, Spain, Britain, America, even Sweden, and you must concede that Islam is no longer on the fringes of the West, but at its center. But what is so threatening about that presence? Buried in the collective culture are memories of the first great Arab-Islamic conquests that began in the seventh century and which, as the celebrated Belgian historian Henri Pirenne wrote in his landmark book *Mohammed and Charlemagne* (1939), shattered once and for all the ancient unity of the Mediterranean, destroyed the Christian-Roman synthesis, and gave rise to a new civilization dominated by northern powers (Germany and Carolingian France), whose mission, he seems to be saying, is to resume defense of the "West" against its historical-cultural enemies. What Pirenne leaves out, alas, is that in the creation of this new line of defense the West drew on the humanism, science, philosophy, sociology, and historiography of Islam, which had already interposed itself between Charlemagne's world and classical antiquity. Islam is inside from the start, as even Dante, great enemy of Muhammad, had to concede when he placed the Prophet at the very heart of his Inferno.

Then there is the persisting legacy of monotheism itself, the Abrahamanic religions, as Louis Massignon aptly called them. Beginning with Judaism and Christianity, each is a successor haunted by what came before: for Muslims, Islam fulfils and ends the line of prophecy. There is still no decent history or demystification of the many-sided contest between these three followers—not one of them by any means a monolithic, unified camp—of the most jealous of all gods, even though the bloody modern convergence on Palestine furnishes a rich secular instance of what has been so tragically irreconcilable about them. Not surprisingly, then, Muslims and Christians speak readily of crusades and jihads, both of them eliding the Judaic presence with often sublime insouciance. Such an agenda, says Eqbal Ahmad, "is very reassuring to the men and women who are stranded in the middle . . . between the deep waters of tradition and modernity."

But we are all swimming in those waters, Westerners and Muslims and others alike. And since the waters are part of the ocean of history, trying to plough or divide them with barriers is futile. These are tense times, but it is better to think in terms of powerful and powerless communities, the secular politics of reason and ignorance, and universal principles of justice and injustice, than to wander off in search of vast abstractions that may give momentary satisfaction but little self-knowledge or informed analysis. The "clash of civilizations" thesis is a gimmick, like "The War of the Worlds," better for reinforcing defensive self-pride than for critical understanding of the bewildering interdependence of our time. This book, in focusing on the "Self" and the "Other" in Jewish and Muslim thought, is an attempt in this direction.

Edward Said

Note: A slightly revised version of an article originally published in *al-Ahram Weekly Online*, no. 555, 11–17 October 2001.

Acknowledgments

The editor wishes to thank the many people who have made this volume possible. First, and foremost, my gratitude to all the authors for their papers, first presented and discussed at the conference "Islam, Judaism, and the Political Role of Religions in the Middle East" (Vienna, 27–29 November 2000), here substantially expanded and revised. I am indebted to the many individuals and organizations who made that conference possible: in particular, my thanks to the German Orient Institute (Hamburg), the Austrian Diplomatic Academy, the Austrian Ministry for Foreign Affairs, the Vienna Municipality, and my colleagues at the Austrian Institute for International Affairs (Österreichisches Institut für Internationale Politik), the principal organizer of the conference. Without their assistance and generous support it could not have become a reality. I am also indebted to the Anniversary Fund of the Oesterreichische Nationalbank for their generous support.

Special acknowledgment to Bill Templer for his meticulous editing of the entire manuscript and the translation of certain passages and to Amy Gorelick at University Press of Florida for her guidance and encouragement in bringing this book project to completion. I have benefited from comments and suggestions from a number of friends and associates on an earlier draft of the introduction. And a final thanks to Edward Said for having agreed to provide an insightful foreword for this collection of timely studies.

Introduction

In God's Name?

John Bunzl

As experience shows, diplomatic agreements between the elites of conflicting parties are not sufficient to achieve lasting peace between their societies. Conflicts of long duration marked by ideological "overdetermination" highlight the limits of a pragmatic approach to their solution.

Hindrances on the path to an understanding in the Middle East often appear in a religious guise. We need but recall the names of Baruch Goldstein (Hebron massacre, 1994), Yigal Amir (Yitzhak Rabin's assassin, 1995), Ariel Sharon's provocative visit to the Temple Mount/Haram al-Sharif in Jerusalem (2000), or the Islamic suicide bombers of Hamas and Islamic Jihad. In all these instances, the actors cited guidance from religious commandments and the blessing of religious authorities. The eruption of the al-Aqsa Intifada in October 2000, as well as the events of 9/11—although with very different meaning—were a powerful confirmation of the political explosiveness of religious symbolism.

But it would be a crude simplification to limit the political role of religion to these extreme examples. In both Jewish-Israeli and Islamic-Arab societies, religious categories and concepts are central to identity and legitimacy, and even secular individuals, movements, and regimes must pay tribute to religious influences. That is why it is imperative to study the sociopolitical perception of religious traditions and their selective interpretation and utilization for diverse strategies (on behalf of freedom and human rights as well as war and violence).

In the West, interreligious studies and conferences are customarily dominated either by the relations between Christianity and Judaism or relations between Christianity and Islam. Aside from their generally Western and Eurocentric perspective, encounters of this type have yielded few practical results. Due to their predominantly diplomatic and theological character, they have had little real discernible impact on political conflicts.

Our project aims to be different. We hope to contribute to a reduction of violence and potential violence in a region where the religious overdetermination of conflicts is a concrete, seemingly insuperable political problem. To achieve this goal it is necessary to analyze the role and function of religious discourse in its own context. Initially, we proceed from two theses. First, there is no necessary connection between the politicizing of religion, the sacralization of politics, and the quest for coexistence and peace in the Middle East. And second, the politicization of religion and sacralization of politics unavoidably tends to heighten conflict. Consequently, ways have to be found to uncouple politics from religion, religion from politics.

Religion and Politics in the Middle East

This book is based on the assumption of a reciprocal dynamics between religious and political behavior and consciousness. But the character of that relation differs depending on time and place. That caveat also holds for the role of religious patterns of argumentation and rhetoric in a given political discourse. The phenomenon of a "politicized religion" (Bielefeldt and Heitmeyer 1998) can be seen as something distinctively modern, even in the Middle East, to the extent that it appears as a mode of confronting new challenges. The phenomenon of fundamentalism is associated today almost exclusively with the Middle East. Who still recalls the origin of the term? Who associates it today with its specifically American Protestant matrix of genesis and elaboration (Marty and Appleby 1996)?

Indeed, the Middle East is not only the cradle of the three great monotheistic world religions, it also seems to be the area most intensely affected by the present global (re)surgence in religions. One of the reasons is probably historical: in the past, except for Turkey, a relative secularization was either the product of colonial influences or failed political movements (nationalism, socialism) (Gerner 2000; Halliday 2000; Steinbach 2000). For this reason alone, despite Westernization and globalization, religious structures of thought and action have retained a central role in public consciousness and the self-identity of the state, both in the Arab-Islamic world and in Israel, albeit for different reasons.

Judaism and Zionism

The relation between Zionism and the Jewish religion was and remains contradictory because the Jewish national movement was born as an antithesis to traditional messianism. Indeed, most Jewish Orthodox leaders admonished the Zionists that they were wrong in seeking to "hasten the end" (i.e., messianic redemption), traditionally termed *dehikat ha-kets*. Rather, it was necessary to wait patiently for the Messiah's coming. At most one might bring that day closer by a life of piety and strict adherence to the commandments of the Torah. The Zionists in any case could not claim they were living such a life of reverence since they had replaced the Torah with a secular national concept and did not keep the religious commandments, and their leaders were totally secular (Ravitsky 1993; Timsit 1996). Yet even traditional and religious Jews could not fail to be impressed by the practical success of Zionism, especially in the wake of repeated calamity for the Jews in Europe, and its progress in constructing a new society in Palestine. Thus, within the movement in Europe, Palestine, and, later, in the young state, a national-religious (Mizrahi) current developed. Initially it was interested solely in serving the cultural needs of its adherents and so sought a role in the political structures of the state. Until 1967 this current was basically pragmatic in outlook and action; Zionism and the state were not sacralized. That was to change after 1967 and the "miraculous" conquest of the Old City in Jerusalem and the biblical core area (Judea and Samaria). Already during the mandate, Chief Rabbi Abraham Isaac Kook had espoused the thesis that the nonreligious Zionists were unintentional tools of redemption. His son, Zvi Yehuda Kook, citing older sources such as the book of Joshua and the views of Moshe ben Nachman (Nachmanides, 1194–1270 C.E.), provided an ideological rationalization for the religious-settler movement Gush Emunim (Bloc of the Faithful), whose leadership were among his students at the rabbinical seminary Merkaz Harav. The 1967 and 1973 wars as well as proactive settlement in the Occupied Territories were seen as part of a divine plan of redemption. Israeli soldiers fell as martyrs *al kiddush ha-shem* (sanctifying the Holy Name), and Palestinians, latter-day Canaanites, were to be treated like the ancient biblical adversaries of the Israelites. Israel, they argued, had to struggle against cultural Westernization, opposing it with a "Jewish" codex of morality (Demant 1995; Lustick 1988; Silberstein 1993; Sprinzak 1991; Prior 1997). Yet the national-religious camp sacralized the Zionist state only so long as it adhered, as they saw it, to the divine plan of redemption. In their eyes, the 1993 Olso Accords were heinous treason and the 1995 murder of Rabin rightful retribution (at least in the mind of the perpetrator).

While a small group (Neturei Karta, Edah Haredit) stuck to the original positions of Orthodox anti-Zionism (Ravitzky 1993), the great majority of the *haredim*—ultra-Orthodox in Israel, represented by Agudat Israel (Ashkenazic) and Shas (Sephardic) political parties—came to occupy a middle position somewhere in between. On the one hand, the state (like all other states) continued to be regarded as a neutral entity. Exile *(galut)* was not a geographical concept but rather the absence of the Shekhina (Divine Presence); galut could thus also continue to exist unabated even in the State of Israel. On the other hand, the parties of the haredim were adept at instrumentalizing the state to further their special interests (mainly in the area of religious education) and to gain certain select posts and even bailiwicks within the political system (Knesset, ministries) for their own. Most successful in this enterprise was Shas, whose phenomenal growth has made it currently the third largest party in the Knesset. Shas was able to galvanize a kind of "Oriental revolution" in the milieu of the haredim, becoming a magnet for Jews from socially underprivileged backgrounds. Led by the former Sephardic chief rabbi, Ovadiya Yossef, the party initially championed moderate positions on the peace process, serving for a time as a coalition partner in the Rabin and Barak governments. However, the party's differences with the Zionist-Ashkenazic-Western-secular left parties (especially Meretz) drove Shas ever further to the right. This is partially due to a standing practice on the Israeli right (Likud and other nationalist parties) to exploit imagery drawn from Jewish tradition. Moreover, the question of holy sites such as the Western Wall, Rachel's Tomb, or the Machpela (Tomb of the Patriarchs) in Hebron cannot be ignored, nor can the presence in the territories of the Torah-true settlers. On the other hand, Israeli sovereignty is somehow secondary for haredi groups like Agudat Israel or Shas, important only insofar as it assures access to the holy sites and the freedom to practice the Jewish Orthodox religion. Unlike the radical Temple Mount Faithful, they do not, for example, make an express demand for Israeli sovereignty over the Temple Mount (Har ha-Bayit, Haram al-Sharif) (Maul 2000; Neugrat 2000; Shragai 2001).

We can thus distinguish between various functions fulfilled by religion in Israel. Ravitzky (1993) proposes a distinction between fundamentalists and quietists, referring to the shifting relation between state/politics and religion. While the fundamentalists utilize religious categories in order to "sacralize" a state/political battery of aims, the quietists mobilized the secular profane state for their "sacred" agenda: the continuity of their congregations, way of life, and education. Although this distinction is valid in ideal-typical terms, it gives too little consideration to the intersections (such as the Chabad Hassidim) and other marginal currents. These encompass not only the ultra-Orthodox anti-Zionist sects but also efforts for a new synthesis between religion and politics influenced by Reform Judaism in the United States (e.g., Netivot Shalom or "Rabbis for Human Rights"). In any event, Israel's political system as a whole would appear to be constrained to fashion a religious justification for existence that springs primarily from the difficulty of constructing a purely secular Jewish identity.

Islam and Islamism

In contrast with the European-Zionist attempt to nationalize and secularize Judaism, analogous efforts in Islam have less importance. Nonetheless, within the context of the current politicization of religion, there are similarities deriving from the legalistic core *(halakha/shari'a)* of these traditions. On this basis, it is possible to legitimate claims to subordinate individual and collective behavior to a sacrally legitimated code.

Nonetheless, the concerns promoted by reference to Islam are as a rule quite modern and political. The use of an Islamic language serves to reduce complexity and is quite selective in trying to cope with problems of modernity. One example is the use of the concept *jahiliyya,* coined for pre-Islamic societies lacking moral values and legitimate rule—and challenged by the prophet Muhammad—but applied to contemporary ones. In any event, Islam is a cultural system open to an array of diverse interpretations (Halliday 1995, 2000; Beinin 1997; Humphreys 1999; Sivan 1985; Zubaida 1993).

The phenomenon of repoliticization of Islam and its mobilization on behalf of a politics of authenticity begins at the end of the nineteenth century as a reaction of Oriental intellectuals like Jamal al-Din al-Afghani (1838–1897), Muhammad Abduh (1849–1905), Rashid Muhammad Rida (1865–1935), Hassan al-Banna (1906–1949), or Sayyid Qutb (1906–1966) to the inordinate influence and power of the imperial West. Their approaches flow into those of current fundamentalisms but are modified depending on the situation. This is why generalizing statements on fundamentalism are so problematic. It is necessary to look at the distinctive specific features of each movement, analyzing them from a comparative perspective, such as in contrast to melds of nationalism and religion in places like Ireland, Poland, Greece, Serbia, and Macedonia.

While the first wave of Islamicist politics began at the turn of the last century, the current wave is bound up with the years 1967 (Six Day War) and 1979 (Iranian Revolution). The loss of the June 1967 war against Israel, perceived as a Western outpost in the Arab East, catalyzed a search for the causes of this traumatic defeat. Criticism soon singled out the defective character of the existing Arab regimes. Nationalism and "socialism" were viewed as apparently failed enterprises and "Islam" was (re)discovered as internal therapy and a weapon toward the hostile outside. The Iranian Revolution appeared to confirm that only an Islamic uprising could achieve true emancipation from the yoke of Western imperialism (Abu-Rabi 1994; Ayubi 1991; Choueiri 1990; Esposito 1998).

The loss of Iran triggered shock in the West. After all, the regime of the shah had been the most important regional ally of the West. Now Khomeini became an exporter of an Islamic revolution *against* the West (and Israel). Although the revolution's export ran into difficulties due ultimately to its distinctively Shi'ite character, it more than sufficed to resurrect and rejuvenate anti-Islamic images of the adversary in the West. This was vigorously abetted by the seizure of hostages at the U.S. embassy in Tehran (1979), the kidnappings and bombings in Lebanon (1983/84), and the growing presence of Egyptian extremists or Hamas in Palestine. Although Western policies did not always target Islamic forces—one need but recall Washington's support for the anti-Soviet Afghan Mujahiddin, the regimes in Saudi Arabia and the Gulf, the Bosnian Muslims, and the Kosovars (Esposito 1999; Tibi 1999)— "Islamic fundamentalism" remains a central image of the current enemy in Western societies, especially after September 11, 2001.

This review should help clarify the relative function of religious or "cultural" (Huntington 1993) affiliations or democratic concerns. There is apparently no clear-cut connection between religion as such and democracy or peace, although there tends to be a contrast between religious extremism on the one hand and liberal democracy and pacifism on the other (Kurzman 1998; Monshipouri 1998; Rejwan 2000).

Relations between Judaism and Islam

To assess the relations between Judaism and Islam, it is necessary to look at their encounter in theological and historical terms. The prime distinction is between theological correspondences and differences on the one hand and the political-historical relevance of such similarities and contrasts on the other.

As numerous authors (Bouman 1990; Bunzl 1989; Busse 1991; Katch 1954; Lewis 1984; Peters 1982) have noted, Muslims over the course of fourteen centuries were not anti-Semites—not because they themselves were Semites (an irrelevant argument), but because they were not Christians. In Islam, the concept of a son of God or murder of God is inconceivable. Jesus, as Muhammad himself, is considered in Islam to be a human being and prophet, not a "savior." The crucifixion, which in the Qur'an is considered an act the Jews were incapable of, is regarded as an illusion: God simply took Jesus unto Himself. While Christianity regarded itself as the sublation and supplanting of Judaism, and saw the survival of Jewish congregations as a provocation and threat, Islam never regarded the Jews as a challenge of comparable salience and severity. Naturally there was Muhammad's dispute with the Jewish tribes in Arabia and his rancor over the fact that they did not accept his prophecy, a teaching that contains many elements of Jewish tradition (see below). But the cosmic exaggeration of the importance of these disputes is part of current Islamic rhetoric, something quite contemporary and novel by any historical yardstick.

Islam and Judaism share many theological and sociocultural features (see Geiger 1970; Rosenthal 1961; Wasserstrom 1995; Brinner and Ricks, 1989; Kramer 1999; Nettler 1993; Nettler and Taji-Farouki 1998), such as the following:

- —strict monotheism
- —analogous role for religious law *(halakha/shari'a)*
- —dietary laws (Sunnis permit kosher food)
- —circumcision
- —rabbi/*'ulema:* scholars, sages of the Law, theologians, but no priests
- —Abraham/Ibrahim: "Jew before the Torah" and "Muslim before the Qur'an"
- —acceptance of the biblical genealogy of the Arabs via Ishmael
- —Abraham as builder of the Ka'ba
- —Moses as role model for Muhammad
- —original direction of prayer *(qibla)* to Jerusalem

This list could be continued (and can be found in what is probably its most detailed appearance in Katch 1954), but should suffice for our purposes here as a bridge to the next section.

On the Historical Experience

In evaluating the history of Jewish minorities in Islamic societies, two extremes should be avoided: the image of idyllic coexistence, often sketched by Islamic apologists, and the image of an eternal hell sometimes propagated by Zionist propagandists (Cohen 1994; Stillman 1979, 1991; Ye'or 1985; Deshen and Zenner 1996; Braude and Lewis 1982; Rejwan 1998). Summarily, one can say that though the historical experience differed at times, there was doubtless an Islamically grounded dualism of discrimination and protection, though the situation of Jews in predominantly Shi'ite societies was generally worse than in Sunni societies. In the latter, there was occasional but rare persecution, though violence against Jews never took on the proportions it achieved in the Christian Occident (before emancipation of the Jews following the French Revolution of 1789). There are no parallels to the mass expulsions, Inquisition, and pogroms, not to speak of the Holocaust. Bernard Lewis (1984) has determined that the situation of minorities in Islamic lands was better in periods of rise than decline. There are references again and again of course to the flowering in Spain after the Islamic conquest (eighth century C.E. to 1492) and in the Ottoman Empire after

1492 (acceptance of Sephardic immigrants) (Goitein 1967; Shaw 1991; Levy 1992; Ashtor 1973–84; Rodrigue and Benbassa, 1995). The legal status of the "People of the Book" (*Ahl al-Kitab,* i.e., Jews and Christians) was basically regulated by their *dhimmi* (protected) status, according to which a certain security, internal autonomy (*millet* system in the Ottoman Empire), and exemption from military service were granted to these minorities in return for recognition of the dominance of Islam and the payment of a poll tax, the so-called *jizya.* Since Jews, in contrast to Christians, were not perceived as actual or potential rivals, a kind of benign neglect or condescending toleration was practiced toward them.

The decline of the Islamic world, represented by the Ottoman Empire, and the rise of the European colonial powers offered Christian minorities (and to a lesser extent Jewish minorities as well) the possibility of overcoming their inferior status by drawing closer to a Europe that in the wake of the French Revolution had developed forms of minority emancipation beyond the dreams of non-Muslim minorities in the Orient. The relative weakness and impotence of the Islamic state reduced its tolerance toward Christians and Jews as well, who were often accused of disloyalty and collaboration with the West. Now the groundwork was laid for a possible deterioration in Jewish-Islamic relations. These preconditions did not spring from religion or religious differences but were rooted in the following historical circumstances:

—the appearance of Zionism; conflicts in and over Palestine
—the percolation of European anti-Semitism, initially via Christian minorities and competitors of the Jews
—the attraction exercised by European ethnonationalisms and later by Nazi propaganda
—shock over the emergence of a Jewish military might

Initially it was believed that the Jews, associated with the traditional stereotype of cowardice, were incapable of creating a state themselves. The creation of the State of Israel in 1948 constituted a shock. Consequently, it had to be rationalized as a creature of the machinations of imperialism—and then, reversing the classic stereotype, defamed as the product of a Jewish "world conspiracy" (see Sivan 1985). This conspiracy theory, actually Christian anti-Semitic in origin (see the classic *Protocols of the Wise Men of Zion*), is now Islamicized (cf. Nüsse in Nettler 1993). The successive process of termination of the Jewish presence in the Arab-Islamic world in the wake of the establishment of the State of Israel intensified an estrangement rationalized in part by both sides in terms of "religion."

On the Structure of This Volume

In the spirit of Edward Said's remarks at the beginning of this book, but more focused on Jewish and Islamic dimensions of contemporary Middle Eastern politics, we refuse to ignore the "internal dynamics and plurality of every civilization." We pay conscious attention to the "exchange and cross-fertilization" between cultures, especially in the present globalizing world. It follows logically from this that we must warn against generalizations and constructions of the "other" as totally different and alien, combined with associated exclusionary practices. Instead of a "clash of civilizations," we prefer to look at "clashes within civilizations."

As for the clash over Palestine, our contributors agree that the origins of the conflict are not religious: rather, in the course of a long and passionate struggle, actors on both sides have sacralized the dispute. Those least able and willing to reach an accommodation have hijacked the discourse on the conflict. Millenarian Jewish and Jihadic Muslim interpretations and politics have gained acceptance in nearly direct proportion to the disappearance of hope for "earthly" solutions. One might add that Evangelical Christian support for right-wing Israeli agendas has been strengthened, especially after 9/11, to a large extent by the dubious attractiveness of these developments, which seem in the eyes of the Evangelical Christians to corroborate their pro-Israel and anti-Islamic attitudes.

While one task of the book consists of an analysis of these troubling phenomena, another looks into alternative interpretations of the same religious-cultural traditions. For broad masses of people in the Middle East, the element of the "religious" plays a significant role in their lives and identity; thus, a struggle over the meaning of this heritage assumes a major political importance.

These concerns flowed into the conception of a conference on which this volume of essays is based: held on 27–29 November 2000 in Vienna, its participants included a number of prominent scholars from the Middle East, Europe, and North America. Organized jointly by the Austrian Institute for International Affairs (Österreichisches Institut für Internationale Politik, Vienna) and the German Orient Institute (Deutsches Orient-Institut, Hamburg), the conference was entitled "Islam, Judaism, and the Political Role of Religions in the Middle East."

The essays presented can be usefully grouped in terms of four thematic research foci within the general subject of the conference:

1. Theological and historical relations between Muslims and Jews, Islam and Judaism, with an emphasis on issues of exchange and cross-fertilization

2. The dynamics of ethnic, cultural, and religious identities in the context of the Israeli-Palestinian encounter and within the Palestinian National Movement itself, where the issue of Muslim-Christian relations is examined
3. Sources within religious traditions that can be given an emancipatory meaning and constitute a potential for progressive politics
4. Issues of contemporary instrumentalization of religions for political purposes in the sense of a "clash of civilizations"

Accordingly, the essays by Hans-Michael Haussig (University of Potsdam) and Nissim Rejwan (Hebrew University of Jerusalem) investigate theological and historical aspects subsumed under the first focus. Haussig elaborates on the differing status of the concept of religion within Judaism, Islam, and Christianity, exploring not only the status of belief systems within each tradition but also the recognition and comparability of other denominations. Rejwan's essay, on the other hand, centers on the most productive periods of the Muslim-Jewish intellectual and cultural symbiosis, especially in medieval Muslim Spain, stressing that these traditions could have renewed political relevance today. The concept of a Judaeo-Christian tradition as opposed to the World of Islam can be thus understood as a relatively recent construction.

Within the second focus, Herbert Kelman (Harvard University) draws on comprehensive research on the political psychology of the Israeli-Palestinian conflict as well as on extensive experience in interactive workshops where Israeli and Palestinian personalities participated unofficially. In addressing the centrality of the identity of the Other, Kelman conceives of religion as an important element of identity. Helga Baumgarten (Birzeit University, Palestine) draws our attention to the relevance and irrelevance of religious (Muslim-Christian) identities and cleavages within the Palestinian National Movement. She shows how secular and Islamist concepts of political struggle affect the status of Christians within Palestinian society in different ways.

The third thematic complex revolves around the issue of alternative political potentials within Jewish, Christian, and Muslim traditions, "alternative" in the sense of "counterhegemonic" under the present circumstances. The contributors in this section focus on Jewish and/or Islamic traditions in order to substantiate emancipatory, intercultural, or democratic approaches. Raja Bahlul (Birzeit University, Palestine) examines this attempt within a Muslim framework, investigating sources and conceptions of democracy in Islamic thought. Uncovering Muslim roots of democratic concepts imbues the idea of democracy with greater authenticity in the Middle East, distinguishing it from a discourse and practice of democracy as imported from the West. In a similar vein, Adam Seligman (Boston University) explores the religious roots of tolerance with special reference to Judaism and Islam. His point of departure is the conviction that for the predictable future, religious forms of consciousness will remain predominant and valorized among peoples in the Orient. Seligman suggests that given this configuration, political change should best be sought from armatures of these traditions.

The fourth focus is addressed in the essay by Joel Beinin (Stanford University). He stresses pluralism and syncretism, pointing to the relevance of multiple identities in the region. In a powerful analysis he gives examples of how the hegemonic "clash of civilizations" can be undermined by subversive forms of popular culture. Writing about the Palestinian National Movement, Alexander Flores (University of Bremen) explores the extent and limits of its "Islamization." Referring to the al-Aqsa Intifada, he emphasizes that in spite of the religious significance of Jerusalem's sacred places, the character of the uprising has remained primarily political. On the other hand, a constant deterioration of living conditions and political prospects (especially after 9/11) increases the dangers of "essentializing" the conflict, that is, seeing it as an uncompromising cultural confrontation. A similar development is observed by Avishai Ehrlich (Tel Aviv University) for the Israeli side. He presents a predominantly pessimistic account of the way religious themes enter political discourse and/or mass consciousness, citing empirical data indicating a reverse relationship between religiosity and readiness for peace and reconciliation with the Palestinian Other. Moreover, he suggests that an "Israeli Judaism" has developed, reflecting conditions other than those that led to the emergence of traditional "Diaspora Judaism." Nonetheless, Ehrlich cautions us not to trivialize secular nationalisms by overemphasizing religious fundamentalisms.

References and Selected General Bibliography

Abu-Amr, Ziad. *Islamic Fundamentalism in the West Bank and Gaza: Muslim Brotherhood and Islamic Jihad.* Bloomington: Indiana University Press, 1994.

Abu-Rabi, Ibrahim, ed. *Islamic Resurgence: Challenges, Directions, and Future Perspectives.* Tampa, Fla.: World and Islam Studies Enterprise, 1994.

Ahmad, Mumtaz, ed. *State Politics and Islam.* Indianapolis, Ind.: American Trust Publications, 1986.

Andrews, Richard. *Blood on the Mountain: A History of the Temple Mount from the Ark of the Covenant to the Third Millennium.* London: Phoenix, 2000.

Arkoun, Mohammed. *Der Islam: Annäherung an eine Religion.* Heidelberg: Palmyra, 1999.

Armstrong, Karen. *Holy War: The Crusades and Their Impact on Today's World*. New York: Doubleday, 1991.

———. *Jerusalem: One City, Three Faiths*. New York: Ballantine Publishing Group, 1997.

Ashtor, Eliyahu. *The Jews of Moslem Spain*. 3 vols. Philadelphia: Jewish Publication Society, 1973–84.

Ayubi, Nazih. *Political Islam: Religion and Politics in the Arab World*. London: Routledge, 1991.

Bayoumi, Mustafa, and Andrew Rubin, eds. *The Edward Said Reader*. New York: Vintage Books, 2000.

Beinin, Joel, and Joe Stork, eds. *Political Islam: Essays from Middle East Report*. Berkeley and Los Angeles: University of California Press, 1997.

Benvenisti, Meron. *City in Stone: The Hidden History of Jerusalem*. Berkeley/Los Angeles/London: University of California Press, 1997.

———. *Sacred Landscapes: The Buried History of the Holy Land since 1948*. Berkeley/Los Angeles/London: University of California Press, 2000.

Bernstein, Reiner. *Der verborgene Frieden: Politik und Religion im Nahen Osten*. Berlin: Jüdische Verlagsanstalt, 2000.

Bielefeldt, Heiner, and Wilhelm Heitmeyer. *Politisierte Religion: Ursachen und Erscheinungsformen des modernen Fundamentalismus*. Frankfurt am Main: Suhrkamp, 1998.

Bouman, Johan. *Der Koran und die Juden: Die Geschichte einer Tragödie*. Darmstadt: Wissenschaftliche Buchgesellschaft, 1990.

Braude, Benjamin, and Bernard Lewis, eds. *Christians and Jews in the Ottoman Empire*. 2 vols. New York and London: Holmes and Meier, 1982.

Brinner, William M., and Stephen D. Ricks, eds. *Studies in Islamic and Judaic Traditions*. Atlanta, Ga.: Scholars Press, 1989.

Bunzl, John. *Juden Im Orient: Jüdische Gemeinschaften in der islamischen Welt und orientalische Juden in Israel*. Vienna: Junius, 1989.

Burke, Edmund, III, and Ira M. Lapidus, eds. *Islam, Politics and Social Movements*. Berkeley/Los Angeles/London: University of California Press, 1988.

Busse, Heribert. *Die theologischen Beziehungen des Islams zu Judentum und Christentum: Grundlagen des Dialogs im Koran und die gegenwärtige Situation*. Darmstadt: Wissenschaftliche Buchgesellschaft, 1991.

Choueiri, Youssef. *Islamic Fundamentalism*. Boston: Twayne, 1990.

Cohen, Asher, and Bernard Susser. *Israel and the Politics of Jewish Identity: The Secular-Religious Impasse*. Baltimore and London: Johns Hopkins University Press, 2000.

Cohen, Mark R. *Under Crescent and Cross: The Jews in the Middle Ages*. Princeton, N.J.: Princeton University Press, 1994.

Courbage, Youssef, and Philippe Fargues. *Christians and Jews under Islam*. London: I. B. Tauris, 1997.

Cragg, Kenneth. *The Arab Christian: A History in the Middle East*. Louisville, Ky.: John Knox Press, 1991.

Cutler, Allan Harris, and Helen Elmquist Cutler. *The Jew as Ally of the Muslim: Medieval Roots of Anti-Semitism.* Notre Dame, Ind.: University of Notre Dame Press, 1986.

Demant, Peter. *Jewish Fundamentalism in Israel: Implications for the Mideast Conflict.* Jerusalem: Israel/Palestine Center for Research and Information, 1995.

Deshen, S., and W. Zenner, eds. *Jews among Muslims: Communities in the Precolonial Middle East.* New York: New York University Press, 1996.

Duran, Khalid. *Children of Abraham: An Introduction to Islam for Jews.* Hoboken, N.J.: KTAV Publishing House, 2001.

Endelman, Todd M. *Comparing Jewish Societies.* Ann Arbor: University of Michigan Press, 1997.

Esposito, John L. *Islam and Politics.* 4th ed. Syracuse, N.Y.: Syracuse University Press, 1998.

———. *The Islamic Threat: Myth or Reality?* 3d ed. New York: Oxford University Press, 1999.

———, ed. *Voices of Resurgent Islam.* Oxford: Oxford University Press, 1983.

Esposito, John L., and John Voll. *Islam and Democracy.* Oxford: Oxford University Press, 1996.

Firestone, Reuven. *Children of Abraham: An Introduction to Judaism for Muslims.* Hoboken, N.J.: KTAV Publishing House, 2001.

Friedman, Menachem. "Jewish Zealots: Conservative versus Innovative." In *Fundamentalism in Comparative Perspective,* ed. Lawrence Kaplan, 159–76. Amherst: University of Massachusetts Press, 1992.

Fuller, Graham, and Ian Lesser. *A Sense of Siege: The Geopolitics of Islam and the West.* Boulder, Colo.: Westview Press, 1995.

Geiger, Abraham. *Judaism and Islam.* Reprint, New York: KTAV Publishing House, 1970.

Gellner, Ernest. *Postmodernism, Reason, and Religion.* London: Routledge, 1992.

Gerner, Deborah J. *Understanding the Contemporary Middle East.* Boulder, Colo., and London: Lynne Rienner Publishers, 2000.

Goitein, S. D. *Jews and Arabs: Their Contacts through the Ages.* New York: Schocken, 1967.

Gurr, Ted Robert, and Barbara Harff. *Ethnic Conflict in World Politics.* Boulder/San Francisco/Oxford: Westview Press, 1994.

Hafez, Kai, and Udo Steinbach. *Juden und Muslime in Deutschland: Minderheitendialog als Zukunftsaufgabe.* Hamburg: Deutsches Orient-Institut, 1999.

Halliday, Fred. *Islam and the Myth of Confrontation: Religion and Politics in the Middle East.* London: I. B. Tauris, 1995.

———. *Nation and Religion in the Middle East.* London: Al Saqi Books, 2000.

Haynes, Jeffrey. *Religion in Third World Politics.* Boulder, Colo.: Lynne Rienner Publishers, 1994.

Hertzberg, Arthur. "Jewish Fundamentalism." In *Fundamentalism in Comparative Perspective,* ed. Lawrence Kaplan, 152–59. Amherst: University of Massachusetts Press, 1992.

Heuberger, Valeria. *Der Islam in Europa*. Frankfurt am Main/New York/Vienna: Peter Lang, 1999.

Hourani, Albert. *A History of the Arab Peoples*. Harvard University Press, 1991.

Humphreys, Stephen R. *Between Memory and Desire: The Middle East in a Troubled Age*. Berkeley/Los Angeles/London: University of California Press, 1999.

Huntington, Samuel P. "The Clash of Civilizations?" *Foreign Affairs* 72, no. 3 (1993): 22–49.

Johnston, Douglas, and Cynthia Sampson, eds. *Religion, the Missing Dimension of Statecraft*. Oxford: Oxford University Press, 1994.

Katch, Abraham I. *Judaism and the Koran: Biblical and Talmudic Backgrounds of the Koran and Its Commentaries*. New York: A. S. Barnes and Co., 1954.

Kepel, Gilles. *Die Rache Gottes: Radikale Moslems, Christen und Juden auf dem Vormarsch*. Munich and Zurich: Piper, 1991.

Kepnes, Steven. *Interpreting Judaism in a Postmodern Age*. New York: New York University Press, 1996.

Khalidi, Walid. *Islam, the West, and Jerusalem*. Washington, D.C.: Center for Contemporary Arab Studies, Georgetown University, 1996.

Kramer, Martin. *The Jewish Discovery of Islam: Studies in Honor of Bernard Lewis*. Tel Aviv: Moshe Dayan Center for Middle Eastern and African Studies: Tel Aviv University, 1999.

Kurzman, Charles. *Liberal Islam: A Sourcebook*. New York: Oxford University Press, 1998.

Lerch, Wolfgang G. *Halbmond, Kreuz, Davidstern: Nationalitäten und Religionen im Nahen und Mittleren Osten*. Frankfurt am Main: Eichborn, 1992.

Levy, Avigdor. *The Sephardim in the Ottoman Empire*. Princeton, N.J.: Princeton University Press, 1992.

Lewis, Bernard. *The Jews of Islam*. London: Routledge and Kegan Paul, 1984.

———. *Islam and the West*. New York: Oxford University Press, 1993.

———. *The Multiple Identities of the Middle East*. London: Schocken Books, 1999.

Liebman, Charles. "The Jewish Religion and Contemporary Israeli Nationalism." In *Religious Radicalism and Politics in the Middle East*, ed. Emmanuel Sivan and Menachem Friedman, 77–94. New York: State University of New York Press, 1990.

Liebman, Charles, and Eliezer Don-Yehiya. *Civil Religion in Israel*. Los Angeles: University of California Press, 1983.

Lustick, Ian S. *For the Land and the Lord: Jewish Fundamentalism in Israel*. New York: Council on Foreign Relations, 1988.

Marcus, Amy Dockser. *The View From Nebo: How Archeology Is Rewriting the Bible and Reshaping the Middle East*. Boston/New York/London: Brown and Co., 2000.

Marty, Martin E., and R. Scott Appleby. *Herausforderung Fundamentalismus: Radikale Christen, Moslems und Juden im Kampf gegen die Moderne*. Frankfurt am Main: Campus, 1996.

Maul, Stephan. *Israel auf Friedenskurs? Politischer und religiöser Fundamentalismus in Israel. Wirkungen auf den Friedensprozess im Nahen Osten.* Münster: LIT Verlag, 2000.

Milton-Edwards, Beverley. *Contemporary Politics in the Middle East.* Cambridge: Blackwell Publishers, 2000.

Monshipouri, Mahmood. *Islamism, Secularism, and Human Rights in the Middle East.* Boulder, Colo., and London: Lynne Rienner Publishers, 1998.

Nardin, Terry. *The Ethics of War and Peace: Religious and Secular Perspectives.* Princeton, N.J.: Princeton University Press, 1996.

Nettler, Ronald L., ed. *Studies in Muslim-Jewish Relations.* Chur, Switzerland: Harwood Academic Publishers, 1993.

Nettler, Ronald L., and Suha Taji-Farouki, eds. *Muslim-Jewish Encounters, Intellectual Traditions, and Modern Politics.* Amsterdam: Harwood Academic Publishers, 1998.

Neugart, Felix Gregor. *Die alte Herrlichkeit wiederherstellen. Der Aufstieg der Shas-Partei in Israel.* Schwalbach/Taunus: Wochenschau Verlag, 2000.

Nieswandt, Reiner. *Abrahams umkämpftes Erbe: Eine kontextuelle Studie zum modernen Konflikt von Juden, Christen und Muslimen um Israel/Palästina.* Stuttgart: Verlag Katholisches Bibelwerk, 1998.

Nüsse, Andrea. "The Ideology of Hamas: Palestinian Islamic Fundamentalist Thought on Jews, Israel, and Islam." In *Studies in Muslim-Jewish Relations,* ed. Ronald Nettler, 97–125. Chur, Switzerland: Harwood Academic Publishers, 1993.

Palestine-Israel Journal 2 (Spring 1994).

Peters, F. E. *Children of Abraham: Judaism, Christianity, and Islam.* Princeton, N.J.: Princeton University Press, 1982.

Philipps-Heck, Ulla. *Daheim im Exil: Orientalische Juden im Exil.* Schwalbach/Taunus: Wochenschau, 1998.

Prior, Michael. *The Bible and Colonialism: A Moral Critique.* Sheffield, U.K.: Sheffield Academic Press, 1997.

Ravitsky, Aviezer. *Messianism, Zionism, and Jewish Religious Radicalism.* Chicago: University of Chicago Press, 1993.

Rejwan, Nissim. *Israel's Place in the Middle East: A Pluralist Perspective.* Gainesville: University Press of Florida, 1998.

———. *Israel in Search of Identity: Reading the Formative Years.* Gainesville: University Press of Florida, 1999.

———. *The Many Faces of Islam: Perspectives on a Resurgent Civilization.* Gainesville: University Press of Florida, 2000.

Rodinson, Maxime. *Marxisme et Monde Musulman.* Paris: Editions du Seuil, 1972.

Rodrigue, Aron, and Esther Benbassa. *The Jews of the Balkans: The Judeo-Spanish Community, 15th to 20th Centuries.* Oxford: Blackwell Publishers, 1995.

Said, Edward. *The End of the Peace Process: Oslo and After.* London: Granta Books, 2000.

Shahak, Israel. *Jewish Fundamentalism in Israel.* London: Pluto Press, 1999.

Sharif, Regina. *Non-Jewish Zionism: Its Roots in Western History.* London: Zed Press, 1983.

Shaw, Stanford J. *The Jews of the Ottoman Empire and the Turkish Republic.* New York: New York University Press, 1991.

Shragai, Nadav. "Religious, right-wing and realistic. In ultra-Orthodox right-wing politics, it's practical considerations that matter, not ideology." *Ha'aretz,* English ed., 15 February 2001.

Sidahmed, A. Salam, and A. Ehteshami, eds. *Islamic Fundamentalism.* Boulder, Colo.: Westview Press, 1966.

Silberstein, Lawrence J., and Robert L. Cohn. *The Other in Jewish Thought and History: Constructions of Jewish Culture and Identity.* New York/London: New York University Press, 1994.

Silberstein, Lawrence, ed. *Jewish Fundamentalism in Comparative Perspective: Religion, Ideology, and the Crisis of Modernity.* New York: New York University Press, 1993.

Sivan, Emmanuel. *Radical Islam: Medieval Theology and Modern Politics.* New Haven, Conn.: Yale University Press, 1985.

Sprinzak, Ehud. *The Ascendance of Israel's Radical Right.* New York: Oxford University Press, 1991.

Steinbach, Udo. *Geschichte der Türkei.* Munich: C. H. Beck, 2000.

Stillman, Norman, ed. *The Jews of Arab Lands: A History and Source Book.* Philadelphia: Jewish Publication Society of America, 1979.

———. ed. *The Jews of Arab Lands in Modern Times.* Philadelphia and New York: Jewish Publication Society of America, 1991.

Tibi, Bassam. *Kreuzzug und Djihad: Der Islam und die christliche Welt.* Munich: Bertelsmann Verlag, 1999.

Timsit, Martine. "Le nouveau militantisme religieux en Israel: L'analyse culturelle en questions." Thesis, Université Paris X–Nanterre, Sciences Juridiques, Administratives, et Politiques, 1996.

Von Grunebaum, G. E. *Classical Islam: A History, 600 A.D.–1258 A.D..* New York: Barnes and Noble Books, 1996.

Walzer, Michael. *Exodus and Revolution.* New York: Basic Books, 1990.

Wasserstrom, Steven M. *Between Muslim and Jew: The Problem of Symbiosis under Early Islam.* Princeton, N.J.: Princeton University Press, 1995.

Wertheimer, Jack. *The Uses of Tradition: Jewish Continuity in the Modern Era.* Cambridge: Harvard University Press, 1998.

Ye'or, Bat. *The Dhimmi: Jews and Christians under Islam.* Cranbury, N.J., and London: Fairleigh Dickinson Press and Associated University Presses, 1985.

Zerubavel, Yael. *Recovered Roots: Collective Memory and the Making of the Israeli National Tradition.* Chicago and London: University of Chicago Press, 1995.

Zubaida, Sami. *Islam, the People and the State: Political Ideas and Movements in the Middle East.* London: I. B. Tauris, 1993.

I

On Islam and Judaism, Muslims and Jews

A Religion's Self-Conception of "Religion"

The Case of Judaism and Islam

Hans-Michael Haussig

One of the fundamental assumptions of the history of religions *(Religionswissenschaft)* as an academic discipline is that something we may term "religion" exists in many if not all parts of the world and in different cultures. Adherents of these various religions share the belief that our life is not restricted to the mundane world, that there is something transcendent that imbues life with ultimate meaning. This assumption has characterized the study of religion from its very inception in nineteenth-century Europe; many specialists in the study of religion still deem it valid. The idea of different religions in all parts of the world is highly modern and did not exist in medieval times. Moreover, it has few equivalents in other cultures or religions, and one may discern in it primarily a modern Christian conception of what religion is and must be. Thus, this view ignores the concepts that the religions themselves employ. In this essay I offer distinctive categories for describing the concepts used by the religions themselves to express their self-understanding and general conception of religion. Applying these categories, I deal with the concepts of religion in classical and medieval Judaism and Islam.

The concept of "religion" as used today was derived from the religious discourse of post-Enlightenment Christianity. In medieval times, religion as a general concept was unknown. As Ernst Feil has shown, the medieval term *religio* had the meaning of "devotion to God," that is to say, a concept with primarily cultic signification; yet the term *religio* was restricted to Christianity and never used to designate other non-Christian kinds of devotion that we might define today as religions. If one compared Christianity with other faiths, such as Islam, the terms *secta* or *lex* were used. In contrast with *religio*, these terms do not express devotion to God in any sense but signify a mere organizational or judicial aspect. One did not want to concede devotion to God to another secta—understood as mere superstition, not as an adequate expression of divine worship.

The Enlightenment led to a new attitude toward other religions, now viewed in a certain way similar to Christianity (Feil 1986). In the concept of religion, Christianity had a conception that was broader: it not only expressed its own way of devotion to God but served as a more general notion for possible comparison between itself and other religions. For this reason, we may characterize religion as a comparative concept—"comparative" in the sense that it renders interreligious comparison possible. Comparative concepts may refer to a single religious phenomenon, for example, when the term *priest* serves as a general cover concept for all kinds of religious specialists in a variety of religions. They may also denote the whole complex of religion, as does the Western concept of religion. Not all religions have such comparative concepts. The Hindu term *Brahmin,* for example, would never have been used by traditional Hinduism as a comparative concept, notwithstanding the fact that some scholars of comparative religion deem it virtually identical with the religious specialist of the Catholic Church and therefore might denote both by the term *priest*. In the case of Brahmin, we may thus speak of an "exclusive concept." Both "exclusive concepts" and "comparative concepts" may denote individual religious phenomena as well as general concepts of religion. In their traditional form, most of the world's great religions have developed exclusive concepts of self-reference, that is, they have a proper name for autodesignation. For example, the proper names of various religions—Judaism, Christianity, Islam—are exclusive. Some religions also developed comparative concepts, though less encompassing in their comparative scope than the Western term *religion*. Most tribal religions neither have comparative concepts of religion nor exclusive concepts to denote their own tradition.

These categories are useful for a simple model for classifying the various concepts that religions employ in formulating their own self-understanding and their general idea of religion. It is necessary to go further and distinguish between different aspects as well, namely, the diverse connotations associated with the religious concepts. Whereas religion in its contemporary use may be understood primarily by associations with "God" or "faith," other religions might best be comprehended by aspects such as "ritual" or "behavior."

I distinguish five aspects of religious concepts: belief, faith, the cultic-ritual aspect, the aspect of (ethical) conduct, and the sociological aspect. *Belief* entails the objective content of the religion, the beliefs a certain religion demands from its adherents. It contains the tenets of the official religion, whereas *faith* involves the subjective feelings and religious emotions of believers. The *cultic-ritual aspect* encompasses all features of ritual and cult, whereas the *aspect of (ethical) conduct* comprises all prescriptions regulating interaction between individuals not included under the rubric of cult and ritual. It often encompasses ethical commands, such as the injunction "Thou shalt not kill," and may also embrace the sphere of law, which in the contemporary, more-general Western context is not subsumed under religion. The *sociological aspect* describes the religion from its institutional side. It comprises the way in which a religious community is distinguished and separated from its competitors.

These aspects are ideal types. In practice, a given concept of religion may encompass at least two or more of these aspects. The aspects also differ in respect to the context and historical development of the various concepts of religion. Some of the terms in contemporary use as concepts of religion may not have been so employed in the past, such as the Hindu term *dharma*, which in its origins designated only the system of castes and stages of life. Religions have developed quite different concepts regarding their own nature and that of other religions. They may be understood primarily by cultic-ritual aspects or by a comparative aspect of faith, conceiving religion as a certain feeling for the holy. One should also take into account that, at least at the beginning of their development, most religions did not define their key concepts in a systematic way. This was generally the elaboration of later religious specialists.

Let me illustrate these more abstract statements by concrete examples drawn from classical and medieval Judaism and Islam (Haussig 1999).[1] Biblical Judaism had no exclusive or comparative concept of religion. The term *Ioudaismos*, from which our "Judaism" is derived, was coined by Greek-speaking Jews of the first century. The Bible and rabbinical literature did not yet know its Hebrew equivalent *yahadût*, which first occurs in medieval literature, though infrequently. Although the word *yehudî*, from which the abstract noun *yahadût* is derived, occurs in the Bible, it primarily denotes a descendant from the tribe of Judah, and later, after the destruction of the Northern Kingdom of Israel, it became the general designation for all descendants of the tribes that lived in the Southern Kingdom of Judah. Comparative concepts of religion used in contemporary Hebrew are taken from the Bible; however, they do not function as religious concepts there. Although the religion of Ancient Israel competes with alien cults, as the Bible reports, this competition is not conceptualized by a notion of vying religions. In the Hebrew Bible, the contestation we find is between different gods. This is evident from the prophet Jeremiah (2:11): "Hath a nation changed its gods, which yet are no gods? But My people hath changed its glory [i.e., the glory of God] for that which doth not profit."

The same holds true for rabbinical Judaism. Moreover, here we can note a clear distinction between Israel and the "nations of the world" *(yisra'el we umôt ha'ôlam)* (Stern 1994). Like biblical Judaism, rabbinical Judaism does not argue with other religions by means of religious concepts. Instead, we find comparisons as to habits and feasts, as in the following story related in *Midrash Bereshit Rabbah* (13:6):

> A certain Gentile asked R. Joshua, observing to him: "You have festivals and we have festivals; we do not rejoice when you do, and you do not rejoice when we do. When then do we both rejoice together?" "When the rain descends." What is the proof? (Ps. 65:14) "The meadows are clothed with flocks"; what follows? (Ps. 66:1) "Shout unto God, all the earth. Not priest, Levites, or Israelites is written here but, "All the earth." (*Midrash Rabbah: Genesis 1,* 1983)

There are numerous occurrences of the expression *avodah zarah* in rabbinical literature, which literally means "foreign cult." But it is not always clear whether this expression denotes the foreign cult, or the object of worship of this cult, that is, an idol.[2] In general, one can say that rabbinical sources concerning foreign cults or other religions are vague in their historical value. It is evident from them that rabbinical Judaism had neither a comparative concept of religion nor an exclusive one.

Islam seems to be the first great religion credited to have had concepts of religion from its very beginning that were in some sense comparable to our own modern ideas of religion. In the Qur'an, we find both a comparative and an exclusive concept of religion. The exclusive concept of religion is expressed by *islam*, whereas we encounter the term *din* for the comparative concept.[3] Yet islam in its original meaning may not have been understood as an exclusive concept, that is, the name used by Muslims to denote their own religion, discriminating it from other faiths. The basic meaning of islam is submission (to God). We may indeed wonder whether islam in its Qur'anic occurrences should be understood by its basic meaning or in the sense of "Islam," that is to say as a proper name. Since most of its occurrences are in connection with din, it seems to me quite evident that at least in these cases, it should be interpreted in the latter sense, as in 3:19, which offers a polemic against other religions: "Lo! The *din* with God (is) the *islam*. Those who (formerly) received the Scripture differed only after knowledge came unto them" (Pickthall 1930).[4]

This verse follows the dictum of the preceding one, namely, that there is no god but God. Because of its contrasting use in respect to other scriptural religions, one may assume that the term *islam* is used here as an exclusive concept of religion, a proper name for the religion of the Muslims in dissociation from other religions. This self-definition implies the aspect of belief, as one may conclude from the former verse, as well as sociological aspects, evident by its contrasting use over against the other scriptural religions.

Regarding the comparative concept *din,* Wilfred Cantwell Smith, the first scholar to have pointed out the shortcomings of the Western concept of religion and its contradictions, argues that the original meaning of the word was "piety." According to our classification of religious concepts, he understands din primarily under the aspect of faith (Smith 1963: 81).[5] An examination of various sections of the Qur'an suggests that in some verses din indeed has this aspect but is in no way restricted to it.

One of the central occurrences of the term *din* is contained in the very short sura 109: "Say: O disbelievers! I worship not that which ye worship; Nor worship ye that which I worship. And I shall not worship that which ye worship. Nor will ye worship that which I worship. Unto you your *din,* and unto me my *din.*"

"Din" is used here to denote Muhammad's own view as well as the view of the polytheistic Meccans; thus, it can be analyzed as a comparative concept of religion. However, it is not quite obvious whether we have to understand the concept by theological, cultic, sociological, or other aspects. "Your *din*" and "my *din*" may be understood as denoting different beliefs in respect to God as well as different ritual practices, different communities, or a combination of these. Other occurrences of "din" offer a much clearer picture of its meaning, as in 4:171. The Christians, called here simply "People of the Book," are addressed with the following exhortation: "O People of the Scripture! Do not exaggerate in your *din* nor utter aught concerning God save the truth. The Messiah, Jesus son of Mary, was only a messenger of God, and His word which He conveyed unto Mary, and a spirit from Him. So believe in God and His messengers, and say not 'Three.'"

The Christians are asked to renounce their belief in the Trinity. In this case, we may conclude that the aspect of belief is present. Verse 6:137 speaks of ritual practices, noting that the gods of the polytheists made their followers think it a virtue to kill their own children: "Thus have their (so-called) partners (of God) made the killing of their children to seem fair unto many of the idolaters, that they may ruin them and make their *din* obscure for them." This seems to be a reference to cultic practices of the Arabian heathens. One thus can assume the presence here of a primarily cultic aspect of din.

Although we are unable to find a clear-cut definition of din in the Qur'an, we may at least conclude that it has an unrestricted comparative meaning. "Din" may denote the true monotheism of the revelation received by Muhammad as well as the polytheistic religious practices of his Meccan adversaries. This was to change in the later medieval period, when theologians elaborated a clear definition of din, one that would subsequently come to exert its influence on the medieval Jewish conception of religion as well.

One of the most important representatives in this respect was perhaps the twelfth-century Iranian scholar Abu al-Fath Muhammad ibn 'Abd al-Karim al-Shahrastani. According to Eric Sharpe, one can ascribe to him the honor of having written the first history of religion in world literature. His main opus, *Religious Parties and Schools of Philosophy,* describes and systematizes all the religions of the then-known world and far surpasses anything Christian writers were capable of producing in the same period (Sharpe 1986: 11). Shahrastani offers a distinct definition of the concept of din, yet one far less comparative than in its Qur'anic use. According to Shahrastani, in respect to their beliefs *(madahib)*[6] men can be classified into followers of din (literally here *ahl al-diyanat)* and those who follow their own inclinations *(ahl al-ahwa').* Shahrastani now defines din as obedience *(ta'a)* and submission *(inqiyad).* This means that believers must submit themselves to the teaching and conclusions of someone else.[7] This applies to the prophetic religions, Islam as well as Judaism and Christianity, whose adherents submit themselves in obedience to the teaching of prophets and revealed scripture. Those who follow their own inclinations neither submit to a prophetic revelation nor do they acknowledge any laws or precepts ordered by God. Rather, they base their teachings solely on reason. In this category, the author includes various heterogeneous and sometimes even contradicting groups of religions and philosophies, such as Hinduism, Buddhism, the Greek philosophers, or pre-Islamic Arab religions. Whereas the Western conception designates Islam, Judaism, Christianity, Hinduism, Buddhism, and pre-Islamic Arabian heathenism as religion, medieval Islam would never have categorized the last by the concept of din. We may thus conclude that medieval Islam had a comparative concept of religion, albeit far less comparative in its scope than the Western concept of religion and even the Qur'anic "din."

Unlike Islam, Judaism had no concepts of religion from its earliest beginnings. Since the first Jewish treatises dealing with religion from a comparative perspective were written in Judaeo-Arabic, it is not surprising that the Islamic conception of religion exerted its influence in Judaism. The later Hebrew comparative concepts of religion were coined in accordance with Islamic-Arabic concepts. Unquestionably, the most important apologetic work of medieval Judaism was Judah Halevi's *Book of the Kuzari (Kitab al-Hijja wal-Dalil fi Nasr al-Din al-Dhalil).* It owes its title to the Khazars, a Turkic people living on the steppes of the Volga between the seventh and tenth centuries C.E., whose elite class was converted to Judaism. Notwithstanding its foundation in factual history, the story of *The Book of the Kuzari* is a fictitious dialogue between the king of the Khazars and a philosopher, a Christian, a Muslim, and a Jew about the true religion. The arguments put forward by the Jew prove to be the most convincing to the king and he converts to Judaism. The work was originally written in Judaeo-Arabic but gained greater popularity in its classical medieval Hebrew translation by Jehuda ibn Tibbon. Already the book's first paragraph (I:1) is useful for understanding the concept of din used by Halevi:

> I was asked to state what arguments and replies I could bring to bear against the attacks of philosophers and followers of other religions *(ahl al-adyan)*, and also against (Jewish) sectarians who attacked the rest of Israel. This reminded me of something I had once heard concerning the arguments of a Rabbi who sojourned with the King of the Khazars. The latter, as we know from historical records, became a convert to Judaism *(al-dakhil fi din al-yahud)* about four hundred years ago. To him came a dream, and it appeared as if an angel addressed him, saying: "Thy way of thinking is indeed pleasing to the Creator, but not thy way of acting." Yet he was so zealous in the performance of the Khazar religion *(fi din al-khazar)*, that he devoted himself with a perfect heart to the service of the temple and sacrifices. Notwithstanding this devotion, the angel came again at night and repeated: "Thy way of thinking is pleasing to God, but not thy way of acting." This caused him to ponder over the different beliefs and religions *(al-adyan wa-al-nihal)*, and finally become a convert to Judaism *(tahawwada)* together with many other Khazars. (Halevi 1964)[8]

There is no question that din functions here as a comparative concept of religion. It denotes the Jewish religion *(din al-yahud)* as well as other competing religions. With regard to its semantic content, the aspects of belief are evident at the beginning of the paragraph: on the one hand, through the juxtapositioning of the religions and philosophers and, on the other, by inquiring what arguments Halevi has to counter their attacks against the Jewish religion. When talking about conversion to Judaism, one has to understand the term primarily in terms of sociological aspects. These are more evident in the original Arabic text, where it is stated literally that the king "enters" the Jewish religion *(al-dakhil fi din al-yahud)*. Finally, we may note "din" in its cultic aspect, with mention of the zeal of the Khazar king in his performance of the rituals of the Khazar religion, exemplified in his participation in the Khazar temple sacrifice ceremony. The use of din in Halevi's *Kuzari* is not restricted to these aspects.

On closer scrutiny, all possible aspects of my classification of religious concepts are discernable in the book. However, one of the most interesting features is that Halevi does not only depend on the religious conceptions of his Islamic contemporaries in form but in content as well. This becomes evident when the king asks the scholar (1:60) what he thinks about the claims of the Indians: namely, that their buildings or cities are more than 100,000 years old. The scholar replies that one cannot trust the Indians: they are an unruly nation and there is nothing one can verify of what they say. They annoy the followers of other religions *(ahl al-adyan)* by these claims; and likewise incense them by their use of idols and talismans and their disregard for revealed scripture. Thus, Halevi and his Muslim contemporary Shahrastani do not categorize the Indians as followers of din, since they fail to base their claims on divine revelation.

Since biblical and rabbinical Judaism had no comparative concepts of religion available, the translator of *The Kuzari*, Jehudah ibn Tibbon, encountered difficulties in finding appropriate Hebrew equivalents for the comparative concept of din. Jehudah ibn Tibbon did not invent or coin a new word, as one might have assumed, but made use of the biblical terms *dât, tôrâh,* and *emunâh*. Dât and torâh may denote a single law as well as a corpus of law, whereas emunâh has the meaning of "confidence" or "reliability." There is, however, no discernable reason why the translator used different terms in Hebrew for the Arabic concept of din. One might assume that he preferred to render the various aspects of din by different concepts in Hebrew, yet this is not the case. The concept of emunâh serves only to render the aspect of belief, but the concepts of dât and torâh are interchangeable and not restricted to a single aspect. With time dât would eventually become the chief comparative concept in Hebrew.

In conclusion, it is clear that some religions do not, from their inception, have comparative concepts to refer to themselves and other religions. If a religion employs such concepts, that does not necessarily mean they have the same meaning as the comparative Western concept of religion. In order to come to a better understanding of one religion or the other, it is necessary not just to emphasize the common shared ground but also to probe the differences in discursive concepts and strategies for portraying each other.

Notes

1. My arguments on comparative and exclusive concepts of religion and their various aspects are discussed at greater length in Haussig 1999.

2. See *Mishnah Sanhedrin* VII, 6. The words *"ha-'obed abodâh zarâh"* may be understood as "a person who commits idolatry" or "who serves an idol."

3. In addition to *din,* we also have the term *milla,* which I must exclude from consideration here for reasons of time.

4. The translation is according to Pickthall, 1930. However, I use the word "God" instead of "Allah" and have left the words *din* and *islam* untranslated.

5. Smith bases his argument on the fact that din in the Qur'an never appears in its plural form.

6. The term *madahib* can be understood in different ways. I would argue the correct interpretation here is in the sense of "belief" or "doctrine."

7. Moreover, the concept of din as obedience and submission calls for joining together with other followers of din in the milla, which according to Shahrastani is the form, the vessel of this conjunction.

8. The original Arabic text is found in Judah Halevi, *The Book of Refutation and Proof on the Despised Faith (The Book of the Khazars)*, ed. by David H. Baneth, prepared for publication by Haggai ben-Shammai. Jerusalem: Magnes Press, 1977 (Arabic in Hebrew characters with short introduction in Hebrew).

References

Feil, Ernst. *Religio: Die Geschichte eines neuzeitlichen Grundbegriffs vom Frühchristentum bis zur Reformation*. FKDG 36. Göttingen: Vandenhoek & Ruprecht, 1986.

Halevi, Judah. *The Kuzari (Kitab al-Khazari): An Argument for the Faith of Israel*. Translated from the Arabic by Hartwig Hirschfeld. New York: Schocken, 1964.

Haussig, Hans-Michael. *Der Religionsbegriff in den Religionen: Studien zum Selbst- und Religionsverstandnis in Hinduismus, Buddhismus, Judentum und Islam*. Berlin und Bodenheim: Philo-Verlag, 1999.

Midrash Rabbah. Genesis 1. Translated into English with notes, glossary, and indices, eds. Rabbi Freedman and Maurice Simon. 3d edition. London and New York: Soncino Press, 1983.

Pickthall, M. M. *The Meaning of the Glorious Koran: An Explanatory Translation*. New York: Amana Publications, 1930.

Sharpe, Eric J. *Comparative Religion: A History*. LaSalle, Ill.: Duckworth Publishers, 1986.

Smith, Wilfred Cantwell. *The Meaning and End of Religion*. New York: Augsburg Fortress Publishers, 1963.

Stern, Sacha. *Jewish Identity in Early Rabbinic Writings*. Leiden: Brill Academic Publishers, 1994.

2

Islam and Judaism

Cultural Relations and Interaction through the Ages

Nissim Rejwan

The Historical Record

The present sorry state of relations between Arabs and Jews calls for a methodical, consistent, and conscious restatement of the history of these relations through the ages, and for an earnest reexamination of the elements that the religio-cultural traditions of Judaism and Islam have in common.[1] The effects of four major wars in the span of three decades, coupled with the virtual evacuation, since 1949, of the Jewish communities from Muslim-Arab countries, make such a historical recapitulation essential if the present generation of Jews and Arabs is not to lose all perspective.

Jakob Burckhardt once wrote that history was, on every occasion, "the record of that which one age finds worthy of note in another." I would add, in the same vein, that each generation has not only the right but also the obligation to restate and reinterpret its collective history for itself and in the light of its own specific needs and concerns. Indeed, if any subject has been in need of reinterpretation for the present generation of Jews and Arabs, it is the history of their peoples' relations in the past, especially the period in which a true cultural and even religious symbiosis was attained between the two cultures and the two faiths.

Fortunately, history has a long breath, and a few decades of Arab-Jewish conflict and strife are not as long and as decisive a period of time as it may seem to those of us who have lived through them. A brief glance at the history of Arab-Jewish relations, cultural contacts, and fruitful cooperation and interaction may help us gain a more balanced perspective. Even though history may not be a safe guide for the future, such perspective does seem to point to far less bleak prospects for Jewish-Arab coexistence and cooperation than the state of tension and mutual fears that continue to prevail between Israel and most of the neighboring Arab states.

Encounters between Jews and Arabs date back to before the rise of Islam. Indeed, from the advent on the stage of history of a people called "Arab," there has been a connection of some kind between the Arabs and the People of Israel. The ties between the Israelites and their immediate southern neighbors are well established historically. On the origin, extent, and broad human context of these encounters, some historians go very far indeed, some suggesting that the sons of 'Eber (the Hebrews) peopled the whole of the Arabian Peninsula—and that Habiru, Hebrew, and Arab are interrelated much more closely than might otherwise be supposed. Shortly after the fall of Jerusalem in 105 C.E., when Rome incorporated Arabia into its imperial structure, contacts between Jews and Arabs intensified even further. Finally, about the year 358 C.E., the entire area between the Red Sea and the Mediterranean was united with Palestine, probably for Christian as well as administrative reasons, and henceforth appeared in the records as the province of Palaestina Tertia.

The closeness of relations between the two peoples is demonstrated by the fact that, centuries before Muhammad, Jews began to settle all over the peninsula. It was inevitable that such settlements should attract outsiders. To quote Salo Baron (1957: 65):

> By slow infiltration several Arab tribes drifted into Medina and its vicinity, and were hospitably received by the Jewish farmers. By the sixth century, these new arrivals . . . eventually prevailed over their hosts. Nevertheless, Muhammad still found vigorous Jewish tribes in and around that center of northern Arabia, probably constituting the majority of the settled population. Of course, they were not all of Jewish extraction. In large part they were descended from Arab proselytes, as indicated, for example, in the remarkable story of the Banu Hishna in Teima.

These arrivals "were prevented by the Jews," says al-Bakrin, "from entering their fort as long as they professed another religion, and only when they embraced Judaism were they admitted" (Baron 1957: 65).

The contributions made by the Arabian Jews in the material, cultural, and spiritual fields were important and lasting. In particular, the Jews of Yathrib, Khaibar, and Teima, as Baron notes (1957: 70–74), "seem to have pioneered in introducing advanced methods of irrigation and cultivation of the soil. They also developed new arts and crafts from metal work and dyeing and the production of fine jewelry, and taught the neighboring tribes more advanced methods of exchanging goods and money."

The contribution of Arabian Jews in the cultural sphere was no less significant. Along with the art of writing, they also communicated to their neighbors, consciously or unawares, certain rudiments of their religious and ethical outlook. Always captivated by their effective storytelling skills, Arabs used to gather in Jewish and Christian inns and listen to the exploits of one or another biblical hero. By the time their predominance waned following the appearance of Muhammad (571–632 C.E.), the Arabian Jews, Baron asserts (1957: ibid.), "had injected enough of their restless quest of religious values into the tribes of both the Peninsula and the borderlands between Persia and Byzantium to help prepare the ground for a new effervescence of religious and cultural creativity."

This interaction between Jews and Arabs was not confined to the inhabitants of the Arabian Peninsula. Commercial relations on a large scale between Arabia and Palestine go back to the days of Solomon, and many books of the Old Testament show that the connection was steadily maintained until the seventh century, when Peninsula Arabs, under the triumphant banner of Islam, were to overrun the whole of the Levant. Though his emergence and rise to power was to be inextricably connected with the decline of Jewish predominance in the peninsula, Muhammad had originally set out to win the Jews of Arabia over to his new faith. For this reason, he adopted many of their religious beliefs, customs, and practices. The depth of the impression made by these Jews on the Prophet's mind is easily discernible in most of the chapters of the Qur'an: the uncompromising monotheism, the centrality of Abraham *(Ibrahim al-Khalil)*, the insistence on formal prayers, fasting, and almsgiving, the adoption of the Day of Atonement, and the introduction of dietary laws (such as the prohibition of pork).

When one turns from the Qur'an proper to the religious rules and laws that comprise the body of the shari'a, one finds that the rules prescribed in the Qur'an are often translated into everyday practices virtually identical to those laid down in the Law of Moses as it had been developed, expanded, and articulated in the Talmud. Many students of Judaism and Islam have remarked on the astonishing similarity between the content and form of the Talmud and the *Hadith* (the body of the traditions as to what the Prophet said and did, and on which all laws and rules not formally articulated in the Qur'an are theoretically based).

Like the Talmud in respect to Judaism, the Hadith is an authoritative exposition of Islam. The more deeply the two sources are explored and studied, the plainer their similarities become, despite some superficial differences. The effect of Judaism on the new religion was indeed so profound that, in the words of Guillaume (1969: 154), it has become "impossible to determine the limits of the latter except in the categories of the former."

Physically and materially, the lot of the Arabian Jews in the early years of Islam was on the whole not an unhappy one, with the exception of a brief later period of rift and hostility. When he discovered that the Jews refused to accept him and acknowledge his mission, Muhammad turned his fury against them and proceeded to persecute and expel them from Arabia. This policy was followed for a brief period by some of Muhammad's first successors; but, as Isidore Epstein writes, before long these rulers' inherited fanaticism "gave way to almost boundless toleration" (1959: 180). They eventually saw in the Jews a people much akin to them in race and religion, and they also found that the Jews could be of great use to them in the consolidation of their world conquests. Their control of commerce, especially foreign trade, their contacts with fellow Jews everywhere, and their knowledge of Hebrew made the Jews indispensable as interpreters and mediators for the new and energetic conquerors.

Thus, wherever the Crescent had hegemony, the lot of the Jews began to improve. This was especially the case in Palestine and in Egypt, where the Byzantine rulers had interfered not only in the economic and social life of the Jews but also in the internal affairs of the synagogue and its services. In Babylonia, which was still the heart of the Jewish Diaspora, and where the Jews enjoyed a privileged existence, the onset of Islam served only to increase their influence and augment their position. There, in the Islamic capital, Baghdad, the secular Jewish authority of the Prince of the Captivity, also known as Resh Galuta and Exilarch, was revived and clothed with renewed magnificence, while the spiritual authority remained vested in the Geonim, the heads of the two major Babylonian academies of Sura and Pumbeditha. The institution of the Geonate, which was regarded by Jews all over the world as the highest authority in all religious matters, became so prominent in Jewish life during the first five centuries of Islam that these are labeled in Jewish history as the Geonic Period (Epstein 1959: 181).

Islam and the Jews

In recent years—and especially after the rise and growth of Islamic fundamentalism—it has become customary for Israeli and Western observers to speak of Islam and Judaism as two irreconcilable faiths, and of Jewish life under Islam as a continuous record of unrelieved persecution, humiliation, and murder. Talk of "Arab anti-Semitism" has also become common. However, there has been no consensus among scholars as to the two most elementary starting points for any serious study of the phenomenon: its definition and its genesis.

Writing on anti-Semitism in pagan antiquity, Leon Poliakov, the author of a standard work on the subject, touches on the problem of dating its beginnings. Can we infer the existence of a generalized anti-Semitism during the period of the Roman Empire? In Poliakov's view, "the Jewish question" as a whole does not seem to have had more than secondary importance for the men of those times. Yet he cautiously avoids making any definite judgment, preferring, as he puts it, "to establish our investigation on more positive bases"(Poliakov 1975: vi–viii).

Poliakov makes it abundantly clear that what in antiquity was nothing more than normal xenophobia developed into what we have come to know as anti-Semitism only after the establishment of the Christian Church; that in pagan antiquity one finds none of those collective emotional reactions that would subsequently render the lot of the Jews so hard and so precarious. He notes that the Roman Empire in pagan times knew no "state anti-Semitism," despite the frequency and violence of Jewish insurrections, and that the attention of contemporaries, especially that of the intellectuals, in fact oscillated between aversion to Jewish "exclusiveness" and attraction to the monotheistic religion whose proof was furnished by the success of Jewish proselytism. It was not, in fact, until the beginning of the third century that the thesis of the divine punishment of the Jews, which was to become a basis of anti-Semitism proper, was coherently formulated.

Poliakov draws an instructive comparison between the lot of Jews living under Christendom and those who lived under Islam. He shows how the Crusades were to add a new popular venom to the original theological variety of the contagion and how the favorable status of the Jews in the Carolingian Empire was whittled away. He explores how the calamities and depressions of the fourteenth century added economic motives to the various religious and cultural ones; and how the Jews' own reactions to persecutions—the "collective trauma" that left an indelible stamp upon Jewish mentality—invited even greater Christian animosity.

Turning to the Jews who lived in Muslim lands, Poliakov examines the fortunes of three Jewish colonies that were destined, each in its own way, to play leading roles over the centuries, namely, the Jews of Mesopotamia, of North Africa, and of Spain. He quotes from the Qur'an to show that Islam proclaimed both freedom of conscience and the inalienable right of the People of the Book (the Jews and the Christians) to worship the Eternal in their own (admittedly imperfect) fashions. What, then, about the Qur'anic injunction "Kill the infidels wherever you find them; take them, lay siege to them"—that is, the holy war, the *jihad?* In Poliakov's view (1975, vol. 2: 23–24): "Certainly that too is in the Koran; but these imprecations and this violence were expressly reserved for the polytheists, for the Arab idolaters who refused to accept the theocratic order instituted by the Prophet for his people . . . Muhammad was merciless towards these wrongdoers whose opposition endangered his work." For the rest, "Islam is a religion of tolerance above all."

Further enlarging on this theme, Poliakov writes: "Nothing could be farther from the truth than the traditional conventions that depict Islam as shattering all resistance by fire and steel. On the whole, it is a religion to the measure of man, taking his limits and weaknesses into account." He quotes with approval the judgment of a great Orientalist, Snouk Hurgronje: "There is in Islam something interreligious," and he concludes with this observation: "The gentle precepts of Christ preside at the birth of the most combative, the most intransigent civilization that human history has ever known, while the warlike teachings of Muhammad gave rise to a more open and more reconciliatory society. For it is true, once again, that where too much is demanded of man, he is subjected to astonishing temptations, and that he who tries too hard to play the angel, plays the beast" (ibid.: 24–25).

This, however, is all in the realm of theory. Touching on practice, Poliakov observes that the theology of Islam was developed chiefly in Baghdad, "that is, in that Mesopotamia which for centuries was the fortress of Jewish tradition." Jews who had converted to Islam helped determine the form and methods of that faith, and in addition to the obvious similarities in construction between the Talmud and the Hadith, the religious folklore of the first centuries of Islam was abundantly fed by Jewish sources. Those legends, known in the Qur'an under the significant title of *Israiliyyat,* have remained popular to this day. From this and a wealth of other sources, Poliakov draws the following conclusion concerning relations between Judaism and Islam and how they differed from those prevailing between Jews and Christians in the same period of history. "In addition to affinities of language and culture . . . the religious teaching itself of Islam made cohabitation with the Jews easy to the point where it was hard to avoid the conclusion that there was nothing incompatible between the two religions and that one could belong to both at the same time" (Poliakov 1975, vol. 2: 27).

Again, writing about the status of the non-Muslim minorities—the "Protected People" or *dhimmi*s (*Encyclopedia of Islam:* 229–30)—during the "classical centuries" of the Middle Ages, the distinguished Islamic historian Claude Cahen compared their treatment to the experience of the Jews in medieval Christendom. "There is nothing in medieval Islam which could specifically be called anti-Semitism," he wrote, adding: "Objectivity requires us to attempt a *comparison* between Christian and Muslim intolerance, which have partial resemblances and partial differences. Islam has, in spite of many upsets, shown more toleration than Europe toward the Jews who remained in Muslim lands" (quoted in Cohen 1994: xvii).

Jewish historians likewise have often noted certain comparative facts. As Haim Hillel Ben-Sasson (quoted in Cohen 1994: 36) observes: "The legal and security situation of the Jews in the Muslim countries was generally better than in Christendom, because in the former Jews were not the sole 'infidels,' since in comparison to the Christians, Jews were less dangerous and more loyal to the Muslim regime. In addition, the rapidity and territorial scope of the Muslim conquests brought with it a reduction in persecution and a greater possibility for the survival of members of other faiths in their lands."

Muslim-Arab writers and historians writing on this subject usually also insist on drawing a comparison between the attitudes of Islam and attitudes of Christianity toward the Jews. To cite only one example, the Egyptian Islamic scholar Abdul Fattah 'Ashoor, in a paper read at the Fourth Conference of the Academy of Islamic Research at al-Azhar University in 1968, observes (quoted in Cohen 1994: 7–8):

> It may be sufficiently evident that Jews throughout history received no better or kinder treatment than that of Muslims. The egoism and greed of Jews subjected them to persecution by the Romans in early times and by various peoples of Christian Europe in the Middle Ages. They found in Muslims—*as Jewish writers themselves admit*—tolerant and merciful brothers who regarded them as fellow believers and did not allow religious differences [to] affect their treatment or attitude toward them. Spain provides a clear example of the great difference in the treatment of Jews by Muslims and Christians.

To sum up, it may safely be said that Islam's attitude to Jews and Judaism never produced anything like the strongly felt hatred and the ingrained venom that characterized the pronouncements of the Christian churches. For Islam, being Jewish or Christian was a forgivable sort of perversity rather than an offense. The People of the Book, *Ahl al-Kitab,* were not regarded by Muslims as nonbelievers, since they all shared belief in one God. But Christians and Jews were not regarded as true believers, either, because they failed to acknowledge the mission of Muhammad and did not accept the Qur'an as divine revelation. Consequently, these Ahl al-Kitab, while allowed to live in the Islamic state unmolested, were granted this privilege on condition that they pay a poll tax *(jizya)* and accept the status defined in treaties and charters as that of dhimmi. However, as a protected minority, the dhimmis were exempted from payment of *zakat,* the tax imposed on Muslims as one of Islam's five precepts or "pillars." In this way, the jizya may be seen not as a levy or penalty for religious nonconformance but as a kind of substitute for zakat. No less significant is the fact that the dhimmis were also supposed to pay this special poll tax as a levy on their exemption from military service in the wars of the Muslims.

It is important to note that in principle, Muhammad did not consider the Arabian Jews a nation or community *(umma)* separate from their Muslim neighbors. In the famous Treaty of Medina—signed before the heightening of tension between Muhammad and the Jews caused by their refusal to accept his mission, and concluded circa 625 with the tribes of 'Aws and Khazraj and to which the Jews adhered as a party—it was stipulated that the various Jewish tribes "form a nation *(umma)* with the believers." They were to have their own religion and the Muslims their own religion. This particular provision in the Treaty of Medina is of special historical and constitutional significance, rendering that document much more than a mere treaty. Majid Khadduri (1962: 209–10) calls it "a constitution for the Islamic state in its embryonic stage." In accordance with its provisions, a kind of confederation was established between the Arab and Jewish tribes, with the state of Medina taking the leading and prominent position. This, Khadduri adds, was achieved through the provision that, while each Jewish tribe constituted "a nation with the believers," the "Jewish tribes as a whole were not seen as forming a nation by themselves."

Interesting in this connection is that as far as Palestine is concerned, the right of Jews to return to live in this small area of land was accepted by all the successive Muslim rulers from the Muslim conquest right to the end of the nineteenth century, when Zionist settlement there became entangled in European *Weltpolitik*. Gibb and Bowen relate how, when the Jews of Europe "learned of the paradisiacal life awaiting them in Turkey" and many of them set out for (Ottoman) Palestine, it was not the Muslims who objected but the Franciscans of Jerusalem, "who talked the Pope into forbidding the Venetians to carry Jewish passengers to the Holy Land." This was not the first time Jerusalem Christians tried to prevail on Muslim rulers to ban Jews from living in the city. A similar attempt was made first when the second caliph, Omar, entered Jerusalem at the time of its conquest by the Muslim army in the seventh century, and again when Salah al-Din drove out the Crusaders in the twelfth century. On both of these occasions, the Christian patriarch of the city tried to persuade the Muslim conquerors to prevent Jews from living in or, as in the latter case, returning to Jerusalem after they had been expelled from it by the Christians. Both Omar and Salah al-Din refused to heed their pleas (Gibb and Bowen 1957: 225).

In conclusion, a word of caution is advised. For if such was roughly the record of Arabic Islam in its dealings with Jews and Judaism, it must be pointed out that the picture has not been uniformly so rosy, and that instances of religious intolerance toward and discriminatory treatment of Jews under Islam are by no means difficult to come by. This point is of special relevance at a time in which, following a reawakening of interest in the history of Arab-Jewish relations among Jewish writers and intellectuals, certain interested circles have been trying to counter talk of a Judaeo-Arabic tradition or symbiosis by digging up scattered bits of evidence to show that Islam is essentially intolerant, that Muhammad himself was responsible for expelling and exterminating those Arabian Jews who refused to embrace the new faith, and that the Muslims' contempt for Jews was even greater and more deep-rooted than that manifested by the Christians.

Significantly, the contrast between Christian enmity and Muslim tolerance toward the Jews is nowhere more emphasized than in the writings of Jews, especially from the time of their expulsion from Spain in 1492. After the expulsion, Ottoman Muslim Turkey was to become a haven for the Jews, not only those from Spain but many who were to flee from Christian persecution in Central and Eastern Europe. This was reflected in the writing of Jewish historians. Heinrich Graetz, the prominent nineteenth-century Jewish historian, stresses this point in his *History of the Jews* (quoted in Cohen 1994: 3–4):

> Wearied with contemplating the miserable plight of the Jews in their ancient home and in the countries of Europe, and fatigued by the constant sight of fanatical oppression in Christendom, the eyes of the observer rest with gladness upon their situation in the Arabian Peninsula. Here the sons of Judah were free to raise their heads, and did not need to look about them with fear and humiliation, lest the ecclesiastical wrath be discharged upon them, or the secular power overwhelm them. Here they were not shut out from the paths of honor, nor excluded from the privileges of state, but, untrammeled, were allowed to develop their powers in the midst of a free, simple and talented people, to show their manly courage, to compete for the gifts of fame, and with practiced hand to measure swords with their antagonists.

Citing Graetz and a number of other Jewish historians, Mark R. Cohen (1994) writes that, in its nineteenth-century context, "the myth of the interfaith utopia" was used as an attempt "to achieve an important political end, to challenge supposedly liberal Christian Europe to make good on its promise of political equality and unfettered professional and cultural opportunities for Jews." First, he adds, if medieval Muslims could have so tolerated the Jews that a Samuel ibn Nagrela (d. 1056) could rise to the vizierate of the Spanish Muslim state of Granada, or a Maimonides to a respected position among Muslim intellectuals, "could not modern Europeans grant Jews the rights and privileges promised them in the aftermath of the French Revolution?" Second, "did not the Christian world owe this to the Jews, to compensate for its history of cruelty toward the Jews?" Third, "just as Jews in Spain (and elsewhere in the Muslim world) benefiting from liberal treatment, had benefited Arab society, so would the Jews of modern Europe, if treated with equality, contribute to European civilization" (Cohen 1994: 4–5).

The Cultural Heritage

Although encounters and intercultural influences between Jews and Arabs date back to pre-Islamic times, it was during the Middle Ages that the meeting between Jews and Muslim Arabs produced the most interesting, fruitful, and durable results. In Spain, where they had lived for centuries, the lot of the Jews had been unhappy; the Christian Visigothic kings were harsh and merciless. When the Muslims came to the Iberian Peninsula early in the eighth century, they brought the Jews of Spain not only relief from their oppressors but, in the words of Isidore Epstein (1959: 181), "also encouraged among them a culture which in richness and depth is comparable to the best produced by any people at any time."

The majority of the Jewish people at that time came under Arab rule, and now commenced that long and brilliant period of Arab-Jewish symbiosis, described as the most flourishing in Jewish history, and whose significance for the Jews and for Judaism to this day cannot be exaggerated. In his *Judaism and Islam* the Cambridge historian and Orientalist Erwin Rosenthal (1961: ix) notes, "The Talmudic age apart, there is perhaps no more formative or positive period in our long and chequered history than that under the empire of Islam from the Mediterranean to the Indian Ocean."

During the four centuries in which they ruled Spain, the cultural, artistic, and commercial activities of the Arab invaders turned the country into by far the most enlightened in Europe. Jewish and general history books speak with awe about Cordova, the capital of the Umayyad caliphs, which became a magnificent seat of culture, with lakes and parks, glittering palaces and mosques.

But the splendor was not all material. The Court attracted and lavishly patronized poets and philosophers, men of letters and scientists. The Jews responded wholeheartedly, throwing themselves and their talents eagerly into the general culture and drawing from it inspiration to revive their own language and culture. Thus the flickering light of Jewish culture in the East was rekindled in the West; and when the great Babylonian center finally crumbled, Jewish cultural hegemony passed on to the Jews of Muslim Spain, to be maintained and nurtured by them for half a millennium.

Eliyahu Ashtor, author of the three-volume history *The Jews of Moslem Spain*, notes that in the eleventh century, scholars who were steeped in Jewish lore and familiar with all areas of Jewish literature "lived in every Jewish community on the Iberian Peninsula." Throughout the entire first half of that century, he adds, "the leaders and rabbis of the Spanish Jewish communities maintained close contacts with the Near Eastern academies—particularly with the eminent heads of the Talmud schools in Iraq," sending contributions to them and seeking guidance from them in legal and religious matters. During the second half of the eleventh century, when the level of scholarship at the Babylonian academies began to show clear signs of decline, Jewish scholars in Muslim Spain were already attaining high degrees of learning (Ashtor 1973: 3–6).

Works produced by Jewish writers in Muslim Spain at this stage, Ashtor states, demonstrate to what a large degree the Jewish intellectuals were rooted in Arabic culture. "The profound influence of Arabic literature," he adds, "is conspicuous in the ennobled type of Jew found in many of their works who is both loyal to the heritage of his forebears and permeated with the general culture" (Ashtor 1973: 7).

In fields other than literature, the degree of interaction and mutual influence was even greater. "Within the area of the exact sciences, the contact between Jewish and Arabic scholars developed into collaboration." Treatises by Jewish scholars on the natural sciences all derived from the classical works of the Arabs. "The calculation of the 'cycles' in the Jewish calendar drawn by Hasan b. Mar Hasan, the Jewish astronomer from Cordova, was made in accordance with the system of the renowned Arab astronomer al-Battani. In the eleventh century quite a number of Jewish intellectuals from Spain were astronomers, and all of them depended upon the tables and studies of the Arabs" (Ashtor 1973: 7).

Another example of interaction in the cultural sphere cited by Ashtor is that of the study of Hebrew grammar, in which Jewish intellectuals in Muslim Spain showed great interest: "Just as the Arabs ascribed much importance to a perfect knowledge of their language, including all its rules and principles, and just as they would discuss its problems at their gatherings, so did the Jewish intellectuals concern themselves seriously with the structure of the language of the Bible" (Ashtor 1973: 11–12). They discussed questions of Hebrew grammar and philological interpretations of biblical verses, and any innovations that some Arab philologist brought forth prompted them to do the same for their own language.

Jewish intellectuals interested in questions of philosophy and who devoted themselves to philosophical meditation also abounded in the communities of eleventh-century Spain. "They too followed in the footsteps of the

Arabs—poring over books available to Arab philosophers and discussing the problems that engaged them." According to one tradition cited by Ashtor, the prominent Jewish leader and benefactor Samuel the Nagid, who was also a poet, addressed an inquiry to the Gaon rabbi Hai of Iraq as to whether it was permissible and worthwhile to engage in philosophy. According to this story, the rabbi's response was in the negative. Whether this story is authentic or only apocryphal, Ashtor asserts that many of the Jewish intellectuals in the cities of Spain in that period were influenced by philosophical views, and this provoked the wrath of the fundamentalists. "Some of these intellectuals freely professed religious scepticism," Ashtor reports, "whereas others attempted to strike a compromise between the conclusions of the philosophers and religious belief, which is based on belief in divine revelation." Here, too, the influence of their Arab neighbors and fellow intellectuals was evident.

As Ashtor writes in a reference to this group of Jewish intellectuals and philosophy students, whose members sought to reconcile reason and faith: "It was the ideal of the latter group to reconcile Arabo-Spanish science with Judaism, by basing Jewish thought on the systems of the philosophers and the cultural creations of the Jews on the principles of Arabic writers and scholars. In short, they sought to develop a Jewish culture that would dovetail with the great syncretic Arabic culture" (Ashtor 1973: 11–12). In carrying over ideas, concepts, and points of view from the world of Arabic thought to Jewish literature, these intellectuals "succeeded for the most part in choosing those conceptual elements that harmonized with the Jewish spirit—consequently retaining their spiritual identity and producing works of distinction" (ibid.).

The influence of Arab culture on the intellectual life of the Jews in Muslim Spain expressed itself primarily in the development of Hebrew poetry, whose level "mounted ever higher from one generation to another until it scaled the very heights of artistic creativity." As it was for the Arabs, so too did poetry become for the Jews the most beautiful means of expression in all things relating to etiquette and personal sentiments. "Even a rabbinical scholar who wrote his colleague a letter would append some verse composed by him or would intersperse rhymes throughout the letter." Apart from their aesthetic and sentimental value, the poems composed by the Jews of Muslim Spain also filled an important role in the social consciousness of the upper strata of the Jewish society, as "they demonstrated that Hebrew was no less eminent than other languages and that it could also be employed to express the sentiments and desires of the people of that era" (Ashtor 1973: 13–14).

Nor did this amalgamation or symbiosis carry with it any danger of what today we call assimilation. The Jews of Muslim Spain, with the help of

Jewish scholars hailing from the famous Iraqi academies, adopted the language of the Muslim conqueror and with it, inevitably, many of his patterns of thought and ideas. Nevertheless, as Rosenthal (1961: xi) points out, "Despite all assimilation to Muslim ways of thought, the Jews under Islam maintained, even enriched, their distinctive character as Jews with a vigour and determination hitherto unknown."

In this unprecedentedly congenial environment, the Jews of Muslim Spain, like the Babylonian Jews before them, were able to embark on a great enterprise, namely, to define and describe Judaism with a clarity and force unknown in the entire history of the Jewish people. As Rosenthal states: "The basic tenets of Judaism, its formative concepts and ideas, were combined into a system intended to sustain the Jews, to demonstrate their distinctiveness, to secure survival and instill hope and the expectancy of redemption. The form of this exposition was largely borrowed from Muslim theology and religious philosophy. Even the newly developing codification of the *Halakhah* and the *Responsa* literature of the Geonim owe their form to Muslim patterns."[2]

The amalgamation, symbiosis, collaboration, and interaction discussed above were by no means confined to intellectual and literary pursuits. Quoting contemporary sources, Ashtor relates that the Jews of Cordova actively participated in the long struggle for dominance between the ruling factions of Muslims, which took place in the middle of the eleventh century: "During that period, the Jews in the Spanish states believed that they had a share in Spain's destiny. They did not regard themselves as wayfarers or aliens and therefore took part in all the conflicts and intrigues among the rulers and the various factions. In the eleventh century the Jewish community of Cordova was one of the most important in Andalusia. The Jews were deeply and actively involved in the affairs of the city, as were their brethren in other cities of Muslim Spain" (Ashtor 1972, vol. 3: 17).

How mutual were these influences? What, for one, did Muslim theologians and historians know about the Old Testament—besides, that is, the rather fragmentary accounts given in the Qur'an? In other words, did these Muslim scholars engage in what has come to be known as Bible criticism? In its broadest sense, biblical criticism as we know it today is the application to the books and texts of the Jewish Bible of certain techniques generally used in the examination of many kinds of literary writings, in an attempt to establish such aspects as their original wording, the manner and date of their composition, their sources, authorship, and revisions of their texts.

However, while this endeavor in all its forms is generally associated with the names of nineteenth-century Christian students of the Old Testament, mainly Wellhausen and Graf, in her book *Intertwined Worlds: Medieval Islam and Bible Criticism,* Lazarus-Yafe (1992: xi) shows that Muslim medieval authors developed "a kind of Bible criticism very close in nature and detail both to earlier pre-Islamic Bible criticism and to the beginnings of later scholarly European Bible criticism." She also shows how these Muslim writings on the Bible, and the use their authors made of biblical texts, may well have influenced early Western critical Bible studies.

The attitude of Muslim authors to the Old Testament and to its study differed markedly from that of their Christian counterparts. Whereas medieval Christian authors "concentrated mainly on the typological interpretation of the commonly shared divine text of the Bible," their Muslim contemporaries "put the Biblical text itself, and its ways of transmission, to polemical scrutiny, believing that it had been falsified or tampered with." It was thus that an "almost scholarly" Muslim critical study of the Old Testament, as well as of the New Testament, came about.

In these "almost scholarly" critical studies, Muslim authors developed arguments in four somewhat contradictory and overlapping areas: falsification *(tahrif)*, abrogation *(naskh)*, lack of reliable transmission *(tawatur)*, and Bible exegesis *(tafsir)*. Only three of these four arguments are based directly on charges made in the Qur'an, while the one that developed in the most scholarly fashion, the lack of *tawatur,* has no clear Qur'anic basis. This is not to say that the three Qur'an-based arguments were not enlarged upon and elaborated by later Muslim authors. They were, especially by the Spaniard Ibn Hazm (d. 1064) and the Jewish convert to Islam Samau'al al-Maghribi (d. 1175) (Lazarus-Yafe 1992: 19).

Two more points made by Lazarus-Yafe about Muslim biblical exegesis are worth mentioning here. Like the Christians before them, and most probably under the influence of Christian converts, Muslim polemicists against the Bible make use of the text as a prophecy of the coming of Muhammad and the rise of Islam. However, this never became as important to Islam as the typological and allegorical interpretation of the Old Testament was for Christians. Another problem that medieval Muslim polemicists and interpreters encountered, and which has inevitably made the study of Muslim Bible criticism especially difficult, is the unavailability of or the lack of access to any kind of authoritative Arabic translation of the texts. This was why, rather than perusing and comparing different translations of the Bible, Muslim authors of the time consulted Jews and Christians orally "and received different ad hoc translations of specific verses, even from the same person" (Lazarus-Yafe 1992: 47–48).

The Case of Judaeo-Arabic

In the sphere of language, the influence of Arabic on Hebrew and the phenomenon known as Judaeo-Arabic are of central interest. Although no Jewish literary or philosophical works in Arabic written prior to the ninth century have been preserved, it is almost certain that many urban Jewish populations spoke Arabic as far back as the seventh century, that is, as soon as they came under Islam's rule following the great Arab conquests. By the tenth and eleventh centuries, Arabic became the language of Jewish writers throughout the Muslim-Arab empire, extending from Spain to Iraq and the Arabian Peninsula. In his introduction to the translation of Bahya ibn Paquda's *Duties of the Heart,* Judah ibn Tibbon, the doyen of Hebrew translators from Arabic, asserts that most of the Geonim under Islam in Babylonia, Palestine, and Persia spoke Arabic. "Most of the commentaries they wrote on the Bible, the Mishnah and the Talmud," he reports, "they wrote in Arabic, as they did with other works, as well as with their *responsa,* for all the people understood the language."[3]

This readiness on the part of the Jews under Arabic Islam to adopt Arabic as the language of their prose writings has led many modern scholars to wonder how it came about that Hebrew and Aramaic were so rapidly superseded by Arabic even in works dealing with the most sacred matters of Judaism—why, for example, Maimonides wrote most of his theological works in Arabic: *Sefer Ha-Mitzvot* (The book of prescriptions), *Hakdamot la-Mishnah* (Introductions to the Mishnah), and *Shemonah Perakim* (Eight chapters), among others. Joshua Blau (1965) concludes that in addition to the author's desire to reach the widest possible audience, there were two factors at work here (as Abraham Halkin has also demonstrated, 1956, 1963): the inadequacy of Hebrew as a vehicle for religio-philosophical and other, scientific writings, and the fact that Arabic was considered by the Jews to be their genuine and natural language and consequently nothing seemed to them to be more natural and effortless than to use it as the language of their religious and other writings.

What sort of language was Judaeo-Arabic and where did it originate? There are no conclusive data as to the origins of Judaeo-Arabic literature. According to both Zunz and Steinschneider, Judaeo-Arabic literature originated in Babylonia, spread to Palestine and Syria, and eventually encompassed the other countries of the Arab-Muslim empire, such as Egypt, North Africa, and Spain. In his *The Emergence and Linguistic Background of Judeo-Arabic,* Joshua Blau traces the origins and characteristics of "Middle Arabic," which he maintains is the linguistic result of the great Arab conquests of the seventh century. This Middle Arabic, he suggests, constitutes the missing link between classical and modern Arabic dialects. Yet he himself admits that "were it not for extra-linguistic considerations, we might forgo the term 'Middle Arabic' and speak only of modern Arabic, perhaps designating the period after the Arab conquests as the older epoch of modern Arabic."

Blau asserts, nevertheless, that Middle Arabic and modern Arabic have quite different cultural significance: "Middle Arabic is usually transmitted in literary texts, mingled, as a rule, with classical elements and often very important culturally, whereas modern Arabic, as a rule culturally inferior, has not produced literature in the true sense of the word." Blau here seems to be speaking of modern Arabic vernaculars as contrasted with written Middle Arabic. Yet there is a written modern Arabic that has produced "literature in the true sense of the word," whether culturally "important" or "inferior" (Blau 1965: 3–4).

The truth, however, is that written modern Arabic is hardly distinguishable from written Middle Arabic in any significant sense, while both still attest to a remarkable continuity with classical Arabic. This continuity is, of course, attributable almost solely to the enduring influence of the Qur'an. Such continuity is not encountered in any other language spoken today, with the significant exception of biblical Hebrew, which has also been preserved almost intact, thanks to its being the language of the Jewish Scriptures.

This point has considerable bearing on the nature and style of Judaeo-Arabic. While the Jewish-Arabic authors originally aimed at writing in classical Arabic, "It was deficiency in mastering classical Arabic that gave rise to a Judeo-Arabic literature teeming with Middle Arabic elements," Blau asserts. However, this does not seem to be borne out by the style and syntax of Judaeo-Arabic as preserved in the works of Jewish-Arabic authors from Saadia Gaon (892–942) to Maimonides. These works were written neither in classical nor in Middle Arabic, but simply in the Arabic that all Arabic-writing authors used at the time, whether Muslim or non-Muslim.

However, that does not imply that a specific Judaeo-Arabic language did not exist. What it suggests is that we must look for that language's distinguishing characteristics mainly outside the purely linguistic sphere. In the course of his analysis, Blau himself contends that three characteristics of the Middle Arabic of the Jews entitle us to speak of a separate Judaeo-Arabic language clearly distinct from all other forms of Middle Arabic. These are the Jewish flavor of the topics dealt with; the almost universal presence of Hebrew elements; and the employment of the Hebrew script. In addition, there are indications that the writers of Judaeo-Arabic themselves felt that they were writing in a separate language. Blau suggests that although it probably originated in the writers' inability to master classical Arabic and its complex grammar, in the course of time Judaeo-Arabic came to be thought of as a literary language in its own right, "employed even by authors who were themselves competent to some degree in classical Arabic." Thus we come to the conclusion that even though Judaeo-Arabic was not in itself very different from the Middle Arabic of Muslims and Christians, "the writings of Jewish authors addressing a Jewish audience must be accorded the status of a language"(Blau 1965: 49).

To sum up, the Arabic that the Jews of the Muslim-Arab empire in the Middle Ages wrote and used in all their varied intellectual pursuits was the same Middle Arabic employed by their Muslim and Christian colleagues. It was, as Goitein (1965: 132) points out, "Arabic as developed in the post-classical period." The deviations from the ancient models of Arabic style found in Judaeo-Arabic literature were thus "not due to a specific Jewish idiom, but to the stage of development reached in the latter Middle Ages, a change more conspicuous in Jewish literature because the Jewish writers who used Hebrew characters felt themselves less bound by the classical models than the Muslims."

It is difficult to establish precisely when Arabic became the language of the majority of the Jewish people then living in the various lands of the Muslim-Arab empire. According to Goitein, the process was completed by the year 1000, but this did not affect the status of Hebrew as a second and literary language. As a matter of fact, the most remarkable aspect of the Jews' adoption of Arabic and their integration into Muslim-Arabic culture was that the almost universal use of Arabic not only did not affect the position of Hebrew adversely, but Arabic actually served to revive and enrich Hebrew and, to a considerable extent, to make it what it is today. The Jewish-Arab symbiosis in its linguistic aspect led to an unprecedented revival of the Hebrew language in all branches of linguistic-philological study.

The implications of the acquisition by Jews of Arabic as the language of their writings in almost all fields of intellectual and literary activity were far reaching and its impact was lasting. Adopting Arabic at a time when the Arabs had already developed a national literature and a comprehensive religious terminology, it was inevitable that the Jews should acquire, together with the language, Arab ways of thinking and Arabic literary forms, and even Muslim religious notions. In the words of Goitein (1965: 134–35): "Arabic was used by Jews for all kinds of literary activities, not only for scientific and other secular purposes but for expounding and translating the Bible or the Mishnah, for theological and philosophical treatises, for discussing Jewish law and ritual, and also for the study of Hebrew grammar and lexicography," all of which was to influence their habits of thought and world outlook profoundly.

In connection with this last field of intellectual endeavor, it is worth pointing to one particularly curious aspect of Jewish cultural history. Prior to their encounter with Muslim-Arab culture, the Jews somewhat inexplicably failed to develop a system of Hebrew grammar and lexicography, even when conditions for such a creative effort seemed ideal—such as in the time of the Mishnah, when the nucleus of the Jewish people was still firmly rooted in its native soil. "Why," Goitein (1965: 136) asks, "did the Jews wait for the Arabs to give them the impetus to study their own language," especially considering the Jews' innate proficiency in this field and the fine work subsequently done by medieval Jewish philologists? A large part of the explanation resides in the fact of the encounter with the Arabs itself. That encounter, with a people whose devotion to their language is proverbial, "directed the Jewish mind to a field of activity for which, as it was subsequently proved, it was particularly gifted, and which bore its mature first fruits to the benefit of the national language of the Jewish people itself." As Rosenthal (1961: 73) puts it, "Without the existence of a well-developed science of the Arabic language which largely arose in connection with the exegesis of the Koran, Hebrew linguistics could hardly have been cultivated." In terminology and arrangement, in the treatment of problems, and in the solution of difficulties, he points out, "the Jews were dependent on Arab grammarians."

It is generally assumed that this revival of the Hebrew language started with the translation of the Jewish Bible into Arabic. Originally, according to Goitein, the reason for this activity "was not so much that Hebrew was no longer understood, but an endeavour to provide by these translations—which had the character of explanatory free renderings—an authoritative interpretation of the text, in particular in theological matters." This is why the most famous of the classical translations, which superseded all the others in popular usage, that of Saadia Gaon, was called by him *Tafsir* (Commentary). The study of the Jewish Bible also led to the study of its language in general: "Writing in Arabic and using Arabic methods and terminology, Jewish scholars assiduously explored and described the Hebrew of the Bible and soon also that of the Mishnah or post-biblical Hebrew. For the first time Hebrew pronunciation, grammar, and vocabulary were scientifically treated and, so to speak, brought under control. Thus Hebrew became a disciplined and well-organized means of expression under the influence of Arabic" (Rosenthal 1961: 73).

There is no doubt that this revival of Hebrew under the influence of Arabic, and during the peak of the hegemony of Arabic, can be attributed to the obvious affinity between the two languages. As Goitein points out, it was then a commonplace among both Jewish and Arab scholars that Arabic, Hebrew, and Aramaic were basically one and the same language. There were, to be sure, many Jews who felt that it was no honor for Hebrew to be treated as part of the same family as Arabic and Aramaic. But the more sober-minded scholars were in agreement on this point. Maimonides believed unqualifiedly that Arabic "is certainly Hebrew somewhat corrupted," as he wrote in a letter to his translator, Samuel ibn Tibbon. Elsewhere he asserts that for anyone who knows both languages, Hebrew and Arabic "are undoubtedly one language, while Aramaic is somewhat akin to them." In *The Book of the Kuzari*, (II:68), Judah Halevi also speaks of Hebrew, Arabic, and Aramaic as related and similar languages. He suggests that Abraham's mother tongue was Aramaic, adding however that Abraham knew Hebrew as a sacred tongue (Halkin 1963: 238–39; Halevi, quoted in Halkin, 239).

It was perhaps in the field of translation that Hebrew was most visibly enriched and benefited the most through its symbiotic encounter with Arabic. It has already been mentioned that Arabic was a far richer and more advanced instrument for philosophical and scientific writing than Hebrew. In an instructive introduction to his translation of Ibn Paquda's *Duties of the Heart*, Judah ibn Tibbon writes candidly and at length on the subject of Arabic and Hebrew in general, and on the problems of translating Arabic works into Hebrew in particular. Explaining why the Geonim in Babylonia and in Islamic lands wrote in Arabic, he adds:

> They did it because it was the language people understood, and also because it is an adequate and rich language for every subject and for every need, for every speaker and every author; its expression is direct, lucid and capable of saying just what is wanted much better than can be done in Hebrew, of which we possess only what has been preserved in Scripture and which is insufficient for the needs of a speaker. It is simply impossible to express the thoughts of our hearts succinctly and adequately in Hebrew, as we can in Arabic—which is adequate, elegant and available to those who know it. (quoted in Halkin 1963: 238–39)

Judah ibn Tibbon was not alone in stressing this point. In their respective Hebrew translations of Maimonides's *Guide for the Perplexed*, both Samuel ibn Tibbon and Judah al-Harizi supply glossaries of "foreign words" used in their Hebrew renderings, the former explaining that he was compelled to do so because Hebrew was limited and because works on demonstrated sciences do not exist among the Jews, "so those foreign words employed by peoples who possess those particular sciences are not found in our language." Even a superficial perusal of the words included in these two glossaries would suffice to show the extent to which Hebrew was enriched by the translations. Today it may sound incredible, but the glossary of "foreign words" appended by al-Harizi includes such words—now in common Hebrew usage—as *eikhut* (quality), *efshar* (possible), *amiti* (true), *dibbah* (libel), *ha-regashim* (the senses), *meyuhhad* (unique), *safeq* (doubt), *kaddur* (ball), *kefirah* (heresy), *naggar* (carpenter), and dozens of other words about which today's Hebrew reader would find nothing "foreign" whatsoever. At the conclusion of his famous commentary on the *Song of Songs,* Abraham ibn Ezra also deplores the poverty of Hebrew, drawing some consolation however from the fact that Hebrew and Arabic "are very akin to each other" (Ibn Tibbon: 57).

Some modern scholars (e.g., Halkin 1956) rightly reject the thesis that the inadequacy of Hebrew was the reason why Jewish writers and philosophers in the Middle Ages preferred Arabic. They point out that Hebrew could, and actually did, do the work of Arabic when the necessity arose, as when a work in Arabic was translated into Hebrew, either contemporaneously or shortly after the death of the author. Nevertheless, it is obvious that the extensive work of translation from Arabic into Hebrew during the Golden Age of Judaeo-Arabic culture contributed greatly toward the creation of modern Hebrew—so much so, indeed, that a whole style of Hebrew writing and syntax has come to be called after the Tibbonides, who undertook the bulk of Hebrew translation in their day (Halkin 1963: 246).

A Treasury of Jewish Thought

In the mid-1960s, a mass-circulation Israeli daily offered its readers what it called *The Treasury of Jewish Thought.* This anthology included six major works of Jewish philosophy, all written between the years 1050 and 1428 in Spain, and all but one in Arabic. Although it may be somewhat exaggerated to present these works as *the* treasury of Jewish thought, they remain the most representative body of philosophical and speculative work from a period justly considered the most fruitful and creative in Jewry's long history. The treasury included works by Solomon ibn Gabirol, Bahya ibn Paquda, Judah Halevi, Moses ibn Maimon, and Joseph Albo.[4]

Only a fleeting impression can be given here of the scope and character of these works, in order to indicate the extent of the mutual influences at work in the creation of the Judaeo-Arabic culture of the Middle Ages. As Charles Singer (1969: 186) has put it, during this period of Arab-Jewish symbiosis "it happened that certain non-Jewish schools of Arabian philosophers had strong affinities with Jewish thought, and deeply affected and were affected by Jewish thinkers.... Many Jewish philosophical works were intended not only for Jews but for the larger Arabic-speaking public, and were widely read throughout the Arabic-speaking world." With the exception of Albo's work, which was written in Hebrew, these remarks apply to all the works included in our "treasury."

A few words may be in order here about the transference of the center of Jewish learning from Iraq to Muslim-Arab Spain. The story is told that during the reign of the Umayyad caliph Abdel Rahman III in Cordova (912–961), a vessel from the East was seized by the caliph's admiral. The ship, headed for Spain, carried among others a Babylonian Jewish family of three: Moses ibn Enoch, his wife, and their young son. Fearing dishonor, the mother threw herself into the sea, while the boy and his father were taken captive and brought to Cordova, where they were ransomed by the influential Jewish community there.

Moses ibn Enoch, one of the most learned teachers at the famous Babylonian academy of Sura, had been sent on a fund-raising mission to Jewish centers in Spain and North Africa. He came to Spain at an opportune moment; the Western caliphs were eager to see their Jewish subjects become independent of the hegemony of Eastern Jewish learning and to stop sending funds to the lands of their archenemies, the Eastern caliphs. Accordingly, with the help of Hasdai ibn Shaprut, a cultured Jew who was the caliph's trusted adviser, Moses ibn Enoch was installed as the head of the Talmudical school in Cordova. With his appointment, and the help of Nunash ben Labrat, another Babylonian scholar, Jewish literature and philosophy entered a new era lasting almost five centuries. During this period, Spanish Jewish philosophers, men of letters, and grammarians produced such a rich and varied body of writing that it came to be known as the Golden Age of Jewish literature or culture. It is thus no coincidence that all the works included in the treasury of Jewish thought should have been written during this period.

In chronological order, two works by Ibn Gabirol come first among the great works of Jewish philosophy produced in Muslim Spain. *Mekor Hayyim* (*Fons Vitae* in its Latin version) was written during the first half of the eleventh century in Arabic; but, unlike subsequent works by Spanish-Jewish philosophers and men of letters of the period, it was never translated into Hebrew, though a Hebrew summary was prepared by Shem Tov Falaquera in the thirteenth century. The current Hebrew text is a translation from a Latin translation rendered about a century before Falaquera at the request of Raymond, Archbishop of Toledo, who was not aware that its author was a Jew, since by this time the author of *Mekor Hayyim* was regarded sometimes as a Muslim, sometimes a Christian, and the Christian scholastics of the thirteenth century made him their own and studied his work diligently. It was only in the middle of the nineteenth century that *Fons Vitae* (whose author's name had been corrupted into Avencebrol or Avincebron) was discovered to be the work of none other than the famous Jewish poet Solomon ibn Gabirol.

This strange circumstance is indicative of a very significant phenomenon, and will also help us understand why *Fons Vitae,* and Ibn Gabirol's philosophy in general, were so neglected by the Jews of his day. It is clear that a work that made it possible for its author to be regarded a Muslim, or even a Christian, could not have contained many indications of a Jewish background or outlook. For the fact is that *Mekor Hayyim* does not contain a single biblical verse or Talmudic saying, and nowhere in the work does its author try to reconcile his philosophical views with his religious faith, as Maimonides, for one, was to do later. The truth seems to be that Ibn Gabirol took his religious convictions so much for granted that he did not see any necessity of reconciling them with philosophy. This later led Abraham ibn Daud, author of *Emunah Ramah* (The exulted faith), to criticize Ibn Gabirol for his failure to take a Jewish attitude, accusing him of holding views that were actually dangerous to Judaism. With *Tikkun Middot Hanefesh,* however, Ibn Gabirol was far more fortunate with his Jewish colleague, though the book itself is far less important than *Mekor.* This is because *Tikkun* (whose Arabic title is *Kitab Islah al-Akhlaq*) was a popular book dealing with manners and morals and contained numerous quotations from the Bible.

Although very little is known about the life of Bahya ibn Paquda, it is fairly certain that his masterpiece, *Hovot Halevavot* (Duties of the heart), was written sometime between 1100 and 1150. Like *Mekor Hayyim,* which preceded it by half a century, it was written in Arabic, as was *Kitab al-Hidaya ila Farayidh al-Qulub*. Research has established that many passages in the book are practically identical in content and expression to similar ideas found in the works of the great Muslim philosopher and mystic Abu Hamid Muhammad al-Ghazzali (1058–1111).

The book's thesis is based on a distinction made by Muslim theologians between ceremony or observance—known as "visible wisdom" and "duties of the limbs" on the one hand—and inward intention, attitude, and feeling, known as "hidden wisdom" and "duties of the heart," on the other. This distinction is hinted at in Isaiah's recurring complaint that while the people were diligent in bringing sacrifices, celebrating the festivals, and offering prayers, their hands were full of blood (Is. 1:11–17). Ibn Paquda explains that while people are very interested in finding out and studying the precepts pertaining to bodily actions—the "visible wisdom"—and how they should be observed, they seldom inquire into the manner in which the second category of precepts—those pertaining to the "hidden wisdom" or the duties of the heart—ought to be carried out. What, he asks, are the precepts of this second division, affecting our thoughts and feelings? For instance, we may mention the precept of believing in the unity of God. Do we really know what it means and what it implies? Or, for another example, the precept of trust in God; do we fully realize what it means? Or take again the question of carrying out an action with sincerity. Do we take the trouble of analyzing what sincerity means, and have we ever tried to find out how it is possible to do a deed without any secondary insincere thoughts? When we speak of the fear of God, or the love of God, have we ever thought out what these concepts truly involve?

It is to such problems that Ibn Paquda addresses himself in his treatise, and the crowning merit of the work is that these questions are dealt with in an orderly and precise manner, so that each thought stands out with the utmost definition and clarity. The reader, after perusing the book a few times, obtains such a clear scale by which to judge his own virtue, or lack of it, and such an unmistakable idea as to where his thoughts and attitudes require improvement, that it is almost impossible to study the work without making at least some spiritual progress. Judah Halevi's *Book of the Kuzari (Kitab al-Hijja wal-Dalil fi Nasr al-Din al-Dhalil)* marks a new and novel phase in Jewish religious writing. A poet first and foremost, Halevi makes no secret of his disdain for philosophers, maintaining that Greek wisdom "has no fruits, but only flowers." His book, a classic defense of Judaism, is in the form of a dialogue between the king of the Khazars, ready to relinquish paganism, and the Jewish teacher whom he summons upon discovering that both Christian and Muslim base their appeal ultimately upon the Jewish Scriptures.

It is worth noting here that Halevi's antiphilosophical stance has much in common with that of al-Ghazzali, from whom there is no doubt that he drew his inspiration. In both Halevi and al-Ghazzali we find open skepticism in respect to the powers of human reason and a deep and personally experienced religious sense. But there is one significant difference: Halevi defended a persecuted race and a despised faith not merely against the philosophers but also against the more powerful professors of other religions.

Maimonides likewise found it necessary to defend Judaism against the assaults of rational philosophy, and his book *Guide for the Perplexed (Dalalat al-Ha'irin* in Arabic, *Moreh Ha-nevukhim* in Hebrew) stands out as the highest monument to this defense. However, all resemblance between Halevi and Moses ben Maimon ends there. For while in the case of Halevi it was the Jew in him who was to be defended against the philosopher without, in Maimonides's case it was the Jew in him who was to be defended against the philosopher within.

A confirmed Aristotelian, Maimonides undertook to find and demonstrate a reason for every precept and commandment of the Law (Torah). He showed he was an opponent of all mysticism, sentimentality, and arbitrariness. For Maimonides, reason is paramount. The intellect determines the will, and not even God's will may be arbitrary. There is a cause for everything that God wills. We may not in every case succeed in finding a reason, where God himself did not choose to tell us; but a reason there always is, and the endeavor on our part to discover it should be commended rather than condemned. In the theological system Maimonides so superbly develops in the *Guide,* the age-old process of welding Hellenic wisdom and the Judaic faith—a process begun in Alexandria with Philo, continued in Baghdad by Saadia Gaon, and maintained in Toledo by Abraham ibn Daud—was completed.

Joseph Albo's *Sefer Ha 'Ikkarim* (The book of roots) is little more than a review of the problems that occupied his predecessors, especially Maimonides, from whose writings he benefited greatly. It must be added, however, that philosophy as such was not Albo's forte, nor was it his main interest. It was religion as such that he investigated. His work, completed in 1428, distinguishes between fundamental dogmas (roots) without which Judaism is unthinkable; derivative beliefs (secondary roots) that follow from fundamental dogmas and a denial of which involves a denial of that in which they are rooted; and, lastly, beliefs that, though obligatory upon the Jews, are merely subsidiary (branches).

It is interesting that among these branches, Albo includes a belief in the Messiah, claiming that it is not central in Judaism. This weakening of emphasis upon the messianic doctrine, a weakening of which we find no trace in the work of Maimonides, was a concession to Christianity—a concession, it will be noted, the like of which no Jewish thinker under Islam felt called upon to make or contemplate. Something was taking place in Judaism: for the first time, the Jews were being called upon not merely to justify but to underplay and even revise some aspects of their faith. Judaism's Dark Ages were at hand.

A Literary Transformation

Beginning from the first decades of the ninth century, the bulk of the literary output produced by Jews in the extensive Muslim-Arab empire, including works on religion and ritual, were written in Arabic. But there was one significant exception: their poetry was generally composed in Hebrew. However, as Goitein has so keenly put it, "The most perfect expression of Jewish-Arab symbiosis is not found in the Arabic literature of the Jews, but in the Hebrew poetry created in Muslim countries, particularly in Spain." This applies especially to religious poetry, which Goitein calls "our most precious heritage from Hebrew-Arab Spain" (Goitein 1965: 131–32).

The reasons why Jewish verse, unlike prose, was written in Hebrew are difficult to establish. Abraham Halkin maintains that the tradition established by liturgy, beginning with the Palestinian initiators who never thought of introducing a foreign language into the divine services, undoubtedly played its part in influencing later poets to continue in Hebrew even for their secular compositions. There is, however, another reason, that Halkin (1956: 230) considers more immediate:

> Poetry among the Arabs served the purpose of displaying the beauties of their language, and they strove to emulate one another in elegance of style and extravagance of metaphor. The finest example of elegance of style was believed by them ... to exist in the Koran. At this, the Jews balked. Their pride in their own language and in their own Bible not only restrained them from displaying the beauties of Arabic and its master-work (the Koran) but also impelled them to do for Hebrew as their neighbors did for their tongue.

As an illustration of this sentiment, Halkin (1956: 232) cites the interesting case of Judah al-Harizi and his motives for writing his famous work *Tahkemoni*. In his introduction, al-Harizi writes:

> When I saw the work of al-Hariri [an Arab poet from Basra, Iraq, who excelled in a special type of poetic composition known as *maqama*, which al-Harizi emulated in *Tahkemoni*, Nissim Rejwan], the heavens of my joy were rolled together and the rivulets of my mourning flowed, because every nation is concerned for its speech and avoids sinning against its tongue, whereas our tongue, which was a delight to every eye, is considered a brother of Cain ... Therefore, I compiled this book in order to display the force of the sacred tongue to the holy people.

In his introduction, al-Harizi further informs us that initially he had translated al-Hariri's *maqamat* into Hebrew, but then he realized that he had "acted foolishly and sinfully by forsaking our book of eloquence and undertaking to translate a book belonging to others." Hence, we are told, he applied himself to the task of creating a similar composition in Hebrew. Incidentally, Goitein considers al-Harizi's rendering of al-Hariri's maqamat into Hebrew to be "the greatest linguistic feat ever performed [in Hebrew]" (Halkin 1956: 232).

Whether or not al-Harizi's case is typical of the other Judaeo-Arab poets of his time, the influence of Arabic language and literature on medieval

Hebrew poetry remains decisive. True, one can read and respond to the work of such poets as Samuel Hanagid, Solomon ibn Gabirol, Moses ibn Ezra, and Judah Halevi without knowing anything about the Arabic language; but it is precisely because Arabic influences on these poets and their work is so subtle, and their absorption in Arab-Muslim culture so complete, that these influences appear all the more significant and vital.

Yet there were apparent as well as subtle influences. Of the former, the most significant was the introduction into Hebrew poetry of nonreligious themes. Jewish literature and thought before the Islamic age were, almost without exception, an uninterrupted flow of sacred writings and their poetic interpretation. There was no place in them for the profane and the secular. Contact with the culture of Arabic Islam changed all this. In the words of Abraham Halkin (1956: 232): "It is a testimony to the profound influence of environment that, beginning with the tenth century, Hebrew poetry and literary prose of a non-religious character underwent an intense development. And it is a further testimony to environment that this new phenomenon caused no surprise or criticism."

The reasons for this literary transformation are not hard to find. Life under Islam, especially in Spain, made new demands on the poets. Many Jews became fond of worldly pleasures; they learned to appreciate the charm of music, the grace of the dance. They participated in drinking bouts, they conversed with women, they joined in literary discussions. They were stimulated by Muslim poets, by their themes, and by their literary forms. "All of these experiences," Halkin writes, "encouraged the development of a secular poetry. It did not replace religious poetry, but grew alongside it. But the standards and characteristics of secular verse influenced liturgical composition."

These secular influences did not affect these poets' religious beliefs or attitudes. That is attested to by the fact that nearly all the Jewish poets of Spain wrote religious as well as secular verse. In both, however, the effect of the Islamic environment is clearly discernible. Halkin (1956: 233) has analyzed one facet of this influence:

> Whereas the Palestinian and Babylonian poets, with their successors in France and Germany, speak mostly anonymously for their own people, their counterparts in Spain speak in their own names. The former treat of Israel's plight, hopes, sinfulness, and her pleas for God's mercy, with no desire to assert themselves... In the Spanish poets, on the contrary, the personal note is very much in evidence. They compose religious lyrics which are a direct expression of their feelings toward God and so bear the stamp of a particular religious experience. Even when their themes are the national [Jewish] ones they share with their brethren in

Christian lands, their treatment of them is their own ... So it is not difficult in the case of an anonymous liturgical verse to determine whether it is the product of the Islamic or the Christian environment.

It has already been suggested that the religious poetry of the Spanish Jews is of universal and permanent value—and it is precisely here that the contribution of Arabic literature and of Muslim-Arab culture was pivotal. According to Goitein, "The most important contribution of Arabic literature toward the development of Hebrew religious poetry does not consist in the provision of actual models, or even in the formal elements, but in the spirit which pervaded Islamic civilization as a whole and which enabled the Jews within it to develop an intensive, completely harmonious spiritual life of their own. Muslim philosophy and theology, pietism and mysticism, through their Jewish counterpart, are mirrored in the Hebrew poetry of the Middle Ages." The result was perfect: "The Hebrew poet could draw in full measure from a civilization which was closely akin to his own, while at the same time cherishing a strong transcendental belief in the mission of Israel" (Halkin 1956: 233).

Maimonides's Legacy

The theological and philosophical works of Moses Maimonides are universally acknowledged as representing the crowning achievement of the great epoch of Jewish-Arab symbiosis in the Middle Ages. After his death, religious philosophical thinking in general, and Jewish philosophy in particular, were reduced to something akin to a commentary on his work. The *Guide* practically closed the circle of philosophical speculation and reflection. The problems posed by Maimonides in this work were taken up again and again by his successors, who like him sought to establish the unity of religion and philosophy, though not always along the same lines. This process, which continued for three centuries, was entirely dominated by Maimonides and his work. According to Guttmann (1966: 172), Maimonides's work "not only laid the foundation for subsequent philosophic inquires, but actually influenced them by its continued vitality and immediate relevance. Discussions of the problems that he raised continued beyond the Middle Ages, sometimes by critical development of his position, at other times by radical opposition to it, but always with reference to him."

Maimonides's influence extended beyond Judaism. The founders of Christian Aristotelianism, Albertus Magnus and Thomas Aquinas, found that he had shown the way to a system of theistic Aristotelianism, and traces of his influence upon Christian philosophy can be followed right into the first centuries of the modern era (Guttmann 1966: 173).

One point about Maimonides's work that deserves particular attention is the extent to which it actually influenced Muslim-Arab thought. According to Goitein (1965: 170), *The Guide for the Perplexed* is a great monument of Jewish-Arab symbiosis "not merely because it is written in Arabic by an original Jewish thinker and *was studied by Arabs,* but because it developed and conveyed to large sections of the Jewish people ideas which had so long occupied the Arab mind" (emphasis added). It has been pointed out, however, that since their Arabic was written in Hebrew characters, the works of the great Jewish writers of Arab Spain could not have been studied by Muslim Arabs; that Maimonides was hardly known among the Arabs; and that, in fact, there was no real intellectual dialogue between the Jews and the Arabs of those days.

This raises the question as to whether and how the various cultural, linguistic, and literary influences between Arabs and Jews in Muslim Spain were reflected in works of theology and philosophy written by Muslims in the Middle Ages. Comparatively little is known about this aspect, although a few Arab authors do make reference to such effect. One of the more interesting of these comes in a most unexpected context. Abu Hamid Muhammad al-Tusi al-Shafi'i, better known as al-Ghazzali, was born in Tus in Khurasan in 1058 and is considered the most original thinker Islam has ever produced and its greatest theologian. Ibn Taymiyya, himself a great Muslim theologian and philosopher, makes the interesting statement that al-Ghazzali was to the Muslims what Maimonides was to the Jews.

Ibn Taymiyya compares the two religious thinkers "in commingling the dicta of the prophets with the philosophers and allegorically interpreting the former according to the latter," and this is precisely where both al-Ghazzali and Maimonides were to be subjected to criticism on grounds of inconsistency in their attempt to reconcile reason with revelation. Both were to be accused of contradictions and lack of logic, and in certain cases of dishonesty. In her *Studies in Al-Ghazzali,* Lazarus-Yafe (1975: 439–40) comments: "It is only [we] living in the twentieth century who find it hard to accept [al-Ghazzali's] somewhat naive combination of religious faith and free reasoning."

From this, of course, the road was not long to the kind of cultural ambiguity that characterized our "compunctious poet" (Brann 1991).

Notes

1. In preparing this essay I have drawn heavily on my *Israel's Place in the Middle East: A Pluralist Perspective.* Thanks are due to the Board of Regents of the State of Florida, the holders of the copyright, for permission to quote.

2. On the codification of Jewish law along the lines of the Hadith, see Rosenthal 1961: xi.

3. The quote from Ibn Tibbon is taken from his translator's introduction to Bahya ibn Paquda, *Hovoth Ha-Levavoth,* ed. E. Tzifroni (Tel Aviv: Yedi'ot Aharonot, 1964), 56–57.

4. The set was published by Yedi'ot Aharonot, Tel Aviv, 1971.

References

Ashtor, Eliyahu. *The Jews of Moslem Spain.* 3 vols. Philadelphia: Jewish Publication Society, 1974–1985.

Baron, Salo. *A Social and Religious History of the Jews.* Vol. 3. New York: Columbia University Press, 1957.

Ben-Sasson, Haim Hillel. *On Jewish History in the Middle Ages* (in Hebrew), translated and quoted in M. Cohen, q.v., 36.

Blau, Joshua. *The Emergence and Linguistic Background of Judeo-Arabic.* Oxford: Oxford University Press, 1965.

Brann, Ross. *The Compunctious Poet: Cultural Ambiguity and Hebrew Poetry in Muslim Spain.* Baltimore, Md.: Johns Hopkins University Press, 1991.

Bunzl, John. *Israel's Place in the Middle East: A Pluralist Perspective.* Gainesville: University Press of Florida, 1998.

Cohen, Mark R. *Under Crescent and Cross: The Jews in the Middle Ages.* Princeton, N.J.: Princeton University Press, 1994.

Encyclopedia of Islam, s.v. "dhimma."

Epstein, Isidore. *Judaism: A Historical Presentation.* Harmondsworth, U.K.: Penguin, 1959.

Gibb, Hamilton, and Harold Bowen. *Islamic Society and the West.* Vol 1. London: Oxford University Press, 1957.

Goitein, S. D. *Jews and Arabs: Their Contacts through the Ages.* New York: Schocken Books, 1965.

Guillaume, Alfred. "The Influence of Judaism in Islam." In *The Legacy of Israel,* ed. Edwin R. Bevan and Charles Singer. London: Oxford University Press, 1969.

Guttmann, Julius. *Philosophies of Judaism.* New York: Anchor Books–Doubleday, 1966.

Halkin, Abraham. "The Judeo-Islamic Age." In *Great Ages and Ideas of the Jewish People,* ed. Leo Schwarz. New York: Schocken Books, 1956.

———. "The Medieval Jewish Attitude toward Hebrew." In *Biblical and Other Studies,* ed. Alexander Altmann. Cambridge, Mass.: Harvard University Press, 1963.

Khadduri, Majid. *War and Peace in the Law of Islam.* Washington, D.C.: Middle East Institute, 1962.

Lazarus-Yafe, Hava. *Studies in Al-Ghazzali.* Jerusalem: Magnus Press, 1975.

———. *Intertwined Worlds: Medieval Islam and Bible Criticism.* Princeton, N.J.: Princeton University Press, 1992.

Poliakov, Leon. *A History of Antisemitism.* Vol. 1. London: Oxford University Press, 1975.
Rosenthal, Erwin. *Judaism and Islam.* London: Thomas Yoseloff, 1961.
———. *Studia Semetica.* Vol. 1. Cambridge, U.K.: Cambridge University Press, 1973.
Singer, Charles, ed. *The Legacy of Israel.* London: Oxford University Press, 1969.
———. "The Jewish Factor in Medieval Thought." In *The Legacy of Israel,* ed. E. R. Bevan and George Singer. London, 1969.

II

Negotiating Religions and Identities

3

National Identity and the Role of the "Other" in Existential Conflicts

The Israeli-Palestinian Case

Herbert C. Kelman

My work and that of my colleagues as scholar-practitioners has focused on analysis and resolution of protracted, seemingly intractable conflicts between national, ethnic, religious, or other kinds of identity groups, best exemplified by intercommunal conflicts such as those in Cyprus, Northern Ireland, Sri Lanka, Bosnia, and apartheid South Africa.[1] My own most intensive and extensive experience, over some thirty years, has been with the Israeli-Palestinian conflict, and my analysis will draw primarily on that experience. In this conflict, as in most of the other conflicts mentioned, the religious dimension is an integral part of the collective identities that fuel that dispute.

Using the Israeli-Palestinian conflict as a case in point, I shall examine the way in which issues of national identity can exacerbate an international or intercommunal conflict and the way in which such issues can be addressed in conflict resolution efforts. I start by describing the struggle over national identity between the two peoples, which has led them to perceive their conflict in zero-sum terms, not only with respect to territory and resources but also with respect to national identity and national existence. Next, I argue that long-term resolution of this and similar deep-rooted conflicts requires changes in the groups' national identities, such that affirmation of one group's identity is no longer predicated on negation of the other's identity. Such identity changes are possible, as long as they leave the core of each group's national identity intact. Furthermore, such changes *need* to be and *can* be "negotiated" between the two groups. One venue for negotiating identity is provided by the problem-solving workshops between Israeli and Palestinian elites that my colleagues and I have convened for many years.

The Struggle over National Identity

In the Israeli-Palestinian conflict, as in other such conflicts, the threat to collective identity is a core issue, integrally related to the struggle over territory and resources. Both peoples and their national movements claim the same territory, and each seeks ownership of that territory and control over its resources as the basis of an independent state that gives political expression to its national identity. The integrity of this collective identity is critical to each group for several reasons. First, the integrity of the national identity is an end in itself, in that the identity serves as a source of distinctiveness, unity, and continuity for the group and of a sense of belongingness for its members. Second, the national identity constitutes the ultimate justification of the group's claim to ownership of the land and control of its resources. And third, the national identity provides a focus for developing and maintaining the group's distinctive culture, religion, and way of life. The collective identity of each group is bolstered by a national narrative—an account of the group's origins, its history, and its relationship to the land—which explains and supports its sense of distinctiveness, its positive self-image, and the justice of its claims and grievances.

In conflicts such as that between Israelis and Palestinians, in which the two sides live in the same space and claim ownership of the same territory, it is not only the actions of the other, but the identity and the very existence of the other that are a threat to the group's own identity. The other's identity and its associated narrative challenge the group's claims to ownership—at least to exclusive ownership—of the land and its resources. The other's presence in the same space, particularly if it is accompanied by demands for a share of the power and for recognition of the other culture, religion, and/or language, is perceived as a threat to the integrity and cohesiveness of the group's society and its way of life.

These dynamics lead to a view of the conflict as a zero-sum struggle, not only around territory but also around identity (Kelman 1987). Acknowledging the other's identity becomes tantamount to jeopardizing the identity—and indeed the national existence—of one's own group. Thus, over the course of the Israeli-Palestinian conflict, there has been a systematic tendency on each side to deny the other's identity as a people, the authenticity of the other's links to the land, the legitimacy of the other's claims to national rights, and the very existence of the other as a national group (Kelman 1978, 1982). Negation of the other's identity and of the narrative in which it is embedded becomes so important to the conflict that negation of the other is incorporated in the identity that each group constructs for itself and in the narrative that the group presents to the world (Kelman 1999).

The contrasting Israeli and Palestinian narratives about the creation of the State of Israel in 1948 both rely on the negation of the other to bolster the justice of their own cause. For Israelis, the creation of Israel represented a rightful return of the Jewish people to their ancestral homeland. Establishment of a Jewish state in Palestine did not, in their eyes, constitute an injustice to the Arabs who resided there, because—according to the Israeli narrative—Palestinian Arabs were not a people, distinct from the Arab inhabitants of surrounding countries, and they had never exercised sovereignty in Palestine. Moreover, in the Israeli narrative, the responsibility for the Palestinian refugee problem and the suffering of the Palestinian Arab population rests with the Palestinians' aggressive and incompetent leadership, which rejected all compromise and initiated violent attacks in the effort to block the establishment of Israel. The Palestinians, by contrast, regard the creation of Israel as an act of usurpation by European settlers who forcefully displaced the indigenous population and destroyed its society, property, and way of life. In the Palestinian narrative, Jews are a religious group, not a nation entitled to its own state, and Zionism is a form of settler colonialism that imposed itself on a region in which it has no roots. Each identity thus gains some of its strength and legitimacy from negating and delegitimizing the other.

The sense of existential threat and the consequent negation of the other gain additional strength when the ethnic differences correspond to religious differences. In such a situation, the other comes to be seen as a threat to the ultimate meaning of personal and collective existence. Moreover, an unlimited violent response to the threat is often justified by obedience to the highest authority.

Identities that rest in part on negation of the other inevitably take on an exclusivist and monolithic character (Kelman 1997b). In the Israeli-Palestinian conflict, exclusivist and monolithic definitions of identity have begun to give way in recent years. For significant segments of the two populations, however—and in some respects even for large majorities—such definitions still prevail.

In the Israeli-Palestinian case, a defining element of each group's identity is its relationship to the land and its history. Insofar as this relationship is *exclusive*—that is, insofar as the group's identity rests on the view that the land and its history belong to it alone and that the other's claims on them as part of its own identity are illegitimate and inauthentic—there is little room for conflict resolution. Conflict resolution becomes an option when the parties accept the possibility that certain elements of identity may be *shared* with the other, acknowledging that the other also has a profound attachment to the land, anchored in authentic historical ties. Israelis and Palestinians have been gradually moving toward acceptance of shared elements of identity as they have been searching for a political formula for sharing the land. It has proven more difficult for the two sides, so far, to accept Jerusalem as a shared element of the two identities and to develop a political formula to reflect that view. For a long time the Israeli rhetoric treated Jerusalem as an exclusive property of Israel, although public opinion data (e.g., Segal 1999) suggest some flexibility that was also reflected in the Israeli offers at the Camp David and Taba negotiations in 2000 and 2001. Palestinians have been prepared to concede West Jerusalem to Israel, but they have treated the Old City and particularly the Temple Mount/Haram al-Sharif as an exclusive property of their state.

Identities that rest on negation of the other also take on a *monolithic* character; that is, all dimensions of the group's identity—such as ethnicity, religion, and language—tend to be viewed as highly correlated. The ideology calls for complete correspondence between ethnic boundaries, political boundaries, boundaries of emotional attachment, and boundaries of intensive interaction. Self and other are, in principle, completely separated along all of these lines. The Israeli-Palestinian conflict, as well as other protracted conflicts, particularly between identity groups living in close proximity within a small space (such as Northern Ireland or Cyprus), might be more amenable to resolution if there were some degree of disaggregation of the monolithic identity, based on distinctions between different types of boundaries. Such distinctions would allow for the development of a *transcendent* identity—not in place of the particular ethnonational identities, but alongside of them. In the Israeli-Palestinian case, a transcendent identity could be fostered by separating the concept of the state as a sovereign political entity from that of the country as a geographical entity. This distinction would allow the two communities to treat the entire country (Eretz Israel or Palestine) as an object of common sentimental attachment and as the framework for common instrumental pursuits (in such areas as development and use of water resources, environmental protection, public health, and tourism), while living in and identifying with separate political states within that country.

The zero-sum view of identity and the mutual denial of the other's identity that I have described create serious obstacles to conflict resolution. All issues tend to become existential—matters of life and death for each side. Compromise solutions that involve sharing of the land or agreeing on different boundaries for different purposes are likely to threaten exclusivist and monolithic identities. The demonized other is not trusted to negotiate in good faith and respect agreements. In short, when acceptance of the other's national rights and recognition of the other's national identity are seen as relinquishing the group's own rights and jeopardizing its own identity, distributive solutions based on compromise are hard to achieve. Even if the parties agree to make certain compromises in response to reality demands and external pressures, these compromises are unlikely to lead to durable changes in the relationship between the conflicting groups, conducive to stable peace, mutually enhancing interaction, and ultimate reconciliation. Lasting change requires mutual adjustments in collective identity.

Identity Changes

The stubborn resistance to change in collective identities is widely recognized and taken for granted. Yet identities have to change, at least tacitly, if protracted identity conflicts are to be settled and, certainly, if they are to be resolved in a way that transforms the relationship and opens the way to reconciliation. South Africa provides perhaps the best illustration of an arena of intense, protracted conflict in which fundamental identity changes paved the way to resolution and reconciliation, although it also illustrates the difficulties in changing the worldviews and the structural realities that became entrenched during the apartheid era.

Despite their undeniable rigidities, identities are potentially changeable (and indeed negotiable) for two reasons: First, unlike territory and resources, they are not inherently zero-sum; though they are perceived and debated as such in intense conflicts, it is in fact not the case that A's identity can be recognized and expressed only if B's identity is denied and suppressed.

If the two identities are to become compatible, however, they have to be redefined. And this points to the second reason for the potential changeability of group identities: They can be redefined because they are to a large extent constructed. To view national identity as a social construction does not imply that it is manufactured out of nothing. There may be cases in which one can properly speak of an imagined past, invented to buttress a newly formed identity (Anderson 1983). Generally, however, the social construction of an identity draws on a variety of authentic elements held in common within a group: a common history, language, or religion; or common customs, cultural expressions, experiences, values, grievances, or aspirations (Kelman 1997b). Typically, the social construction of an identity involves a dual process of *discovery* (or rediscovery) and *creation* of such common elements (Kelman 1997a). The social construction of the identity implies a degree of arbitrariness and flexibility in the way the identity is composed (which elements are admitted into it and which omitted from it) and in what its boundaries are (who is included and who is excluded). These choices depend on the opportunities and necessities perceived by the elites that are engaged in mobilizing ethnonational consciousness for their political, economic, or religious purposes (Kelman 1997b). Serbs and Croats, for example, share a common language and culture but differ in religion and historical experiences. Political leaders have at times focused on the similarities in the effort to shape them into a single nation; at other times they have magnified the differences to define them as separate—and mutually antagonistic—nations.

Thus, although national identities are generally constructed out of real experiences, these experiences can be ordered in different ways, resulting in different boundaries and priorities. As a consequence, they can be—and typically are—deconstructed and reconstructed. "In fact, the reconstruction of identity is a regular, ongoing process in the life of any national group. Identities are commonly reconstructed, sometimes gradually and sometimes radically, as historical circumstances change, crises emerge, opportunities present themselves, or new elites come to the fore" (Kelman 1997b: 338). Clearly, therefore, there is room for maneuver in a group's self-definition, particularly with respect to the definition of group boundaries and the priorities among different elements of the group's identity.

Changes in identity over the course of a protracted conflict come about through a combination of changed perceptions of the *necessity* and the *possibility* of resolving a conflict that has become increasingly costly to the parties. The mounting costs and dwindling prospects of French governance of Algeria, white South African continuation of apartheid, Israeli occupation of Palestinian territories, or the Palestinians' armed struggle created the *necessity* for changes in identity. Algeria as an integral part of France, South Africa under exclusive white control, Israel within the borders of Greater Israel, and Palestinian repossession of the entire homeland were assigned lower priority in the national identities of these groups as it became clear to a majority that these aspirations could not be realized at an acceptable cost.

What made it *possible* to change these priorities was often the discovery that accommodation of the other's identity need not destroy the core of the group's own identity and that a compromise solution to the conflict was therefore negotiable. This kind of learning can take place in the course of official or unofficial interactions between the groups or their members, including the problem-solving workshops that my colleagues and I have conducted. In the course of Israeli-Palestinian workshops, for example, participants have learned to differentiate their image of the enemy by discovering that there are potential negotiating partners on the other side, that there is a distinction between the other's ideological dreams and operational programs, and that the other has positive goals beyond destruction of the opposing group (Kelman 1987). They were enabled to enter into the enemy's perspective, thus discovering the historical sources of the other's claims and grievances, the depth of the other's fears, and the authenticity of the other's sense of peoplehood. They began to visualize a different future, discovering possibilities for mutually beneficial coexistence and cooperation. As such experiences multiply, and as the knowledge produced by them is infused into the two political cultures, each group may gradually change its identity by eliminating the negation of the other's identity as an element of its own identity and perhaps even admitting the possibility of a partnership as a new element of its own identity.

Negotiating Identity

The changes I have described are often the result of an explicit or implicit process of negotiating identity. At its core, national identity is clearly nonnegotiable; indeed, the very idea of negotiating identity sounds like an oxymoron. National identity is a collective psychological conception; it cannot be dictated or prescribed by outsiders. A group of people who define themselves as a nation cannot be told that they have no right to do so because their self-definition does not conform to some set of theoretical, juridical, or historical criteria, or because their nationhood is inconvenient to others. Nor does it make sense to tell them how to draw the boundaries of the group: whom to include and whom to exclude. People are a nation if they perceive themselves as such and are prepared to invest energy and make sacrifices in terms of that perception (Kelman 1978). Neither Palestinians nor Israelis will give up the core of their identity: their sense of peoplehood, their attachment to the land, their conviction about the historical authenticity of their links to that land, or their commitment to their national culture, language, and way of life. Nor will they give up the national narrative that substantiates the justice of their cause.

But there are many elements that can be added to or subtracted from an identity without jeopardizing its core. In fact, changes in less central elements of the identity are often advocated precisely in order to protect the core of the identity. It was on that basis that the majority of Israelis and Palestinians came to accept territorial compromise—that is, a shrinking of the territorial dimension of their identity—as the best available option for maintaining their national identity. The Peace Now movement in Israel, for example, advocated withdrawal from the Occupied Territories largely on the grounds that this was the only way in which Israel could maintain its character as both a Jewish state and a democratic state. Yehoshafat Harkabi (1986), a former chief of Israeli military intelligence and a prophetic voice in the debate about Israeli-Palestinian peace, explicitly advocated a smaller

Israel—a "Zionism of quality" rather than a "Zionism of acreage." He argued that Israel had to choose between withdrawing from the West Bank and making way for a Palestinian state there, or annexing the West Bank with the consequence that Israel would eventually become a Palestinian state. On the Palestinian side, the territorial dimension of the Palestinian identity has gradually changed as the movement reflected on its realistic options. The thinking of the Palestine Liberation Organization (PLO) evolved from advocacy of a Palestinian Arab state in the whole of Palestine, to a secular democratic state, and eventually to a Palestinian state alongside of Israel, comprising the West Bank and Gaza (Muslih 1990). Significant segments of both societies still reject territorial compromise on religious or ideological grounds and link their national identity to possession of the land in its entirety. But the Palestinian and Israeli mainstreams have by now come to terms with a national identity that finds its political expression in only part of the land, as evidenced by the opinion polls that are now conducted on a regular basis in both societies.

Such changes in elements of identity are a legitimate subject for negotiation between groups whose identities clash, because the identity that one group chooses for itself has significant implications for the rights, interests, and identity of the other. Whenever one group translates the self-definition of its nationhood into action—"by making territorial claims, by demanding an independent state, by seeking to redraw borders, by declaring who is included in the national identity and who is excluded from it, or even by selecting a name for itself" (Kelman 1997b: 337)—the other is inevitably affected. Each group, therefore, has a legitimate concern about the way the other defines itself, the way it formulates its national identity. It is not surprising, then, that identity issues play an important role in the formal and informal processes of prenegotiation and negotiation.

To some extent, identity issues are part of the subject matter of the official negotiations. I have already referred to the territorial dimension of identity. Insofar as Israelis and Palestinians are negotiating on the basis of a "land for peace" formula, they are accepting territorial limits to their national identities, which have, after all, been historically linked to the whole of the land. Similarly, the mutual recognition between Israel and the PLO, as expressed in the exchange of letters between Yasir Arafat and Yitzhak Rabin—which I regard as the most important breakthrough of the Oslo agreement (Kelman 1997c)—can be viewed as a product of the negotiation of identity: an act of acceptance and legitimization of the Other who in the past had been defined as the antithesis to the self.

Although redefined identities are thus promulgated around the official negotiating table, the negotiation of identity is primarily an informal, unofficial process in which members of the conflicting parties explore and invent ways of accommodating their group identities to one another. The purpose of negotiation in this looser sense of the term is not to produce political agreements but to develop joint understandings and formulations that can help pave the road to political agreements at the official level. Implicitly and explicitly, this kind of negotiation has been a central focus for problem-solving workshops between Israelis and Palestinians that my colleagues and I have conducted over the past quarter century.

Problem-Solving Workshops

Problem-solving workshops are the central instrument of interactive problem solving, an unofficial, third-party approach to the resolution of international and intercommunal conflicts, derived from the pioneering work of John Burton (1969, 1979, 1984) and anchored in social-psychological principles (Kelman 1972, 1979, 1992, 1998). A workshop is a specially constructed, private space in which politically influential (but generally unofficial) members of conflicting communities can interact in a nonbinding, confidential way. The microprocess of the workshop provides them the opportunity to penetrate each other's perspective; to explore the needs, fears, priorities, and constraints of each side; and to engage in joint thinking about solutions to the conflict that would be responsive to the fundamental concerns of both sides. Workshops produce *change*—in the form of new insights and ideas—in the individual participants, and *transfer* of those insights and ideas into the political process at the levels of both public opinion and decision making. The Israeli-Palestinian workshops we carried out until 1990 were all one-time events designed to create a climate conducive to movement to the negotiating table. In 1990, Nadim Rouhana and I organized our first continuing workshop, in which a group of high-level Israelis and Palestinians met periodically over a three-year period (Rouhana and Kelman 1994). In 1994, we convened a Joint Working Group on Israeli-Palestinian Relations, which met regularly over several years and—for the first time in our program—produced several jointly authored concept papers on some of the final-status issues in the Israeli-Palestinian negotiations and on the future relationship between the two societies (Alpher, Shikaki, et al. 1998; Joint Working Group 1998, 1999).

Much of the discussion in our workshops, from the beginning in the 1970s through the 1990s, focused, in effect, on a process of negotiating collective identities. In our experience, such a process can be productive only if it is based on mutual respect for the core of the other's identity and on the principle of reciprocity. Each side must know that the other does not seek to undermine its group identity, and each must take care not to undermine the other's identity. And each must know that the risks it takes in acknowledging the other's claims, rights, and authenticity will be reciprocated by the other's acknowledgment of its claims, rights, and authenticity.

Starting from the understanding that neither side is prepared to negotiate the core of its identity—its peoplehood, its relationship to the land, the basic justice of its cause—or the general lines of its national narrative, there remain various elements of each group's identity that can be negotiated in the interest of mutual accommodation. Let me illustrate some of the possible changes in identity that can and have been discussed in problem-solving workshops and similar encounters and that have, over time, begun to penetrate the Israeli and Palestinian political cultures.

1. Many members of both communities have become able to remove the negation of the other's identity as an integral part of their own identity. Though the other may still be seen as an obstacle to achieving one's own national goals, the other is not as often seen as the antithesis of one's own identity whose demise is a condition for one's own survival. Thus, many Israelis have come to accept the reality of Palestinian peoplehood, particularly after observing Palestinians' readiness to make sacrifices for their national cause during the earlier intifada and Palestinians' celebration of the signing of the Oslo agreement in September 1993. Interestingly, Israelis saw parallels between these events and their own struggle for statehood and celebration at attaining it—a significant degree of identification with the other whose existence had previously been denied. Many Palestinians, on their part, now recognize the right of Israelis to their state, on the grounds that the state has existed for over half a century and that its dismantlement would create a new injustice to the generations that were born into it. Very few Palestinians, on the other hand, are prepared to acknowledge the historical links of Jews to the land, which might be seen as justification for the establishment of the Jewish state in the first place.

2. We have seen signs of softening of the exclusiveness of group identity, which allows for the recognition that—despite the validity of one's own claims—the other too has valid claims. The recognition of shared elements of identity with the other opens the way to political solutions based on sharing territory and resources. In a recent workshop, for example, mainstream Israelis and Palestinians were able to agree—much to everyone's surprise, including their own—

on a formula for sharing Jerusalem: a united city containing the capitals of both states.
3. Workshop participants have experimented with disaggregating the monolithic nature of their identities, recognizing that there are different boundaries of group identity (such as ethnic boundaries, political boundaries, boundaries of sentimental attachment) that do not necessarily coincide. This recognition opens the way to the development of transcendent identities, which might allow the two peoples to maintain a common attachment to the country while "owning" only part of that country as their political state. The concept of a "united country with divided sovereignties" was discussed in one of our workshops in the early 1980s. In a more recent workshop, the idea of establishing different kinds of boundaries was explored in the attempt to find solutions to the problem of Israeli settlements in the areas in which Palestinians hope to establish their state.
4. Workshop discussions can help to identify outdated elements of group identity that refer to maximalist goals and dreams of glory, or self-aggrandizing images that have no current political relevance but poison the climate for conflict resolution. Examples here might be Palestinian references to the armed struggle as the way to eliminate the Zionist entity, or Israeli references to the Zionist project of making the desert bloom. Workshops have often sensitized participants to words and images that humiliate and frighten the other and could be discarded with minimal cost to group identity.
5. In the course of the workshop discussions, participants may decide to reorder the priorities within their national identities, such that certain elements (e.g., territorial ambitions) that may not have been given up but have become too costly to pursue are relegated to low priority and thus become available for negotiated compromise. Thus, over time, Palestinians (in our workshops and in the larger society) decided to give priority to ending the occupation and establishing a Palestinian state over recovering the lost land in its entirety. Israelis gave priority to maintaining the Jewish character of Israel over controlling the whole of the land.
6. Finally, workshop participants may negotiate changes in national narratives that accommodate the other's view of history as much as possible, such as accepting a share of the responsibility for the course of the conflict. A concept paper of our Joint Working Group on Israeli-Palestinian Relations, *The Palestinian Refugee Problem*

and the Right of Return (Alpher, Shikaki, et al. 1998), provides a good illustration of such an effort to negotiate identity. It pointed to the possibilities and difficulties of the negotiation of identity and suggested directions for achieving further progress (see Kelman 2001 for further elaboration).

Conclusion

In the Israeli-Palestinian conflict, as in Cyprus, Sri Lanka, Northern Ireland, and other protracted ethnic conflicts, the ever-present disputes over territory, resources, and political control are exacerbated by perceived threats to national identity and national existence that underlie the actions and reactions of the opposing communities. Threats to identity and existence, particularly when the identity is embedded in a religious framework, create obstacles to the settlement of conflicts, even when both parties have concluded that a compromise agreement is in their best interest. Moreover, even after specific issues in conflict are settled and political agreements signed—often with the mediation of powerful third parties—these agreements may not lead to stable peace, fruitful cooperation, or ultimate reconciliation between the two parties unless they have formed a new relationship based on mutual respect for their national and religious identities.

A central lesson from our experience is that national identity, though very much part of the problem in ethnic conflicts, can also become part of the solution. The way we talk about our identity affects the way we think about it and ultimately the way we act on it. In groups that are caught up in protracted conflict, identity depends on the conflict and is shaped by the conflict: many elements of identity are constructed as vehicles for pursuing the conflict. It should be possible, within limits, to reconstruct these elements as vehicles for peace and reconciliation. What is needed is a change of identity, so that conflict resolution and a transformed relationship with the former enemy become integral parts of the new identity.

Development of such a new, transcendent identity encounters many obstacles. The rapid deterioration of the Israeli-Palestinian peace process in the aftermath of the failed Camp David talks in the summer of 2000 demonstrates the severity of these obstacles. The tentative changes in the identities of the two sides that I described have proven rather fragile. The rhetoric has returned to negation of the other's identity, to exclusivist and monolithic formulations of each group's own identity, to assertion of maximalist goals, and to a hardening of the old narratives. This does not mean, however, that the changes that have taken place over the years have been completely undone. The parties have reverted to the old analysis and rhetoric because they have lost their belief in the other side's commitment to a peaceful solution and readiness to make the compromises required for such a solution. If that belief can be revived—if a new working trust between the two sides can develop—the identity changes that have begun to take shape are likely to reassert themselves. Indeed, I propose that they must and can be mobilized to help revive the peace process.

It is important to keep in mind that the development of a new, transcendent identity cannot bypass the political process of negotiating a mutually acceptable agreement, nor can it be allowed to threaten or undermine the particularistic identity of each group. Parties engaged in a deep-rooted conflict can abandon relatively *marginal* elements of their identity in order to accommodate the identity of the other only if the *core* of their identity is safeguarded and confirmed in the process. But within these constraints, the potential for reconstructing the national identities of former enemies in the service of peace and reconciliation exists and needs to be nurtured. In this task, religious traditions and shared religious commitments can be drawn upon to make constructive contributions.

Notes

1. This chapter draws extensively on an earlier paper, Kelman 2001. Material from that paper is reprinted here by permission of the editors and Oxford University Press.

References

Alpher, J., and K. Shikaki, with the participation of the additional members of the Joint Working Group on Israeli-Palestinian Relations. *The Palestinian Refugee Problem and the Right of Return.* Working Paper no. 98-7. Cambridge, Mass.: Weatherhead Center for International Affairs, Harvard University, 1998. Reprinted in *Middle East Policy* 6, no. 3 (February 1999): 167–89.

Anderson, B. *Imagined Communities: Reflections on the Origins and Spread of Nationalism.* London: Verso, 1983.

Burton, J. W. *Conflict and Communication: The Use of Controlled Communication in International Relations.* London: Macmillan, 1969.

———. *Deviance, Terrorism, and War: The Process of Solving Unsolved Social and Political Problems.* New York: St. Martin's Press, 1979.

———. *Global Conflict: The Domestic Sources of International Crisis.* Brighton, England: Wheatsheaf, 1984.

Goitein, S. D. *Jews and Arabs: Their Contacts through the Ages.* New York: Schocken Books, 1965.

Harkabi, Y. *Israel's Fateful Hour.* New York: Harper and Row, 1986.

Joint Working Group on Israeli-Palestinian Relations. *General Principles for the Final Israeli-Palestinian Agreement.* PICAR Working Paper. Cambridge, Mass.:

Program on International Conflict Analysis and Resolution, Weatherhead Center for International Affairs, Harvard University, 1998. Reprinted in *Middle East Journal* 53, no. 1 (1999): 170–75.

———. *The Future Israeli-Palestinian Relationship.* Weatherhead Center for International Affairs Working Paper no. 99–12. Cambridge, Mass.: Harvard University, 1999. Reprinted in *Middle East Policy* 7, no. 2 (February 2000): 90–112.

Kelman, H. C. "The Problem-Solving Workshop in Conflict Resolution." In *Communication in International Politics,* ed. R. L. Merritt, 168–204. Urbana: University of Illinois Press, 1972.

———. "Israelis and Palestinians: Psychological Prerequisites for Mutual Acceptance." *International Security* 3 (1978): 162–86.

———. "An Interactional Approach to Conflict Resolution and Its Application to Israeli-Palestinian Relations." *International Interactions* 6 (1979): 99–122.

———. "Creating the Conditions for Israeli-Palestinian Negotiations." *Journal of Conflict Resolution* 26 (1982): 39–75.

———. "The Political Psychology of the Israeli-Palestinian Conflict: How Can We Overcome the Barriers to a Negotiated Solution?" *Political Psychology* 8 (1987): 347–63.

———. "Informal Mediation by the Scholar/Practitioner." In *Mediation in International Relations: Multiple Approaches to Conflict Management,* ed. J. Bercovitch and J. Rubin, 64–96. New York: St. Martin's Press, 1992.

———. "Nationalism, Patriotism, and National Identity: Social-Psychological Dimensions." In *Patriotism in the Lives of Individuals and Nations,* ed. D. Bar-Tal and E. Staub, 165–89. Chicago: Nelson-Hall, 1997a.

———. "Negotiating National Identity and Self-Determination in Ethnic Conflicts: The Choice between Pluralism and Ethnic Cleansing." *Negotiation Journal* 13 (1997b): 327–40.

———. "Some Determinants of the Oslo Breakthrough." *International Negotiation* 2 (1997c): 183–94.

———. "Social-Psychological Contributions to Peacemaking and Peacebuilding in the Middle East." *Applied Psychology: An International Review* 47, no. 1 (1998): 5–28.

———. "The Interdependence of Israeli and Palestinian Identities: The Role of the Other in Existential Conflicts." *Journal of Social Issues* 55, no. 3 (1999): 581–600.

———. "The Role of National Identity in Conflict Resolution: Experiences from Israeli-Palestinian Problem-Solving Workshops." In *Social Identity, Intergroup Conflict, and Conflict Reduction,* ed. R. D. Ashmore, L. Jussim, and D. Wilder, 187–212. Oxford and New York: Oxford University Press, 2001.

Muslih, M. "Towards Coexistence: An Analysis of the Resolutions of the Palestine National Council." *Journal of Palestine Studies* 19, no. 4 (1990): 3–29.

Rouhana, N. N., and H. C. Kelman. "Promoting Joint Thinking in International Conflicts: An Israeli-Palestinian Continuing Workshop." *Journal of Social Issues* 50, no. 1 (1994): 157–78.

Segal, J. M. "Defining Jerusalem." *Middle East Insight* 14, no. 1 (1999): 27–28, 51–54.

4

The Politicization of Muslim-Christian Relations in the Palestinian National Movement

Helga Baumgarten

This essay explores Christian-Muslim relations in Palestine in general and in the history of the post-*nakba* Palestinian National Movement (PNM) after 1948 in particular. My analysis is guided by a central question: How has the Palestinian National Movement dealt with the problem of political dynamics in the relationship between different socio-religious communities that in neighboring Lebanon provoked violence and even war in both the nineteenth and twentieth centuries?

I will first briefly analyze the current situation, that is, the ongoing uprising of the al-Aqsa Intifada—also sometimes called the al-Istiqlal Intifada—focusing on the issue of Christian-Muslim relations. I then trace the evolution of the Palestinian National Movement, with particular emphasis on the relations between Christians and Muslims inside the movement and the way the leadership of the PNM has dealt with this issue, politically and ideologically. In this context, the history of religious communities and their interrelationship will be briefly examined in order to identify the historical traditions upon which the modern PNM has built, in the nineteenth century and the mandatory period, that is, in the first half of the twentieth century. In the next part I address the question of what accounts for the difference in the dynamics of intercommunal relations in Lebanon and Palestine. The chapter concludes with several hypotheses concerning the politicization of interreligious and intercommunal relations.

Christian-Muslim Relations during the al-Aqsa Intifada

A brief article published in the Israeli press in November 2000 describes the situation in a village in southern Lebanon, Ain Ebel, where "Christians feel increasingly threatened by Hezbollah. Everyone fears a return to the intercommunal violence of the civil war."[1] The article points in particular to the simultaneous display of two symbols in the village, the church bells of the

Maronite church atop the highest hill in the area, and the yellow and green flag of Hezbollah at the entrance to the village. It interprets the presence of these two symbols in the village as emblematic of attempts at coexistence between the Lebanese Shi'a community, Hezbollah in particular, and the Christian minority in southern Lebanon (a majority in the village of Ain Ebel), and the continuity of a long struggle between the two communities. This last continuity should be viewed "against a complex background of secular hatred, deep-seated religious prejudices, and ancient tribal enmities."

In contrast with this situation of sectarian and intercommunal frictions, Christian-Muslim relations in Palestine seem generally to have been marked by a spirit of harmony, right down to the present. Even when outside forces seek to instigate Christian-Muslim strife, Palestinian Christians and Muslims unite against such interference, rejecting it with a single voice.

For example, on 25 October 2000, the *Jerusalem Post* reported that Israel was "assisting" Palestinian Christians to flee the violence in the Occupied Territories and take refuge abroad. The article quoted a spokesman of the Israeli Foreign Ministry who stated that Christians were frightened and wished to leave because of Muslim sermons in Gaza that had called on Muslims to "attack Jews and Christians." According to the article, the flight was also due to developments in the mainly Christian town of Beit Jala, where Fatah "gunmen" had taken over Christian homes to fire on the Israeli settlement of Gilo, "threatening their occupants if they object."[2] The Palestinian Christian response was unanimous and vocal. I will cite here just one example, "Statement by Christians from amongst the People of Palestine," dated 26 October 2000:

> We, the undersigned, Christians of the Holy Land, as descendants of the Canaanite tribes that inhabited Palestine since times immemorial, as descendants and followers of the first apostles, and as successors of Jerusalem Christians who received the Omar Doctrine from the Great Caliphate Omar Bin *(sic)* Al-Khattab, hereby state unequivocally, at this key juncture in our history, that we are an integral part of the Palestinian national struggle for independence and sovereignty. Our quest for liberty, democracy, and respect for pluralism is a common aspiration we share alongside our Moslem compatriots. Palestinian Christians and Moslems agree on many things, especially when it comes to the issue of independence and the return to Jerusalem.
>
> Accordingly, we utterly condemn any Israeli attempt to deal with us as a separate entity of alien presence in Palestine.
>
> In the *Jerusalem Post* on Wednesday, October 25, 2000, there was

an article claiming that the Israeli Foreign Ministry is helping hundreds of Christian families flee Palestinian Authority areas. We caution against believing such falsity. Israel, as a colonialist entity, after having become morally bankrupt and militarily impotent, is now resorting to an old colonialist tactic: to divide and conquer. Our Palestinian unity is much stronger than any such cheap endeavor. . . . Throughout the conflict, Israel targeted Christians because they constitute a bridge between the Christian West and the Moslem East. . . . As Christian Palestinians and as Arabs, we demand an immediate stop to all Israeli lies and distortions regarding our national unity.³

Numerous statements by different Christian groups and individuals were published in the days after 25 October in the Palestinian press as well as on various Palestinian websites. One example from the Internet, a MIFTAH press release, also from 26 October, "Israel Attempts to Provoke Religious Discrimination between Palestinian Christians and Muslims," is representative.⁴ It begins by expressing its "serious alarm at the recent Israeli attempts to provoke religious discrimination between Palestinian Christians and Muslims, through inaccurate and distorted media reports," and concludes:

> To that end, MIFTAH cautions against this shortsighted attempt to induce a false sense of discrimination within Palestinian society, and provoke religious tensions between the Palestinian Christians and Muslims. Throughout their history, the Palestinian people have unquestionably demonstrated a strong sense of unity under one just cause, and therefore take pride in maintaining a *secular* society based on the principles of justice, freedom, and pluralism. Official responses from the Palestinian Christian community emphasized that Christian Palestinians "are an integral part of the Palestinian national struggle for independence and sovereignty.⁵

Before taking up the question of a secular society as an answer to potential interreligious conflict, I will examine the position of Palestinian Islamist groups regarding Palestinian national cooperation and Christian-Muslim relations. Hamas, the largest and most important Palestinian Islamist organization, describes in detail its position on other Palestinian forces:

1. Hamas maintains that the field of the Palestinian national action is wide enough to accommodate all visions and orientations opposed to the Zionist plot. It believes that the unification of the national Palestinian action is the objective that all forces, factions and detachments should aim to realize.

2. Hamas seeks to coordinate and cooperate with all operating forces and factions out of its belief that common denominators and points of agreement should prevail over points of disagreement. . . .
3. Hamas holds that no matter how far apart the point of view may be in the arena of patriotic action, no party should resort to violence and arms to settle differences or to dictate opinions and persuasions inside the Palestinian camp.
4. Hamas undertakes advocacy for the cause of the Palestinian people *without discrimination between religious, ethnic groups or sects.* It believes in the right of all groups and sects of the Palestinians to defend their territories and defend their homeland. It also believes that the *Palestinians are one people, whether Muslim or Christian.*[6]

Two issues should be discussed when analyzing developments on the ground during the al-Aqsa Intifada since 28–29 September 2000: first, the question of concrete Christian-Muslim cooperation, as perhaps best exemplified in the fighting around Beit Jala, with a brief note on the developments during Prime Minister Sharon's war on the Palestinians ("Operation Defensive Shield" 2002), that is, the long siege of the Church of the Nativity in Bethlehem, and second, the question of a secular and/or openly nationalist interpretation of the present intifada, reinterpreting it as the al-Istiqlal Intifada.

Just as in the first intifada (1987 to the early 90s), there were demonstrations in every single Palestinian community, in cities, towns, villages, and refugee camps. As happened in the 1987 intifada, this included towns that were overwhelmingly Christian (Beit Sahour 80%; Beit Jala 80%; Birzeit 70%), Muslim towns and cities (Muslims being the preponderant majority), and mixed towns and cities like Ramallah/el-Bireh (5% Christian in Ramallah) and Bethlehem (one-third Christian), as well as the Old City of Jerusalem with its Muslim and Christian Quarters (6% Christian among the Arab inhabitants) (Sabella 2001a: 7). This clearly demonstrates that both religious communities in Palestine, the Muslim majority as well as the Christian minority of around 2 percent (ibid.: 3) are participating in this second intifada.

The fighting around the overwhelmingly Christian town of Beit Jala (6,500 Christians, 1,500 Muslims), together with the neighboring refugee camp, Aida, has made headlines, mainly because of shooting incidents originating from Beit Jala and directed against the Israeli settlement of Gilo. The Israeli press (see *Jerusalem Post* article of 25 October 2000, for example) has tried to derive the existence of a Christian-Muslim conflict from this, arguing that Christians were trying to prevent any armed attacks from their village but were forced by armed Muslims (from Fatah in general or from Muslim militants of the neighboring refugee camp of Aida) to surrender. Interviews with residents from Beit Jala[7] as well as numerous statements from Palestinian Christians seem to refute this interpretation. Despite ferocious bombardment by the Israeli army attacking from Gilo or from combat helicopters, the inhabitants have held out. To my knowledge, no incidents of Christian-Muslim confrontations or conflicts have been reported. Opinions are divided, however, as to whether it makes sense to shoot from inside civilian areas and whether this practice should be halted. The predominant views tend toward the notion that it should be stopped because it has proved too costly for the population, both Muslim and Christian.

A comparison with the first months of the second intifada as it unfolded in Ramallah/el-Bireh refutes any claim that the major issue in the Beit Jala/Gilo fighting was sectarian, where Muslim Fatah/Tanzim fighters utilized a predominantly Christian population in Beit Jala as a human shield in their fight against Israeli settlers. In el-Bireh, Ramallah's sister town, a confrontation similar to that in Beit Jala developed between el-Bireh and the Jewish settlement of Psagot, towering on a hill above the exclusively Muslim town of el-Bireh. There, too, Fatah/Tanzim fighters started to attack the settlement; dominating as it does the whole town of el-Bireh, Psagot retaliated with force, causing heavy damage and civilian casualties among the inhabitants. There, too, the same arguments arose as in Beit Jala, yet devoid of any sectarian element in the discussion. People from el-Bireh argued there should be no shooting from heavily populated quarters. And as in the case of Beit Jala, this sometimes worked, and other times did not (Sabella 2001a: 11–13). However, one element that apparently played a major role was the contrast between townspeople and inhabitants of the refugee camp of al-Amari, located in el-Bireh, that is, a social, not a sectarian dichotomy. This dichotomy can also be observed between Beit Jala, a relatively well-off Christian town, and the refugee camps of Aida and, even more, the nearby Dheishe camp.

More important, however, the issue of a united Palestinian front is all-pervasive: a front composed not only of all political stripes ranging from left to right, but also of nationalist and Islamist forces, Christians and Muslims. In the press, political statements, and above all the announcements of the National and Islamic Forces, the joint leadership of the Intifada, there is repeated stress on the concept that all Palestinians, irrespective of their political outlook and religion, are involved in the Intifada; all are fighting the occupation, buoyed by hopes for the establishment of an independent Palestinian state.

The program adopted by the Intifada leadership on 12 November 2000 proclaimed:

> [For a] day of solidarity with our courageous people in Bethlehem, Beit Jala and Beit Sahour, who are facing brutal Israeli shelling with an iron will; it will also be a day of marches and demonstrations led by Muslim and Christian clergy towards the Red Cross and United Nations headquarters to demand international protection for our people; to demand a halt to Zionist aggression and a release of prisoners and detainees in Israeli prisons.[8]

For several reasons, the Palestinian leadership under Yasir Arafat has consistently made a conscious effort to avoid infusing the Intifada with a specific Muslim content. First, Arafat wanted to prevent a possible deterioration in Christian-Muslim relations that might lead to excluding Christians from the common national Palestinian front. This was particularly important in the town of Bethlehem, adjoining Beit Jala, formerly an exclusively Christian town, where a one-third minority of Christians has lived together with a two-thirds Muslim majority. Under such circumstances, problems inevitably crop up (Sabella 2001a: 11 ff.). Second, the Palestinian National Authority projects itself as an inclusive authority for all its citizens. In this respect, changing the name from *Intifada al-Aqsa* to *Intifada al-Istiqlal* or simply *al-Intifada* was a major step in the direction of "de-religionizing the Intifada" and "encourage[d] Christian Palestinians to feel an integral part" (Sabella 2001a: 12) of the current momentous developments in Palestine. Third, "The involvement of Christian Palestinians in the Intifada would advance the image of not simply the unity of the people but also would relay a message to Europe and to other Western countries of the worthiness of a national fight for independence and not one of narrow religious orientations" (ibid.).

How successful the Palestinian leadership under Arafat has been in this respect is borne out by an interview given by one of the Palestinian "hardcore gunmen" in the Church of the Nativity in Bethlehem during the extended siege by the Israeli army in the spring of 2002. Aziz Abayad, a Muslim pharmacist from Bethlehem, spoke about the Church of the Nativity as a "Palestinian" church and continued: "We are all one, there is no difference here, we are united, Muslims and Christians, in this church, like a Muslim church" (CNN interview, 5 May 2002). In this respect, it seems important to mention that the Latin patriarch of Jerusalem, Michel Sabah, consistently stressed the obligation of the church to serve as a refuge for people in distress, while at the same time refuting the Israeli propaganda that Muslim gunmen had taken Christian civilians and clergymen hostage inside the church (*Ha'aretz*, April/May 2002, passim).

In a discussion on the current intifada that *Ha'aretz* reporter Amira Hass had with a group of Palestinian intellectuals and artists in Ramallah,[9] there was discussion of the specific character of the Intifada, particularly the question whether it had any "religious messages." Opinions differed widely. Reacting to Hass's observation that "at every funeral and every demonstration these days, there are several dozen young firebrands—not just Hamas supporters—who cry out "Haybar, Haybar, O Jews, the army of Mohammed will return,"[10] a reference to Mohammed's victory over the Jews at Haybar, members of the group expressed concern about "exhortations that bear a religious message, which could divert attention from the national character of the conflict between Palestinians and Israelis and turn it into a religious conflict."

Some of the discussants maintained that these calls are "a refuge, a comforting expression of natural feelings of anger, understandable 'in a context in which people are killed every day'" and that "despite the religious calls, the majority of the public 'sees the conflict as national and is calling for international protection, for a Palestinian state'—that is, the Palestinians are presenting national, civil demands." They pointed out that the committee coordinating Intifada actions and operations is made up of representatives of the Islamic movements (Hamas, the Islamic Jihad) and all members of the PLO, that is, the national forces *(al-quwa al-wataniya)*. According to this argument, the religious exhortations do not propose an ideology or a program of action. Rather, "the national forces are basically in favor of a two-state solution. The Islamic representatives, basically but not explicitly, share this opinion."

Some discussants expressed divergent views, arguing that these religious exhortations "reflect a Palestinian and Arab political culture in which religious sentiments are strong." According to this argument, perhaps it was not the Islamic forces that had given in to the national forces in the definition of the conflict: "Maybe it is just the other way round. Perhaps it is the national forces that have given in to the religious in the definition of the conflict?" In a variation on the argument, some pointed to "the danger that the religious discourse is becoming part of national discourse: for example, the phrase 'In the name of Allah, the merciful' on posters in memory of the dead, even those from the Democratic Front." All agreed, however, that on the Palestinian street, people would not define the Intifada as a religious jihad. Still, some asked "whether it is the Al Aqsa Intifada or the nationalist Intifada that will determine the direction," while others insisted that there was a general awareness of "the danger that the conflict change its direction from national to religious." There was a general consensus to focus on the national agenda.

While none of the discussants referred to any actual or potential conflicts between Christians and Muslims in the context of the Intifada, they did raise the fundamental question as to whether the Palestinian struggle against the Israeli occupation was national (and national here was automatically equated with secular, without apparent reflection) or religious. Implicitly, the argument expresses fears within the Christian minority of their exclusion within a religious Palestinian struggle against the occupation and for independence. The questions raised in this discourse point to some major traits in the historical post-*nakba* development of the Palestinian National Movement after 1948. Before turning to these I will sketch a brief overview of the history of Christians in Palestine as a basis for the discussion that follows.

Christians in Palestine: A Brief Historical and Demographic Overview

While Christians constituted the majority in Palestine at the end of the Byzantine reign, during the period immediately preceding the Islamic conquest under Omar Ibn al-Khattab they were turned into a minority. Their demographic proportion remained at approximately the same level until the beginning of the project of building the Zionist state and Jewish immigration into Palestine, especially under the British mandate between 1920 and 1948 (Issa 1976; Pacini 1998). Their status was governed by "an entirely new juridical code that has remained in place until modern times under the Ottoman Empire (1516–1918). Millenarian juridical structures of the Christian minority began to develop during these eight centuries," that is, 638 until 1918 C.E., and at the beginning of the British mandate in Palestine (Issa 1976: ch. 2). With the negotiated surrender of Jerusalem to the advancing Arab-Islamic army under Caliph Omar in 638, the status of Christians from that juncture on was governed by the Covenant of Omar Ibn al-Khattab. In this covenant, Omar granted safety to the Christian community in return for their payment of a tax.[11]

At the beginning of British mandatory rule in Palestine, there were approximately 70,000 Christians resident in the country, along with some 600,000 Muslims and over 80,000 Jews. The Jewish population had increased significantly as a result of several waves of immigration. Christians then made up 9.5 percent of the population. Muslims were the preponderant majority, making up about 80 percent, while Jews were some 11 percent of the population. Based on the second British census in Palestine in 1931, Jewish numbers had soared to some 175,000 inhabitants (almost 17 percent of the total population), while Muslims numbered about 760,000 (about 75 percent). Though Christians had enjoyed an absolute increase to the level of some 90,000, their proportion had declined to less than 9 percent of the total population (Sabella 2001a: 1). In 1948, out of Palestine's total population of almost 2 million people, there were 145,000 Christians (7.6 percent of the total).

The Palestinian 1948 "catastrophe" (*al-nakba* in Arabic) refers to the expulsion and flight of Palestinians from their homes, the establishment of the State of Israel, and the concomitant prevention of the establishment of a Palestinian state. In the wake of this, almost 750,000 Palestinians were forced to leave their homeland. Among those refugees, there were between "fifty to sixty thousand Christians, comprising 35 percent of all Christians in pre-1948 mandatory Palestine. . . . The demographics of Palestinian Christians are as much shaped by the politics of the Arab-Israeli conflict, as is the demographics of Palestinians in general. This is confirmed by the fact that at present almost 30 percent of the actual Christian population of the West Bank is of refugee status" (Sabella 2001a: 1).

Most Palestinian Christians live in cities and towns and are thus a predominantly urban population. There are fifteen different denominations, "the largest of which are the Greek Orthodox (52 percent) and the Roman Catholics (31 percent)" (Sabella 2001a: 2). They are distributed over fifteen different localities, "with a concentration in the urban centers of Bethlehem, Jerusalem and Ramallah" (ibid.: 2). Their present number is approximately 50,000. In Israel, by comparison, Christians constitute 11.4 percent of the Arab population and a little more than 2 percent of the overall population: in absolute numbers, some 130,000 out of a total of 1,130,000 Arabs.

Over the centuries and doubtless based on the Covenant of Omar Ibn al-Khattab, good relations prevailed between the Christian minority and the Muslim majority. "This tradition of good Christian-Muslim relations has evolved over the course of centuries of coexistence and exchange in the cities of Jerusalem, Nazareth, Bethlehem, Ramallah and in the rural areas such as Zababdeh, Bir Zeit and other towns and villages where Muslims and Christians live side by side and interact in their pursuit of daily pre-occupations and concerns" (Sabella 2001a: 5).

There are several salient factors that contributed to this tradition of good relations between Christians and Muslims, as contrasted with the problems that repeatedly flared between Christians and Muslims in Lebanon, as elaborated in detail by Sabella (2001a: 5):

1. The historical experience of Palestinians, especially after 1948 (but also during the period of British mandatory rule in Palestine), im-

pacted on Christians and Muslims alike, serving as the great equalizer. Christians and Muslims were driven out of Palestine and lost their homes and homeland, without distinction. Both Christians and Muslims were turned into refugees. As well, Christians and Muslims have jointly experienced the weight of the Israeli occupation since 1967; they have been exposed to its ravages unprotected.
2. Islam in general and Palestinian Muslims in particular recognized and protected Christian holy places, a tradition going back to the Covenant of Omar Ibn al-Khattab of 638 C.E..
3. The millet system of the Ottomans "recognized the autonomy of the Christian communities to run their own internal affairs, especially those related to religious and civil matters" (Sabella 2001a: 5).
4. Christians are held in high esteem in Palestinian society because of the role Christian institutions have played over the decades, most founded by Western colonial powers or Western Christians, such as schools, hospitals, or universities. Without exception, all of these institutions serve society as a whole, not just the Christian minority.
5. "The urban nature of the Christian population and its living in religiously mixed Christian-Muslim neighborhoods [emphasized] openness and neighborly relations. In those instances where Christians lived in villages and rural areas, friendly co-operation and communal sharing always characterized relations" (ibid.).
6. Palestinian Christians took a particular subjective approach to their identity as fusing both the national and religious elements: their identity as "Palestinian" combined the two under the national umbrella.

It is useful to point out one essential difference between the situation in Lebanon and in Palestine: the different demographic composition. In Palestine, Christians constituted a relatively small minority and had no prospect of ever being able to challenge the Muslim majority and its dominant control of affairs. It is interesting that genuine friction and problems between Christians and Muslims have surfaced only in the city of Nazareth. The situation there evinces a precarious numerical balance between the two communities. The former Christian majority in the city is now a minority: in a population of 60,000, Christians make up only some 40 percent. This came to pass in a configuration where the principal political power, embodied in the State of Israel, actively interfered in local communal issues, supporting one or another side to a dispute, as exemplified in the ongoing conflict around the Church of the Annunciation in Nazareth and the question of whether authorities can permit the building of a large mosque just opposite the grand basilica, that is, the issue of Shebab al-Din (Sabella 2001a: 7–9).

Sabella has shown quite perceptively that a similar situation obtains in Bethlehem; here, too, a former Christian majority has been turned into a minority. However, there is no serious active interference by the Israeli occupation, so problems can be kept under control and a serious confrontation avoided. Obviously, outside interference may play a crucial role in stoking sectarian conflicts. Nonetheless, perhaps due to the more mixed urban-rural character of Bethlehem, there is far greater instability in this sphere than in the more urbanized settings of Jerusalem and Ramallah. For example, it has been reported that "Christian Bethlehemites erect fluorescent crosses atop their houses, restaurants, hotels and factories. These crosses, in one sense, are an affirmation of religious bonds but also of family and community bonds that reaffirm the Christian 'tribe' in relation to other 'tribes.' In another sense, these crosses are a yearning for the old times when the town was completely Christian" (Sabella 2001a: 7).

It should be stressed that during the spring 2002 standoff between the Israeli occupying army and the Palestinians trapped (or "holed up," in CNN parlance) inside the Church of the Nativity, all Israeli attempts to stir Christian-Muslim strife or at least sensitivities were successfully foiled: they were thwarted both by the Church, with Latin patriarch Michel Sabah assuming a key role, and on the level of the Bethlehem municipality and the general population.[12]

It seems that Bethlehemites remain aware of the danger to their unity and cohesiveness if they yield to outside interference and its machinations. Perhaps Nazareth played the role of a negative example in this respect. More probably, however, it was the simple fact that the Israeli occupying power had nothing to offer either the Christian minority or the Muslim majority. Both remained under the boot of the occupation, which made no distinctions.

One final example of the eruption of social and sectarian or religious strife is worth mention here. On 31 January 2002, at the major Israeli checkpoint separating the West Bank from Jerusalem, a fracas erupted in the long line of waiting cars (sometimes one has to wait for hours until an Israeli soldier feels inclined to check a car or move it through the checkpoint, so nerves are often frayed and tempers hot around there). In the course of the fight, one man was killed and his brother wounded. The killer fled the scene of the clash and accident (i.e., the homicide); he returned to Ramallah and turned himself in to the Palestinian security there. Within hours of the violence, a large mob from Kalandia moved into Ramallah and began ransacking and burning shops, a youth club, and cars. They even prevented the fire brigade from reaching the scene as they raged.

Now what was the precise background of this murder? The perpetrator was a Christian from Ramallah, his family originating from Birzeit. His victim was from a Muslim family in Kalandia, a refugee camp between Ramallah and Jerusalem. First, rumors spread that this was the beginning of a major Muslim-Christian confrontation, conjunct with a confrontation between the camp in Kalandia and the cities of Ramallah and Birzeit. Both the Palestinian Authority under Yasir Arafat and the civil society and its institutions in Ramallah intervened, seeking to put a lid on the matter and to limit any further damage. The overall goal of everyone was clearly to avoid any risk of an internal Palestinian confrontation. Newspapers carried many announcements, reports, and critiques of what had happened, and within the course of but a few days, the whole matter had been resolved in a very traditional way, supervised by the Palestinian Authority.[13]

This confrontation in early 2002, on the very eve of Sharon's incursion into the territories and open war against the Palestinians, could certainly be read as a sign of the ever-present danger that Christian-Muslim strife can suddenly erupt. By contrast, however, take a similar case: sometime in early 2001, a very similar incident occurred in el-Bireh. There, too, there was a violent confrontation, resulting in injuries and one fatality, bound up with a quarrel involving a family from el-Bireh and another from the Amari refugee camp. There, too, the Palestinian Authority intervened and the problem was quickly resolved. Yet significantly, in this incident both parties were Muslims.[14]

The pattern in these incidents was similar: social problems flare and turn violent. The Palestinian Authority, as well as other organized and institutionalized parties within Palestinian society, intervene and try to achieve a measure of control over the violence. In both cases, this intervention proved successful and restored social calm: the evidence suggests that the difficulties and friction were due far more to social and socioeconomic problems than sectarian, communal, or religious differences or disputes. Whenever the slightest indication appears that sectarian problems may arise, society unites, closing ranks in a common nationalist front. Most evidently, the paramount value for all is Palestinian nationalism, which most believe provides a unifying core identity to *all* Palestinians, whatever their religion. In this ideological and sociopolitical effort, the political top echelon of the Palestinian Authority has assumed the lead.

The Palestinian National Movement and the Question of Christian-Muslim Relations

The historical development of the Palestinian National Movement took on a concrete form, almost a kind of mirror in which to view the discussion between Palestinian intellectuals presented above: two distinct groups emerged, one secular-nationalist, one nationalist with an implicit religious component. Because of the dispersion and ensuing fragmentation of Palestinian society in and after 1948, two new nationalist movements and organizations evolved, in different places and drawing on different traditions.

The first tradition was that of secular Arab nationalism, which had developed historically in *bilad al-sham* (geographical Syria, that is, today's Lebanon, Syria, Jordan, and Palestine), and whose ideological center was Beirut. There, at the American University of Beirut, and influenced by one of its major thinkers, Constantine Zurayk, the Movement of Arab Nationalists *(harakat al-quaumiyin al-'Arab)*, developed, with its roots going back to the year 1948. It stood under the direct impact of both the concrete experience of the war in 1948, especially the expulsion of the Palestinian inhabitants from Lydda and Ramleh by armed force, and the intellectual-ideological role played by Zurayk's small book *The Meaning of the Disaster*, first published in the summer of 1948.

According to this tradition, the Arab defeat (conceptualized as an *Arab* defeat, not a Palestinian one) was a result of Arab backwardness, and was possible because of the simple fact that Arab society had not yet modernized. Modernization was conceived of as a transformation and development of Arab society along the lines of European developments in the eighteenth and nineteenth centuries, which would lead to Arab unification. Islam was considered important as a cultural force, a cultural heritage, not as a religion. Religion had to be separated from the state, analogous to what had occurred in Europe during the Reformation and thereafter.

This predominantly secular Arab nationalist tradition was the ideological and intellectual home for many Arabs and many Palestinian Christians, but never exclusively so. The leadership echelon, however, was dominated by Christians such as George Habash, Wadi' Haddad, and, in our own time, Azmi Bishara. Nationalism in their view was only possible as a secular ideology, thus allowing for the inclusion of all religious communities and backgrounds, whether Muslim or Christian, much in the vein of Azmi Bishara's argument discussed by Raja Bahlul in chapter 6 of this volume: the view that democracy is only conceivable in a secular context. Modernization, and the development of nationalism and modern nation-states as an integral and necessary part of it, was thus conceivable only in terms of the historical model provided by European historical development.

The entire Palestinian Left traces its roots back to this tradition. As a matter of fact, all organizations of the Left that exist today are in effect offshoots of the Movement of Arab Nationalists, including the PFLP, the DFLP, and Fida, and, to a more limited degree, PLF and PFLP-GC. The Palestinian Communist Party, formerly the Jordanian Communist Party (and similarly the Israeli Communist Party), now renamed the People's Party, should be added to this secular-nationalist camp. Again, their leadership included many prominent Christians, such as Suleiman Najjab, and many notable Muslims, such as the late Bashir al-Barghuti and Mustafa al-Barghuti, who played a leading role in the recent intifada. In the ranks of the former Israeli Communist Party, there were personalities such as Emil Habibi and Emil Tuma, on the one hand, and Taufiq Zayyad and others on the other.

This secular, nationalist impact was so dominant that in the case of Taufiq Zayyad, for example, many were unaware he was a Muslim. They had assumed, without much reflection, that as mayor of Nazareth he must be a Christian. The other tradition was the Palestinian-nationalist one, represented by Fatah. It traced its roots back to Cairo, where the old leadership of the Palestinian National Movement from the period before 1948 resided between 1948 and 1959 (when Hajj Amin al-Husayni was forced to leave Cairo and finally settled in Beirut). This tradition was influenced to some degree by the anticolonial spirit and program of the Muslim Brotherhood (MB). A number of Fatah's founders had been members of the MB before becoming involved with Fatah. However, for them it was Palestinian (not Arab) nationalism that formed the basis for their ideology and political program, not religion. The Islamic tradition was carried over and played an implicit rather than direct and explicit role (Johnson 1982).

It is sufficient here to stress Johnson's conclusions: "Islam is one of the many elements of Palestinian identity . . . Islamic symbols form one of the many levels of Palestinian culture. Islamic symbols in Palestinian nationalism as represented by PLO/Fateh are full of ambiguous and implicit meanings. The interpenetration of Islamic and secular-nationalist semantic fields allows . . . a very broad characterization of conflict situations. Thus a high number of interpretations of the enemies, of forms of action and of group identity are made possible. This in turn means, that . . . group solidarity and a distinction of the group from the outside is made possible to a high degree, while at the same time a very broad public can be addressed" (Johnson 1982: 93, 94, 101).

Thus, despite—or, perhaps more accurately, precisely because of—the nonsecular, implicitly religious tradition represented by Fatah, that organization proved to be historically much more successful than the Arab nationalist, and later leftist, secularists in creating an all-embracing nationalist camp, with Christians and Muslims included in the movement on all levels. As a matter of fact, Christians were significantly overrepresented in the middle and upper leadership ranks (Kamal Nasser, Naji Alush, Raymonda Tawil, Ramzi Khoury, Nabil Abu Rudainah, to some extent Hanan Ashrawi, and many others can be named).

The historical traditions Fatah built upon were certain organizational experiences from the early days of Palestinian nationalism under British mandatory rule, especially the Muslim Christian Association that emerged as the first organized Palestinian response to the newly established mandatory role and to Zionist immigration and colonization. This trend was reinforced by the experience of British rule and British policy, which distinguished rigorously between Jews and non-Jews, that is, Palestinian Christians and Muslims. Thus, a colonialist pattern that had been established in the nineteenth century was effectively destroyed in Palestine, while it lived on in Lebanon during French mandatory rule (Makdisi 2000). With the advent of the mandate, the positive privileging treatment accorded minorities, both Christian and Jews, was terminated for the Christians. Those privileges had involved political, economic, social, cultural, and educational benefits (such as establishment of Christian schools; see Sabella 1999: 2–3), a tendency that had begun with the establishment of the first European consulates in Jerusalem around the middle of the nineteenth century (Schoelch 1986). However, it continued only for the Jews, especially during the early mandate period, benefiting the new immigrants from Europe more than the indigenous Palestinian Jews of the Yishuv.

If we trace the development of political programs by the Palestinian movements and organizations, extending from the Arab Nationalists to Fatah and to the PLO, we can find astonishingly few statements explicitly referring to the fact that there was a Muslim majority and Christian minority in Palestinian society. Obviously, the existence of two religious communities (subdivided, of course, into many distinct religious denominations) was not considered politically salient and was thus simply not reflected on the political level.

Only the programmatic idea of a secular democratic state of Palestine, espoused by Fatah in 1969, made specific reference to this aspect. Point 5 of its Seven-Point Program of January 1969 states: "Fateh, the Palestine National Liberation Movement, solemnly proclaims that the final objective of its struggle is the restoration of the independent, democratic State of Palestine, all of whose citizens will enjoy equal rights *irrespective of their religion*" (quoted in Laqueur and Rubin 1995: 224, emphasis added). Interestingly, however, this idea of a secular democratic state was addressed above all to the Jews in Palestine, not the Christians, as is evident from an interview given by Yasir Arafat in August 1969:

> Question: Fateh has offered an alternative to the Jews in Palestine—that is the creation of a progressive, democratic State for all. How do you reconcile this with the slogan "Long live Palestine Arab and Free"?
>
> Answer: A democratic, progressive State in Palestine is not in contradiction to that State being Arab . . . We have offered our solution: that is the creation of a democratic Palestinian State for all those who wish to live in peace on the land of peace. Such a State can only acquire stability and viability by forming a part of the surrounding area, which is the Arab area. Otherwise this State with its Jewish, Christian and Moslem citizens would be another alien and temporary phenomenon in the area . . . The majority of the inhabitants of any future State of Palestine will be Arab, if we consider that there are at present 2,500,000 Palestinian Arabs of the Moslem and Christian faiths and another 1,250,000 Arabs of the Jewish faith who live in what is now the State of Israel . . .
>
> The immediate objective of Fateh is the total liberation of Palestine from Zionism and the destruction of any racial or sectarian notion which might exist among Arabs . . .
>
> We aim ultimately at the establishment of an independent, progressive, democratic State in Palestine, which will guarantee *equal rights to all its citizens, regardless of race or religion.* (quoted in Laqueur and Rubin 1995: 224–25, emphasis added)

It seems obvious that those groups and individuals within Fatah who had developed the notion of the secular democratic state were under the strong influence of European political thinking and of European political concepts. And as the problem for the Palestinians was clearly not the relationship between Palestine's Muslims and Christians but rather the relationship between Palestinians and Jews (i.e., Jewish Israelis), the whole notion was basically addressed to a Jewish audience, projecting Jewish-Arab coexistence within a single binational state. This does not mean, however, that the explicit stating of the notion of a secular democratic state did not have an important and positive impact on the attitude of Palestinian Christians toward a future Palestinian state. Suffice it here to point to the numerous heated discussions and controversies that flared above all in the West Bank after the establishment of the Palestinian Authority, centering on the drafting of a Palestinian constitution, the question of Christian representation in parliament, women's rights, and many other issues.

The Palestinian Declaration of Independence proclaimed by the Palestine National Council in Algiers in November 1988 takes up the issue of religious coexistence within a unitary state; yet there is no longer mention of a secular state, which seems to corroborate this interpretation.

The declaration begins with the following historical statement, a kind of main thread running through the text:

> Palestine, the land of the three monotheistic faiths, is where the Palestinian Arab people was born . . . Nourished by an unfolding series of civilizations and cultures, inspired by a heritage rich in variety and kind, the Palestinian Arab people added to its stature by consolidating a union between itself and its patrimonial land. The call went out from temple, church, and mosque, to praise the Creator, to celebrate compassion, and peace was indeed the message of Palestine . . .
>
> The Palestine National Council, in the name of God, and in the name of the Palestinian Arab people, hereby proclaims the establishment of the State of Palestine on our Palestinian territory with its capital Jerusalem (al-Quds al-Sharif). . . . In it will be safeguarded their political and religious convictions and their human dignity by means of a parliamentary democratic system of governance . . . The rights of minorities will duly be respected by the majority. Governance will be based on principles of social justice, equality and nondiscrimination in public rights on ground of race, religion, color, or sex . . . Thus shall these principles allow no departure from Palestine's age-old spiritual and civilizational heritage of tolerance and religious co-existence.[15]

The writer Anton Shammas, a Palestinian with Israeli citizenship (an Israeli Arab), has written a moving essay on this Declaration of Independence. In this analysis, he focuses on the religious beginning ("In the name of God, the Compassionate, the Merciful . . .") and on the religious ending (with a Qur'anic verse: "In the name of God, the Compassionate, the Merciful. 'Say: O God, Master of the Kingdom, Thou givest the Kingdom to whom Thou wilst, and seizest the Kingdom from whom Thou wilt. Thou exaltest whom Thou wilt, and Thou abasest whom Thou wilt; in Thy hand is the good; Thou art powerful and everything.' Sadaqa Allahu al-'Azim" (ibid.: 216), and concludes that this Islamic religious form and content may implicitly have signified the abandonment of the dream of a secular democratic state in Palestine. He stresses his fear that Palestine might become just one more Middle Eastern polity in which state and church are intermingled in a deadly amalgam (Shammas 1989). Again, we have here the equating of the nationalist and secular, that is, the historical European model, based on a separation of church and state, religion and politics, conceived as the only feasible or realistic basis for the establishment of a modern nation-state.

Particularities of Christian-Muslim Relations in Palestine and Differences in the Dynamic of Intercommunal Relations in Lebanon and Palestine

Although the modern Christian-Muslim relationship began in Palestine along the same lines as in Lebanon, that is, the interference of European colonial powers and their direct collaboration with existing Christian and Jewish minorities in the country, historical developments in Palestine took a different turn. While Lebanon was under the French mandate, which intended to establish a modern Lebanese state dominated by the Maronite community, in Palestine British mandatory rule worked instead toward establishing a modern Jewish nation-state. Such a state, by definition, had no place for the non-Jewish communities living in Palestine, although at the time they constituted the overwhelming majority. Again, both Palestinian Muslims and Palestinian Christians were, by definition, put in the same category; they were not primarily Muslims or Christians but were, over and above all else, non-Jews. The historical, political, and "communal" conflict, to use the terminology of Meron Benvenisti, was thus the conflict between Jews—defined as a national group and simultaneously as a religious community—and Palestinians, made up of a large Muslim majority and a small Christian minority, that is, a national group composed of two religious communities. It seems clear that in such a context there was no space or basis for Muslim-Christian conflicts, and historically these conflicts did not and could not arise.

Over and above this, however, the political leadership of the post-*nakba* Palestinian National Movement focused in its political course on a conscious inclusion of the Christian minority in the nationalist mainstream. As we have seen in the analysis in the previous section, two different trajectories can be distinguished here: a secular nationalist one, which assigns the question of religion to the private realm, that is, removes it from the political arena, and a nationalist agenda with an implicit religious identity—albeit as only one identity among many others. Both Christians and Muslims have participated in the two different trajectories. The secular trajectory always constituted a minority, while the nationalist stream with its religious components formed the majority.

Here, too, the differences with Lebanon are striking, because in Palestine there is a clearly demarcated majority-minority configuration, while in

Lebanon the very question of who is the majority has been an abiding major divisive political issue since the 1930s. Problems in Palestine between Christians and Muslims typically arose in urban contexts where the previous Christian majority had been turned into a minority, that is, in Bethlehem and in Nazareth. In Bethlehem, however, under the conditions of an Israeli occupation that did not differentiate between Christian and Muslim, conflicts could be kept to a minimum and were always under control. This is clearly reflected in the statement by Aziz Abayad, a militant who had sought refuge in the Church of the Nativity in Bethlehem during April/May 2002, mentioned above: "It has become a Palestinian church for the entire people, a kind of Muslim church, because we are one people inside. . . . We are all together here, Muslims and Christians, there is no difference, we are united."

By contrast, Nazareth is spatially inside the state of Israel, where a typical colonial policy (divide and rule) has been applied, even if focusing more on Druze and Bedouin Palestinians than on Christians. Still, in the case of the Shebab al-Din Mosque, precisely this policy has been applied with differing emphasis by subsequent Israeli governments, privileging in turn Muslim and Christian Palestinians. It seems that the "colonial outside" interference does make the decisive difference, determining whether conflicts arise or not. Even in Nazareth, however, with the start of the second intifada in September 2000, the sense of local "Israeli" Palestinians identifying with and sharing the nationalist Palestinian conflict with the Israeli (Jewish) state has proven dominant, serving to unify the population while acting to prevent the conflict from boiling over into violence as in Lebanon.

However, the actual litmus test will only come after an independent Palestinian state has been established: only then will the issue be raised as to what basic aspects underlie the identity of a Palestinian citizen. Already today questions concerning this future decision are being broached, as has been pointed up in the discussions about the first and the second intifadas and in Shammas's analysis of the 1988 Declaration of Independence, and in connection with, for example, Palestinian elections in 1996, when it was decided to assign a fixed number of seats to Christian deputies. This issue will certainly be a major point of controversy once a Palestinian state comes into existence.

Yet I would contend that on the whole, the leadership of the post-1948 Palestinian National Movement has proven quite successful in avoiding the pitfalls of sectarianism. It has been helped by very fortunate historical conjunctures, but it should not be overlooked that the issue was addressed quite openly and courageously whenever it surfaced, especially after the Islamic Revolution in Iran, which catapulted religious discourse to the very center stage of politics.

Arafat is a case in point. A prime concept in his political discourse has been the presentation of Palestine as both Christian and Muslim, focusing consistently on the great historical and religious tradition of both religious communities in the country. It seems plausible to argue that his choice of political advisers and the inclusion of a disproportionately high number of Christians in the higher echelons of the PNM and PA have been a conscious political choice. One might even be tempted to conjecture that his marriage to a Christian Palestinian had some of the makings of the political. What is readily evident is Arafat's concern, in his role as Palestinian president, to participate in the major Christian holidays, especially Christmas celebrations in the Church of the Nativity in Bethlehem. Although the real challenges still loom, the fact that they have already been addressed holds out hope that a solution for a peaceful and unproblematic coexistence between a Christian minority and a Muslim majority might well be feasible.

Conclusion

Ussama Makdisi has suggested an original and stimulating approach to and understanding of sectarianism and religious fanaticism—not as "premodern vestiges that have precluded the development of a modern, democratic, and liberal state in the Middle East" (Makdisi 2000: 173), but rather as something quite modern:

> The beginning of sectarianism did not imply a reversion [i.e., a revival of primordial passions]. It marked a rupture, a birth of a new culture that singled out religious affiliation as the defining public and political characteristic of a modern subject and citizen. To overcome it, if it is at all possible, requires yet another rupture, a break as radical for the body politic as the advent of sectarianism was for the old regime. It requires another vision of modernity.

This clearly entails questions about the nature of fundamentalism, a phenomenon relevant to Lebanon, Palestine, and Israel alike (see Ehrlich, ch. 9). The ongoing al-Aqsa Intifada has posed these questions anew in a fiercely violent form, especially the Palestinian suicide bombings against civilian targets (perceived as mostly Jewish) inside Israel. As Makdisi concludes:

> Finally, by suggesting that the ethnic and religious conflicts in such evidence today are not revivals of primordial passions, we will begin to appreciate that the processes at work in nineteenth-century Mount Lebanon are also at work in other modern societies, albeit in different forms and with different discourses. Therefore, the question that I ask is not why the Middle East has failed to modernize or secularize—

which assumes that the Western model of separation of church and state is the only path toward modernity—but how religion became the site of a multifaceted colonial encounter and why religious violence became a crucial component of national expression. (Makdisi 2000: 174)

In the Palestinian case, there has to date been no religious violence between Christians and Muslims inside Palestinian society. Instead, in the raging encounter with the Israeli occupation over East Jerusalem, the West Bank, and Gaza Strip, an explosive mixture of religious-nationalist violence, a kind of "sacralized violence," has erupted and been directed against the occupying force. As in Lebanon, it has been the outside "colonialist" interference that has led to violence and has contributed to a superimposition of religious identities on national ones. Nonetheless, it would seem that the Palestinian national identity is still the overriding one, with religious identities relegated to a secondary rank.

Notes

1. *Ha'aretz*, 17 November 2000.
2. See also *Middle East International* 637 (10 November 2000): 6.
3. Retrieved 18 July 2002 and quoted from http://www.miftah.org/Other/Letters/christians.htm.
4. MIFTAH (an NGO founded and directed by Hanan Ashrawi) is The Palestinian Initiative for the Promotion of Global Dialogue and Democracy.
5. Emphasis added. See http://www.miftah.org.
6. Emphasis added. See http://www.palestine.info.net/hamas/about/index.htm.
7. *Middle East International* 637 (10 November 2000): 6.
8. Quoted from http://www.jmcc.org/news/00/bayan.htm, retrieved 17 July 2002.
9. *Ha'aretz*, 17 November 2000, B 4.
10. "Khaibar, Khaibar, ya Yahood, Jaish Muhammad saufa yaoud." This victory at Haybar brought about their treaty of submission and certainly not their slaughter, as has been intimated by many press reports quoting this battle cry of the demonstrators as a proof of the bloodthirstiness of Palestinians.
11. "This is the assurance of safety which the servant of Allah, the second Caliph Umar Ibn al-Khattab, the Commander of the Faithful, has granted to the people of Aelia Capitolina. He has granted them safety for their lives and possessions; their churches and crosses; the sick and healthy of the city; and for the rest of its religious community. Their churches will not be inhabited or destroyed by Muslims. Neither they, nor the land on which they stand, nor their cross, nor their possessions will be confiscated. They will not be forcibly converted, nor any one of them armed. No Jew will live with them in Aelia. The people of Aelia must pay the poll tax like the people of the other cities, and they must expel the Byzantines and the robbers." Retrieved

15 July 2002 and quoted from http://www.miftah.org/Documents/documents/omar.html.

12. See daily reports in *Ha'aretz* from Bethlehem during April 2002.

13. *Al-Ayyam,* 1–5 February 2002.

14. Oral communication from *al-Ayyam* journalists and residents from el-Bireh; the exact date of the incident could not be established.

15. Quoted in *Journal of Palestine Studies* 70 (winter 1989): 213–16.

References

Issa, A. O. *Les minorities chretiennes de Palestine à travers les siecles.* Jerusalem: Franciscan Printing Press, 1976. English translation quoted from http://www.al-bushra.org/holyland/chapter2b.htm, retrieved 10 May 2002.

Johnson, Nels. *Islam and the Politics of Meaning in Palestinian Nationalism.* London: Kegan Paul International, 1982.

Laqueur, Walter, and Barry Rubin, eds. *The Israel-Arab Reader: A Documentary History of the Middle East Conflict.* 5th rev. ed. New York: Penguin Books, 1995.

Makdisi, Ussama. *The Culture of Sectarianism: Community, History, and Violence in Nineteenth-Century Ottoman Lebanon.* Berkeley: University of California Press, 2000.

Pacini, Andrea, ed. *Christian Communities in the Arab Middle East: The Challenge of the Future.* Oxford: Clarendon Press, 1998.

Sabella, Bernard. "A Century Apart: Palestinian Christians and Their Churches—from Awakening to Nation Building." In *Out of Jerusalem,* ed. Afif Safieh. 1999. Retrieved 20 June 2002 from http://www.al-bushra.org/holyland/outjerusalem.htm

———. "Palestinian Christians: Population, Interreligious Relations and the Second Intifada. The Demographic Dynamics of Christian Palestinians: Percentage and Presence." Unpublished paper, 2001. (2001a)

———. "Comparing Palestinian Christians on Society and Politics: Context and Religion in Israel and Palestine," accepted for presentation at Middle East Studies Association annual conference in San Francisco, November 2001. Accessible via URL: http://www.al-bushra.org/latpatra/sabella2.html (2001b)

Schoelch, Alexander. *Palästina im Umbruch 1856–1882: Untersuchungen zur wirtschaftlichen und soziopolitischen Entwicklung.* Stuttgart: Steiner, 1986. English translation: *Palestine in Transformation, 1856–1882: Studies in Social, Economic, and Political Development.* Washington, D.C.: Institute of Palestine Studies, 1993.

Shammas, Anton. "Der Tag danach—Fallstricke einer Staatengründung. Palästina und Israel" (The day after). *Lettre International* 4 (spring 1989): 52–56.

Tsimhoni, Daphne. *Christian Communities in Jerusalem and the West Bank since 1948: An Historical, Social, and Political Study.* Westport, Conn.: Praeger, 1993.

Zurayk, Constantine. *The Meaning of the Disaster.* Beirut: 1948 (Arabic); Beirut: Khayat's College Book Cooperative, 1956 (English).

III

Progressive Potentials
within Religious Traditions

5

Democracy without Secularism?

Reflections on the Idea of Islamic Democracy

Raja Bahlul

"Democracy" has become a battle cry in political debates within Arab-Islamic societies.[1] Variously interpreted and understood, it has nevertheless come to represent an ideal that most political movements, even some that identify themselves as Islamic, claim as their own.

What do contemporary Islamic thinkers understand by the term *democracy*? How do they deal with arguments purporting to prove that democracy requires secularism? Do they end up subverting the meaning of democracy, or do they succeed in offering an innovative and coherent understanding of what the term means, a vision of politics in which political and religious elements coexist peacefully?

To examine Islamic approaches to democracy is in part to see how Islam views the "other." In the present case, this other is a victorious, democratic West that claims that, despite its faults, democracy is the only morally defensible political order, the only political option for societies and states that do not want to be left behind in the rapidly evolving world in which we live.

There are at least two reasons why it is useful to explore how Islamic thinkers view democracy. To begin with, there is a purely theoretical interest in seeing how intellectual traditions (or cultures) perceive each other. In particular, what happens to concepts and practices emanating from a given intellectual tradition when attempts are made to graft them onto other intellectual traditions? Here we can find a measure of perceived distance between traditions and their ability (or inability) to recognize in each other an interlocutor from whom to learn.

Second, and perhaps more important, there is a practical interest in seeing the possible form(s) that political practice may assume in countries where Islam is dominant or increasingly influential. For example, are there significant differences between Islamic movements that pledge allegiance to democracy and those that are consciously opposed to it? Better understanding the conceptions and ideas espoused by prodemocracy Islamic thinkers can help us to anticipate the future and perhaps play a part in shaping its evolving contours.

The first section of this chapter centers on an explanation of certain aspects of the "received view of democracy." According to this view, both in Western and Arab-Islamic countries, democracy presupposes (or implies) secularism. Western thinkers, long accustomed to the notion of the separation between religion and the state, tend to presuppose this as part of the intellectual background of discussion. But prodemocracy Arab thinkers opposed to political Islam are acutely aware of the need to convince their readers that no genuine democracy is possible unless religion is relegated to the private sphere. All of this is part of the charged intellectual setting in which Islamic thinkers must contest democracy for Islam or engage in its advocacy.

The chapter's second section seeks to explain the Islamic perspective on democracy. "Islamic democrats" conceptualize democracy as a set of procedures for arriving at political decisions. Moreover, Islamic thinkers view these procedures as basically value free, which is to say they are neutral between different value systems—including Islamic and secularist values or ways of life.

Finally, the last two sections of the chapter explore a number of objections raised in conjunction with the proposed Islamic view of democracy. Such doubts and misgivings about "Islamic democracy" seek to underscore, by means of specific examples and scenarios, the extreme tension if not explicit contradiction seemingly unavoidable between the requirements of democracy and the requirements of the faith. Islamic replies, on the other hand, try to downplay the degree of such tensions, or to show that they are neither inevitable nor peculiar to the Islamic polity.

Secularism and the Received View of Democracy

In the history of ideas, the rich complex concept of democracy has a long course of development during which associations were formed and links to other concepts forged. Consequently, it is not surprising to find that some of the more astute Islamic thinkers who have discovered the concept in recent years do not believe that "democracy" expresses a simple monolithic meaning that must either be accepted or rejected.

Islamic thinkers are fully justified in this attitude, as suggested by the multitude of differing schools of democratic thought, ranging from liberal democracy, social democracy, and participatory democracy to deliberative democracy, in addition to concepts such as elite pacts, pluralism, polyarchy, and others. The existence of different schools of thought, each of which claims to offer a more adequate and perhaps more insightful view of democracy than its rivals, makes it evident that democracy is an "essentially contested concept."[2] Islamic writers who discuss democracy have in effect decided to join the debates on democratic discourse and its central disputed concept, striving to contest or win democracy for Islam.

On the face of it, their task is not an easy one. For despite all the disagreements between proponents of democracy, Western and non-Western alike, and the differences between the various explications of the term, contemporary discussions of democracy commonly assume that religion is firmly within the private sphere and that the public sphere, where political activity takes place, is open to all citizens, without reference to religious convictions.

Indeed, sometimes the need for citizens to meet on neutral, nonparochial ground is advanced as a requirement or presupposition that all but betrays the democratic-cum-secular form of the desired political order. The theorist John Rawls is a case in point, suggesting "political liberalism" as a possible answer to the question: "How is it possible that there may exist over time a stable and just society of free and equal citizens profoundly divided by reasonable, though incompatible, religious, philosophical, and moral doctrines?" (Rawls 1993: xx).

More often, however, it is simply assumed that political debates and arguments that are to be conducted in the public arena, in the presence of all interested citizens, will use what Audi calls "secular rationale." Secular rationale is defined as one whose "normative force, i.e., its status as a prima facie justificatory element, does not evidentially depend on the existence of God (or denying it) or on theological considerations, or on the pronouncements of a person or institution qua religious authority" (Audi 1997: 26).

On the whole, it seems fair to say that what to do with religion is not considered to be a major problem in discussions of democracy in the West. Most of the time debates revolve around issues such as representation, fairness, equality, and participation that put religion somewhat aside. But when democracy is discussed in the context of Arab and Islamic culture, that is not the case: numerous writers remind us of the need to resolve the issue of the relation between religion and politics. The resolution most commonly suggested requires a separation between religion and politics. Democracy, we are told, requires secularism.

For Aziz al-Azmeh, one of the most prolific and insightful writers on political Islam, it is virtually axiomatic that democracy implies secularism. This is evident in the way he bemoans how rare in recent Arab democratist discourse are "positions that underline the necessity of secularism for any democratic order" (al-Azmeh 1994: 127). Elie Kedourie, a firm believer in the hostility of Arab-Islamic culture to democracy, claims that the idea of the secularity of the state (a concept "indispensable to good government and a free society") is "implicit in popular sovereignty" (Kedourie 1994: 5). Given that popular sovereignty is implied by democracy (its etymon underscores rule by the demos), it would seem, according to this argument, that secularism is implied by democracy.

Still a third, Azmi Bishara, appears to infer secularism from the very definition of democracy. According to Bishara, "It is conceptually impossible to entertain a notion of the freedom of thought and expression unless beliefs are placed in the realm of free decision. Freedom to decide, on the other hand, is (by definition) an individual liberty. Thus, if freedom of thought and expression is an essential constituent of democracy, it follows that secularism . . . is an essential constituent of democracy" (Bishara 1993: 78).[3]

This perceived nexus between democracy and secularism, eludable or not, has not been lost on Islamic writers seeking to come to terms with the notion of democracy. The constellation of concepts they grapple with includes not only democracy-related concepts such as the people, popular will, and the common good, but also divine sovereignty, obedience to God's law, and an entire system of moral and aesthetic values that derive from history and religion.

Having seen for themselves the effects, both short and long term, of despotism, and having witnessed, often at close quarters, the well-ordered workings of the polity in stable Western democracies, many Islamic thinkers have begun to yearn for a political order that would in some ways emulate what they observe in the West, without forsaking the living faith of the people. The challenge for them is to decipher the basic components and aspects of this "democratic" method of government, trying to determine how the system functions, what its presuppositions are, and whether and to what extent it can be emulated without doing harm to Islamic religion and culture.

This does not promise to be an easy task, inasmuch as it involves resolving some apparently serious conflicts between religion and democracy. One major problem, hinted at by Kedourie above, is recognizing the principle of popular sovereignty. How can a religion-based political system avoid setting up an office of "religious guardians" with veto power over the will of the people? Another problem area is freedom of thought and expression, referred to by Bishara above. This raises a further question: can the need to preserve a measure of orthodoxy (a hallmark of all religious traditions) be reconciled with freedom of thought and expression? Is that indeed compatible with the spirit of toleration, presumed an essential part of democratic practice and ethos?

An Islamic View of Democracy

Islamic views on democracy are usefully introduced by reference to the writings of three well-known Islamic thinkers: al-Ghannouchi, Turabi, and Khatami. Their views are not universally well received: secularists contend "Islamic democracy" is not sufficiently democratic, while conservative Islamic writers argue that "Islamic democracy" is not sufficiently Islamic. Nevertheless, many find the moderate and reformist views of these three theorists both reasonable and appealing. Considered as a whole, their work represents a quite elaborate attempt to come to grips with the fundamental questions that Islamic thought must face if it is to succeed in arriving at a satisfactory and amicable settlement with democracy.

Their logical move is to distinguish between two ways of thinking about democracy. One is to view democracy as basically a "doctrine of procedure," a method for dispensing, sharing, and managing political power. This view of democratic practice has been classically expressed by Schumpeter: "Democracy is a political method, that is to say, a certain type of institutional arrangement for arriving at political . . . decisions, and hence incapable of being an end in itself, irrespective of what decisions it will produce under given historical conditions" (Schumpeter 1976: 242).

This procedural conception of democracy is broad enough to include Dahl's "institutions of polyarchy," that is, free, periodic elections, inclusive suffrage, associational autonomy, and the like (Dahl 1989: 221). Basically, democracy is a method of government that allows the people to choose their rulers and hold them accountable for what they do in office. The other way is to view democracy as a procedure tied to values and philosophical beliefs that hinge on a certain conception of the "good life," a life that involves, among other things, autonomy, individuality, and free choice—a life lived in dignity within a political community.

Both Schumpeter and, more recently, Rawls reject this view of democracy, though for different reasons. According to what Schumpeter terms the "classical theory of democracy," democracy is an institutional arrangement that aims at achieving "the common good" (Schumpeter 1976: 250). Moreover, this view of democracy has certain religious moorings, in that the belief in the intrinsic and equal worth of all individuals (expressed in some statements of the classical theory of democracy) is basically a political translation of the Christian belief in the equality of all souls before God (Schumpeter 1976: 266).

Rawls, on the other hand, distinguishes between liberalism viewed as a "comprehensive philosophical doctrine" and liberalism viewed as a solution to the problem of how citizens who are divided by "incompatible religious, philosophical, and moral doctrines" can nonetheless manage to live together. This latter Rawls terms "political liberalism," illustrating the difference between these two views of liberalism by reference to the value of individual autonomy: "This value may take at least two forms. One is political autonomy, the legal independence and assured political integrity of citizens and their sharing with other citizens in the exercise of political power. The other form is moral autonomy expressed in a certain mode of life and reflection that critically examines our deepest ends and ideals, as in Mill's ideal of individuality, or by following as best one can Kant's doctrine of autonomy.... Many citizens of faith reject moral autonomy as part of their way of life" (Rawls 1993: xliv–xlv).[4]

The distinctions Islamic thinkers draw between different perspectives on democracy are markedly similar to those made by Schumpeter and Rawls, despite the fact that they differ in details and manner of illustration. Al-Ghannouchi has put forward the clearest formulation of the distinction between two ways of viewing democracy:

> It is possible for the mechanisms of democracy ... to operate in different cultural milieus ... Secularism, nationalism, profit-making, pleasure, power, and the deification of man (these are the values and practices under whose shadow democracy developed) are not inevitable consequences of democracy. Democracy resolves itself into popular sovereignty, equality between citizens, governing bodies which emerge from popular will through free elections, ... recognition of the majority's right to rule ... There is nothing in these procedures which is necessarily in conflict with Islamic values. On the contrary, the democratic apparatus is the best available method for realizing these values. (al-Ghannouchi 1993: 88)

Khatami provides a different formulation: "Democracy is a method of achieving [political] stability. This means that democracy is a mechanism, and that the form of government is to be decided by the popular will. Now, in the West, popular will has led to secularism and liberalism. In Islamic societies, popular will is bound to produce a form of government which is in line with people's Islamic thought" (Khatami 1998: 103).

Statements by al-Ghannouchi, Khatami, and others make clear that to the Muslim way of thinking, democracy has become entangled with certain values and practices that Islam cannot permit. Primary among those questioned values and practices is secularism. Materialism, utilitarianism, skepticism, and liberalism (in the sense of "unfettered freedom") are also somehow intertwined with democracy.

The conceptually innovative move that al-Ghannouchi and Khatami make lies in their claim that democracy as such is only contingently related to the abhorred secular values and practices. For Khatami, democracy is simply the practice of abiding by decisions of the popular will. If people's beliefs and values are Islamic, then by following the democratic method, we are bound to establish an Islamic regime. If, on the other hand, those popular beliefs and values are secular or liberal, then pursuing that same method will naturally lead to the establishment of a secular or liberal regime.

Al-Ghannouchi is even clearer: democracy means popular sovereignty, political equality, representative government, and majority rule. None of these necessarily entails secularism, skepticism, materialism, or utilitarianism. Hence there is no necessity, from an Islamic point of view, to reject democracy. Or, as Schumpeter phrases it, democracy is simply a method of making political decisions. It does not dictate the content of the decisions.[5]

Believing that in a Muslim society the overwhelming majority will want to live in an Islamic way, Khatami and al-Ghannouchi welcome free elections. Their attitude toward political pluralism, party competition, parliamentary debates, and other aspects of the democratic process is equally open and positive. For they imagine that all the competition, opposition, and debate will take place within specified limits established by a national consensus on the essentials of the (Islamic) regime, so that no threat to the integrity of the Islamic society will be posed by these political processes and procedures.

That pluralism and opposition take place within the framework of a lasting fundamental political consensus on essential matters is not an original insight on the part of Islamic writers who have been engaged in examining the presuppositions of democracy. Many Western political writers recognize this. According to Esposito and Voll: "In standard modern Western political thought, acceptable opposition in a democratic system is closely tied to the concept of a constitutional government, in which there is an underlying, fundamental consensus on the 'rules of the game' of politics. Opposition is the legitimate disagreement with particular policies of specific leaders within the mutually accepted framework of the principles of an underlying constitution that is either written or based on long-established practice" (Esposito and Voll 1996: 36).

Islamic thinkers agree with Esposito and Voll in thinking that democratic practice takes place "within the mutually accepted framework of the principles of an underlying constitution." In the case of the Islamic thinkers, though, the constitution derives from the basic principles of the faith. Islamic thinkers consider shari'a (Islamic law) to be that foundation stone.

Turabi, for example, views shari'a as "the higher law, just like the constitution, except that it is a detailed constitution" (1993: 25). Mawdudi, on the other hand, speaks of an "unwritten Islamic constitution," one that already exists, awaiting efforts to codify it, on the basis of its original sources. The sources for this unwritten constitution turn out to be identical with the sources of shari'a (Mawdudi 1975: 11).

Once the binding Islamic constitutional framework is established, political activity can proceed in the familiar democratic manner, allowing for pluralism, opposition, and power contestation. To Turabi, this is a clear feature in Western democracies, exemplified in the logic of "government and loyal opposition":

> Such a consensus on the foundations, which is directly agreed upon, and in whose light details are discussed, is a condition for the stability of all democratic systems. This is how Western democracies have achieved their stability: the people, through a process of cultural and political development, have eventually reached a consensus on the foundations, and have succeeded in delimiting the matters which are subject to consultation and parliamentary debate. . . . If we were to look at partisan debates in Western democratic countries, we would find that the debate takes place within an established framework. For example, the difference between the Labor Party and the Conservative Party in Britain is very limited, and so is the difference between the Republican Party and the Democratic Party in America. (Turabi 1987: 68)

In a nutshell, this is the Islamic perspective on democracy. Democracy must be distinguished from secularism and other "ideological" value-elements with which it has become extraneously entangled in Western practice. Islamic thinkers propose a mode of democracy without or beyond secularism. Freed from secularism, democracy becomes available as a means for Muslim societies to order their political life.

Still, many key questions remain regarding the logical coherence of the resulting proposal, most centering on "rights." What types of rights does the Islamic constitution recognize and protect? Does it legitimize any form of discrimination between citizens? Does it protect the right of opposition and dissent, and to what degree? How does the minority fare within an Islamic polity? But perhaps we should begin by considering the fundamental question whose answer sets theocratic forms of government apart from modern democratic forms. This is the question of popular sovereignty: the collective right that people have to govern themselves by laws of their own making. Is this something that a religion-based system of government can accept?

People versus God: The Question of Sovereignty

Islamic thinkers who want to come to terms with democracy often face a major conceptual difficulty at the outset, summarized as follows: On the one hand, democracy requires the upholding of a principle of popular sovereignty. Islam, on the other hand, seems to require repudiation of popular sovereignty in favor of an institution sometimes referred to as "divine sovereignty" or "divine rulership" *(al-hakimiyya al-ilahiyyah)*. According to Sayyid Qutb, a well-known exponent of this idea: "The right of rulership gives rise to the right to legislate to people, the right to prescribe the way of life which people lead, the right to institute the values which this life is to be based on.... Whoever claims for himself the right to legislate a way of life for a people thereby claims divine authority over them, for he seeks to appropriate the most important attribute of divinity. Moreover, whoever amongst the people accepts this claim has thereby agreed to make this person a God in place of the true God, for he attributes to him the most important attributes of divinity" (quoted in Abu Zaid 1994: 105). This is often understood as illustrating the profound difference between Islam and its Western-secularist "other." With the two sides speaking such different languages, what hope can there be for a real dialogue, much less mutual understanding, to take place?

How can advocates of Islamic democracy reply to this charge?[6] Initially, it should be made clear that Islamic thinkers who speak of divine sovereignty do not usually mean to imply that the Islamic state, unlike other mundane states, has an "invisible president" who rules as mundane potentates do. Sayyid Qutb's statement notwithstanding, God does not rule over the affairs of the Muslim community as human rulers do. As al-Ghannouchi puts it, "Those who uphold the slogan 'Sovereignty belongs to God' do not mean that an Incarnate God comes to dwell amongst us in order to rule over us. God—may His Name be exalted—cannot be seen, nor does He dwell in a person or an institution that can speak for Him. The slogan 'Sovereignty belongs to God' means only 'lawful rule'" (al-Ghannouchi 1999: 155).

Building on al-Ghannouchi's suggestion, one can argue that statements such as "Sovereignty belongs to God" or "In an Islamic state only God rules" should be construed as referring to what political decisions ought to be like if they are to have validity or moral rectitude.[7] The ideal situation is when democratic procedures function within parameters set by divine law. People debate, discuss, and vote. And there is always a way to determine whether the decision was valid: not by the fact that it was accepted by the majority, after discussion and debate, but by checking it against divine law.

To view Islamic calls for divine sovereignty and the application of shari'a as hinting at the idea of "rule of (divine) law," constitutionalism, or an Islamic version of these is not some sort of wishful thinking to interpret Islam in a sympathetic light. This is grasped by more astute Arab secularists, such as Azmi Bishara, who claims that "in times when social consciousness takes a religious form, it is possible that calls for the application of shari'a express a democratic tendency, or (at least) an opposition to despotism, simply because shari'a rule implies restrictions on the exercise of political power over and above mere will of rulers" (Bishara 1993: 83).

This remark, as well as similar statements by Tariq al-Bishri and Nazih Ayyubi,[8] suggest that we should view advocacy of divine sovereignty as a way of referring to the constitutional framework within which the democratic process is to take place, and which is the final arbiter in matters of political validity. This is fully compatible with the Islamic conception of democracy. After all, all democratic procedures, including those in a liberal-secular framework, require an established constitution whose validity is not put to question every time the people go to the polls. In the case of Islamic democracy, the constitutional framework is none other than divine law, which people accept and which is the basis of their consensus.

Still, many difficult questions about the Islamic rule of law, the Islamic constitution, can be raised, pertaining in part to the content of the Islamic law and how it may (adversely) affect the freedoms and the rights of minorities and other specific groups, such as women and non-Muslims. The next section will examine how Islamic writers may deal with questions of this kind. But first we turn to the relation between popular sovereignty and the Islamic rule of law (our basis for explicating the notion of divine sovereignty).

It may be thought that the notion of divine sovereignty, even when taken to mean rule of law, still poses a threat to popular sovereignty. After all, who is to be entrusted with codifying the unwritten Islamic constitution of which Mawdudi speaks? And who is to have a role in interpreting it? Surely not everyone, regardless of religious qualification. The concern here is well expressed by the Egyptian thinker Nasr Hamid Abu-Zaid, who fears that divine sovereignty will easily dissolve into "the sovereignty of the fuqaha' [Islamic jurisprudents]" (Abu-Zaid 1994: 111, 117).

Abu-Zaid's fears seem to have come true in the constitution of the Islamic Republic of Iran (Blaustein and Flanz 1986). This constitution probably represents the first attempt to write a detailed, workable constitution from an Islamic point of view. It is instructive to look at some of the relevant articles of the constitution:

> All civil, penal, financial, administrative, cultural, military, political laws and regulations, as well as other laws or regulations, should be

based on Islamic principles. This principle will in general prevail over all of the principles of the constitution, and other laws and regulations as well. Any judgment in regard to this will be made by the clerical members of the Council of Guardians. (Article 4)

The Islamic Consultative Assembly cannot enact laws contrary to the *usul* [fundamentals] and *ahkam* [judgments] of the official religion of the country or to the Constitution. It is the duty of the Guardian Council to determine whether a violation has occurred in accordance with Article 96. (Article 72)

The determination of compatibility of the legislation passed by the Islamic Consultative Assembly with the laws of Islam rests with the majority vote of the *fuqaha'* of the Guardian Council; and the determination of its compatibility with the Constitution rests with the majority of all the members of the Guardian Council. (Article 96)

The Guardian Council is not a popularly elected body. The clerical members, six in number, are appointed by the religious Leader, while another six are nominated by the head of the judiciary, who is also appointed by the Leader. This prompts Mayer to observe: "In consequence, not even constitutional rights guarantees can have force should the clerics . . . decide that those guarantees are not based on Islamic principles" (Mayer 1991: 37). Surely this cannot be squared with the basic principle of democracy, which gives people (or their duly elected representatives) power to pass legislation. If any agency has veto power over the decisions of the legislative council, which represents the people, how can one possibly speak of "popular sovereignty," much less of democracy?

There are several considerations that Islamic thinkers can underscore here to lessen if not altogether remove the alleged danger posed to democracy by the intrusion of religion. First, with reference to the origination, authorship, or codification of the constitution that regulates political life in society, it is rarely if ever the case that the multitude of the people, in their millions or hundreds of thousands, participate in laying down the foundations of the constitution. More often than not, constitutions have "fathers" who are usually distinguished members of the community, prominent figures who assume a position of leadership. Typically a "people's assembly" or a plebiscite gives a stamp of approval to principles and procedures that have already developed and matured in the guiding hands of the few, the ruling elites. In Islamic history, this class is referred to as *ahl al-hal wa al-'aqd* (those who "loosen and bind"). They include persons knowledgeable in religion, and others as well. If they were to play a dominant role in putting together the constitution according to which the nation lives, this would in no way be inconsistent with the historical practice of elites elsewhere in drafting constitutions.

Second, even if we assume that people (as a multitude) participate in the creation of their constitution (that is, even if we assume that political elites do not play a major role in politics), that still does not mean that constitutions are always based on the free will and free choice of those who live under them. A people creates a constitution that reflects the political will of the generation that created it. But succeeding generations do not re-create the constitution anew. On the contrary, they are in a sense themselves created by the existing constitution, inasmuch as the constitution and the institutions it legitimizes function as a great school of civic instruction for the masses. Constitutional amendments may be approved, but a revolution in a constitution is much less frequent. By their very nature and function, constitutions are on the whole conservative. Thus, seen in broader perspective, we should not attach undue weight to the idea that citizens are basically excluded from the work of creating a constitution in an Islamic republic. There is no reason to think that constitutional politics in Islamic society has to take a radically different form or course of development from that common in other societies.

Third, and most important, neither the office of Guardian Council, found in the Iranian Islamic constitution, nor the "sovereignty of the *fuqaha'*" alluded to by Abu-Zaid, are inevitable consequences of Islamic principles of government. Islamic teachings do not state that some body must have veto power over decisions of the legislative assembly. Islamic thinkers, in common with ordinary Muslims, believe that Islam does not accept any mediation in the relationship between God and man. Enlightened Muslims can and should be wary of ruling elites that aspire to have a monopoly of political power in the name of religion. It is possible, within the bounds of Islam, to conceive of a situation where all believe themselves to be legitimate interpreters of the faith and where all believe that disagreements over questions of interpretation ought to be resolved by putting them to a vote.

Of course, this idea is not likely to be well received by classes of the fuqaha', *'ulema,* or other religious "experts," who often have a vested interest in being viewed as guardians and interpreters of the faith. This is not surprising and can be dealt with in conceptual terms. At most, it calls for a Protestant-like reformation within Islamic society—a transformation that some believe is sorely needed. In other words, the concept of divine sovereignty, suitably interpreted, need not pose a threat to the notion of popular sovereignty. It simply means "rule in accordance with Islamic principles." As long as these principles are freely chosen by the people and applied in a way that does not infringe upon familiar democratic procedures, no one has reason to call into question the logical coherence of the idea of Islamic democracy.[9]

Diversity and Toleration

Another set of difficulties, less philosophical and more pressing, springs from diversity (cultural, religious, and other), an established fact in most societies. Democracy in ideal terms is supposed to be tolerant, even protective, of pluralism and diversity. Democracy guarantees individual rights and liberties for all, regardless of religion, gender, political persuasion, and so on. Minority status is an acceptable situation in a democracy because the system is geared toward protection of individual rights and liberties, regardless of the size of the minority. Can an Islamic polity be trusted to grant and to protect the rights of "others," even when they constitute a small minority in society? If not, what does this portend for "Islamic democracy"?

The approaches Islamic thinkers may take in addressing the issues of pluralism and tolerance are manifold. Take the question of toleration: it is clearly an unresolved problem for all political systems and theories. Bernard Williams underlines that problem:

> The difficulty with toleration is that it seems to be at once necessary and impossible. It is necessary where different groups have conflicting beliefs—moral, political, or religious—and realize that there is no alternative to their living together ... Yet in those same circumstances it may well seem impossible ... In matters of religion, for instance ... the need for toleration arises because one of the groups, at least, thinks that the other is blasphemously, disastrously, obscenely wrong. ... We need to tolerate other people and their ways of life only in situations that make it very difficult to do so. Toleration, we may say, is required only for the intolerable. That is its basic problem. (Williams 1996: 18)

It is thus not surprising to find that toleration continues to be a potential source of embarrassment for various (otherwise plausible) conceptions of democracy. Consider the Rawlsian version of democratic theory, that is, "political liberalism." According to Rawls: "Political liberalism also supposes that a reasonable comprehensive doctrine does not reject the essentials of a democratic regime. Of course, a society may also contain unreasonable and irrational, and even mad, comprehensive doctrines. In their case, the problem is to contain them so that they do not undermine the unity and justice of society" (Rawls 1993: xix).

Liberal democracy is supposed to be tolerant, but, argues Rawls, even liberal democracy has its limits. Unreasonable views, those that are "mad" or "irrational," must be "contained." Presumably containment is not the same as toleration; it is more aggressive. Yet what if we are unable to agree on what to categorize as "irrational," on how to define "madness"? Does this not mean that the question of what to tolerate and what to "contain" will always be an open, unresolved problem for us?

Islamic thinkers face difficult, even perplexing, questions with respect to the toleration of diversity. Yet they differ little from other views, Rawls's included. In fact, it is noteworthy that al-Ghannouchi espouses a view similar to Rawls's notion of "containment" when it comes to ideas al-Ghannouchi considers "beyond the pale." Satisfied that there is a society-wide consensus on a basic Islamic constitution, al-Ghannouchi is able to accept the continued existence and operation of non-Islamic (perhaps even un-Islamic) parties and groups within an Islamic polity. In his analysis, such groups and movements will be largely marginal and ineffective because they are not part of mainstream Islamic tendencies. "Civil society," says al-Ghannouchi, "will see to it that such groups will be marginal. There will be no need to resort to state power [in order to "contain" them]" (al-Ghannouchi 1993: 295).

The above-mentioned considerations constitute one approach available in Islamic democratic thinking for dealing with the difficulty posed by the question of diversity and toleration of difference. Toleration has limits. In every society, in every political system, toleration has a "ceiling." Its height varies depending on the type of measurement we use, as well as our expectations as to how high the ceiling must be if the "house" is to be fit for human habitation. Subjective, culturally relative judgments will abound here, and, short of universally accepted criteria of validity (which experience has shown to be nonexistent), there is no way to resolve disagreements.

Another quite different tack that Islamic writers could follow would be to point out that Islam is not monolithic: it does not mean the same things to all advocates of the Islamic state. Some are hostile to the very idea of speaking of Islam and democracy in the same breath. And those who lean toward Islamic democracy may also differ in their degree of conservatism or liberalism.

A remarkable case in point is the Sudanese thinker Abdullahi an-Na'im, whose approach to ethics and whose daring views on interpreting shari'a are reminiscent of Mu'tazilism at its best. (Mu'tazilism is an Islamic rationalist school of theology; they emphasized the use of reason in the interpretation of religious texts.) An-Na'im accepts all the noncontroversial rights that shari'a offers, such as the right to life, dignity, privacy, and property,[10] but he pushes the frontiers of reform much further, to the extent of seeking to bring Islamic legislation into full conformity with international human rights standards. His understanding of Islam requires the official abrogation of slavery, complete freedom of belief (including freedom to change one's religion), and abolition of all forms of discrimination on the basis of gender (An-Na'im 1990: 179).

In sum, when we say that Islam and democracy are compatible, we mean Islam in some interpretation thereof. Until it is shown that Islam, in each and every possible interpretation, is incapable of displaying tolerance toward those who are different, we have no reason to believe that Islam is intolerant of diversity and pluralism in some monolithic essentialist sense. In short, the issue of tolerance need not be the fatal flaw it is often taken to be as far as Islamic government is concerned.

In connection with the problem of toleration of diversity, there is a kind of last-ditch strategy that Islamic thinkers may resort to when they feel they are at the end of their tether as far as the possibilities of compromise and accommodation are concerned. Imagine a society where Muslims constitute a politically active majority (whether an overwhelming or a small majority) that wants to institute an Islamic state. Suppose, furthermore, that despite all attempts, members of the society are unable to reach agreement on an Islamic constitution that is acceptable to all, Muslims and non-Muslims alike. What is to be done then? The available solutions are limited.

First, there is the secularist solution, which is to remove religion from politics. But contrary to all initial appearances, this has little or no justification from a democratic point of view. For it is hard to think that democracy requires that the majority lead a double life, almost bordering on the schizophrenic: at home you can be religious and you can believe that religion is the most important thing in the world, but out on the street you must hide your religion and pretend that religion does not really matter in the public sphere or civil society.

Furthermore, some religions think it is the epitome of irreligion to live your life in this manner. It is a mistake to think that all religions are like Christianity in being able to separate Caesar's kingdom from that of God. Islam, in particular, may be unable to condone this type of divide between belief and life in society.

Another choice would be to force the minority to lead a life whose pattern is dictated by the Muslim majority. This could engender a situation where Islamic penalties are to be universally applied in a country that has a Christian or other non-Islamic minority. Again, this does not accord with democracy, for the latter cannot accept the idea of people being ruled by a constitution to which they are fundamentally opposed.

Is there a way out of the situation where disagreements cannot be ended except by loss of constitutive identity for one or more party? This is a situation where it seems impossible to agree on a common definition of citizenship. Walzer examines such a situation in the context of his discussion of the collective right that a group exercises with respect to membership: "If a community is so radically divided that a single citizenship is impossible, then its territory must be divided, too, before the rights of admission and exclusion can be exercised. For these rights are to be exercised only by the community as a whole . . . and only with regard to foreigners, not by some members with regard to others. No community can be half-metic, half-citizen and claim that its admissions policies are acts of self-determination, or that its politics is democratic" (Walzer 1995: 62).

Put "half-dhimmi, half-Muslim" in place of Walzer's "half-metic, half-citizen," and you have, in a nutshell, the problem of Islamic political communities that insist on treating individuals of different faiths as "protected citizens" (dhimmi) with diminished political rights. Such politics cannot be democratic. The only way to restore democracy, in line with Walzer's suggestion, is to allow for political separation and the attendant division of territory. Of course, it may be difficult or even impossible to redraw borders and boundaries, especially when communities are intermingled and have been so over generations in the same area. Nonetheless, partition and redivision of territory are sometimes practicable. These options are still feasible, depending on circumstances, albeit at times at a high social price, and not always in the name of a fuller democratic way of life. Yet such solutions are a measure of last resort. Specific circumstances may require looking for other, more innovative options.

So I have put forward three types of considerations to explore for a more adequate perspective on the possibilities of diversity and toleration within an Islamic polity. These considerations are obviously diverse, yet by presenting them in this manner, our primary aim has been to cast doubt on the naive supposition that the Islamic regime is bound to be undemocratic due to the intolerance it entails for those who are "different."

Conclusion

Some continue to think that the Islamic conception of democracy is unviable because it seeks to divorce the democratic procedure from some of the basic values and philosophical beliefs historically associated with it in the West. The fact that Islamic democracy has not been established in most Islamic countries lends further support to the idea that "Islamic democracy" is implausible.

But this harsh judgment is not justified by the hard empirical facts of democracy. The distinctions within contemporary democratic theory between substance and form, method and aim, procedures and result have all been made by Western thinkers. Islamic thinkers recognize the value of the procedure, but they refuse to embrace Western values and definitions of the meaning of life that have sprung and evolved from specifically Western social revolutions. Until it is demonstrated that secularism, liberalism, and relativism derive from the very notion of "government of the people, by the people, and for the people," we cannot dismiss the conceptual possibility of Islamic democracy.

Notes

1. Some of the ideas expressed in this chapter have appeared elsewhere (Bahlul 2000a, 2000b). I would like to thank the publishers for permission to quote passages from these works. My thanks also to John Bunzl (Vienna) and Bill Templer (Shumen, Bulgaria) for comments on an earlier draft of this chapter.

2. "Essentially contested" means there are disputes about the use of the term in question. Different (suggested or actual) uses are sustained by "perfectly respectable arguments and evidence" that nevertheless fall short of settling the dispute about the use of the term. See W. B. Gallie 1964: 14.

3. The missing premise here, of course, is the idea that freedom of thought cannot be ensured in a nonsecular society.

4. Rawls's solution is to give "citizens of faith" (believers in religion) a double identity. Qua political persons, individuals recognize a highest interest in autonomy and individuality. Qua private persons, there is no call for them to separate themselves from their enduring religious attachments, loyalties, or self-definition. For a discussion of some problems that Rawls's view may have, see Kymlicka 1996: 91–95.

5. There is a trivial exception to this, of course. Democracy cannot self-consistently allow the violation of democratic procedures.

6. I have discussed this difficulty in greater detail in Bahlul 2000a and 2000b.

7. By "what political decisions ought to be like" we mean to refer to the *quality* (content) of the political decisions that are taken, as opposed to the *method* by which they are taken. This is a "correctness theory" of legitimacy. It is a member of a family of theories that Estlund refers to as "epistemic theories of democratic legitimacy," which are united in their rejection of the assimilation of validity (rightness) of decisions to the method (procedures) used to reach them, see Estlund 1997: 174.

8. Ayyubi remarks that "[The Islamists] are thus after a kind of 'nomocracy,' not the reign of any particular group in particular (democracy, aristocracy or, for that matter, theocracy)." See Ayyubi 1991: 218.

9. Of course, outside observers may disagree with the principles and values of the Islamic "constitution." We have not said anything to rule out the possibility of their being right in their rejection of such a constitution. But this is a discussion of an entirely different type from the one we are engaged in. We are not attempting to prove either the truth or falsity of Islam, liberalism, or any other doctrine. Our only concern is the possibility of applying democratic procedures within the constitutional frameworks supplied by these doctrines.

10. See Mawdudi (1987: 27–31) for a catalogue of the individual rights that, in his view, are guaranteed by shari'a. Regardless of the strength of his arguments, Mawdudi is not at a loss to cite Qur'anic verses to support his view.

References

Abu-Zaid, Nasr Hamid. *Naqd al-Khitab al-Diniy* (A critique of religious discourse). Cairo: Sina lil-Nashr, 1994.

Audi, Robert. "Liberal Democracy and the Place of Religion in Politics." In *Religion in the Public Square: The Place of Religious Convictions in Political Debate*, ed. R. Audi and N. Wolterstorff. Lanham, Md.: Rowman and Littlefield Publishers, 1997.

Ayyubi, Nazih. *Political Islam: Religion and Politics in the Arab World*. London: Routledge, 1991.

al-Azmeh, Aziz. "Populism contra Democracy: Recent Democratist Discourse in the Arab World." In *Democracy without Democrats? The Renewal of Politics in the Muslim World*, ed. Ghassan Salame. London: I. B. Tauris, 1994.

Bahlul, Raja. *Hukm Allah, Hukm al-Sha'b: Hawla al-Alaqah baina al-Dimoqratiyyah wa-'Ilmaniyyah* (Popular sovereignty, divine sovereignty: On the relation between democracy and secularism). Amman: Dar al-Shurouq, 2000. (2000a)

———. "People vs. God: The Logic of 'Divine Sovereignty' in Islamic Democratic Discourse." *Islam and Muslim-Christian Relations* 11, no. 3 (2000): 287–98. (2000b)

Bishara, Azmi. "Madkhal li-Mu'alajat al-Demoqratiyya wa-Anmat at-Tadayyun" (Democracy and modes of religiosity). In *Hawla al-Khiyar al-Demoqrati* (On the democratic alternative), ed. Burhan Ghalyun et al. Ramallah: Muwatin, 1993.

al-Bishri, Tariq. *Al-Wad'u al-Qanuni baina al-Shari'a al-Islamiyya wa al-Qanun al-Wad'i* (The legal situation in relation to Islamic shari'a and positive law). Cairo: Dar al-Shuruq, 1996.

Blaustein, Albert, and Gisbert Flanz, eds. *Constitutions of the World*. Dobbs Ferry, N.Y.: Oceana, 1986.

Dahl, Robert. *Democracy and Its Critics*. New Haven, Conn.: Yale University Press, 1989.

Esposito, John L., and John O. Voll. *Islam and Democracy*. Oxford: Oxford University Press, 1996.

Estlund, David. "Beyond Fairness and Deliberation: The Epistemic Dimension of Democratic Authority." In *Deliberative Democracy: Essays on Reason and Politics*, ed. James Bohman and William Rehq. Cambridge: MIT Press, 1997.

Gallie, W. B. *Philosophy and the Historical Understanding*. London: Chatto and Windus, 1964.

al-Ghannouchi, Rachid. *Al-Hurriyat al-'Ammah fi al-Dawlah al-Islamiyyah* (Public liberties in the Islamic state). Beirut: Markaz Dirasat al-Wihdah al-Arabiyyah, 1993.

———. *Muqarabat fi al-'Ilmaniyyah wa al-Mujtama' al-Madani* (Approaches to secularism and civil society). London: Magharebi Center for Research and Translation, 1999.

Kedourie, Elie. *Democracy and Arab Political Culture.* London: Frank Cass and Co., 1994.

Khatami, Muhammad. *Mutala'at fi al-Din wal-Islam wal-'Asr* (Readings in religion, Islam and the age). Beirut: Dar al-Jadid, 1998.

Kymlicka, Will. "Two Models of Pluralism and Tolerance." In *Toleration: An Elusive Virtue,* ed. David Heyd. Princeton, N.J.: Princeton University Press, 1996.

Mawdudi, Abu Al-A'la. *Tadwin al-Dustoor al-Islami.* Mu'assat al-Risalah, [n.p.], 1975.

———. *Al-Khilafah wa al-Mulk* (Caliphate and kingship). Kuwait: Dar al-Qalam, 1987.

Mayer, Ann Elizabeth. *Islam and Human Rights.* Boulder, Colo.: Westview Press, 1991.

An-Na'im, Abdullahi Ahmad. *Toward an Islamic Reformation: Civil Liberties, Human Rights, and International Law.* Syracuse, N.Y.: Syracuse University Press, 1990.

Rawls, John. *Political Liberalism.* New York: Columbia University Press, 1993.

Schumpeter, Joseph. *Capitalism, Socialism, and Democracy.* New York: Harper and Row, 1976.

Turabi, Hasan. *Qadaya a-Hurriyyah wa al-Wihdah wa al-Shura wa al-Dimoqratiyyah* (Questions of freedom, unity, consultation, and democracy). Al-Dar al-Su'udiyyah lil-Nashr, 1987.

———. *Islam, Democracy, the State, and the West: A Roundtable with Dr. Hasan Turabi,* ed. A. Lowrie. Tampa, Fla.: World of Islam Studies Enterprise, 1993.

Walzer, Michael. *Spheres of Justice: A Defense of Pluralism and Equality.* Oxford: Blackwell, 1995.

Williams, Bernard. "Toleration: An Impossible Virtue?" In *Toleration: An Elusive Virtue,* ed. David Heyd. Princeton, N.J.: Princeton University Press, 1996.

6

Religious Roots of Tolerance with Special Reference to Judaism and Islam

Adam B. Seligman

Over the course of its many decades, the conflict between Israel and the Palestinians has taken many forms: from interethnic to interstate and, again, to interethnic. On the whole and until relatively recently, the conflict has not assumed an explicit or unambiguous religious dimension, although such dimensions have been present and have, for some on both sides, defined the terms of conflict. The rise of Gush Emunim in Israel after the 1973 war and the more recent increase in the strength of Hamas are of course indications of such religious framing of the conflict. Yet they are also reminders of how circumscribed that idiom has been, and how strongly the conflict has remained rooted in a politics of simple interests and conflicts of interests rather than claims of ultimate religious truth—in the face of which, we should acknowledge, little compromise is possible.

The failure of the Oslo peace accords and the outbreak of the al-Aqsa Intifada and its continuing saliency have all made these issues of increasing relevance on an almost daily basis in the Middle East. For it is clear that articulation of the Israeli/Palestinian conflict in religious terms, to the extent that this has taken place, and the increasing currency of religious arguments make compromise and understanding far more difficult, perhaps even unattainable.

Moreover, the reemergence of religious identities among Jews and Palestinians seems to be a critical component of recent politics in more ways than one. The relative decline of Hadash (the Israeli Communist Party) in Israel has led not only to the rise of Islamic parties and identities but also to a reemergence of the politics of *hamulot* (*hama'il*, extended families) and, at least according to my informants, to a reassertion of religious identities— Christian and Muslim—within the Palestinian population. This is in turn characterized by great tensions, animosities, and sometime murders between villagers. Some of these events have reached the media, but the phenomenon is apparently more widespread than has been reported by the media. The recent Israeli elections (January 2003), with the significant rise in mandates granted to the explicitly anti-religious Shinui Party, is also an indication of just how important religion (and the negative sentiments it can evoke) is within the political arena.

Given these developments, it is critical to take religion seriously. If it is a bedrock of identity and hence cause for conflict and unassailable positions, then perhaps it is also a resource for solutions and alternative forms of politics and understandings, not rooted in an enlightened idiom of individual interests and calculations. In this essay, I present a minimalist argument for the virtue of small dimensions of tolerance. That argument can, indeed must, be predicated on religious assumptions of self and society. I discuss some of the limitations of liberal perspective and certain resources to be found in a religious approach. I certainly do not claim to be presenting an agenda of peace or reconciliation. Rather, I hope to contribute a small building block toward the construction of a new language. For if a religious idiom is returning to the Middle East, as indeed to many parts of the world, it will not help to argue social realities in terms of John Locke or Thomas Jefferson or Adam Smith or Karl Marx. These carry little weight among either the 'ulema or the rabbis. Rather, it is necessary to discuss religion from within religion and recognize its own multiplicity and variability—sometimes perhaps even a pluralism commonly lacking in enlightened models of reason and tolerance. This is conceived at best as only a very modest contribution toward that goal.

In the broader context of global politics, many would counter that the question of toleration is no longer relevant at the beginning of the twenty-first century. They might perhaps even argue that the problems evoked by issues of toleration, insofar as they exist at all, are no more than remnants or traces of insufficiently modernized cultures or subcultures within a broader society. In any case, they would say, these are problems destined to disappear with the final triumph of Enlightenment principles.

Rarely are the myriad examples of intolerance, bloody-mindedness, and evil in today's world seen as part and parcel of modernity itself, as a concomitant of the universalist vision. Rather, most people tend to view these situations as ones wherein the actors are operating according to rules different from those of the modernist worldview. But they also view the situation as amenable to amelioration by proper education, change of political regime, international pressure, or other means. More to the point, certain principles are seen as the hallmark of a properly functioning modern liberal political and social order. These principles are *the privatization of religion, a politics of rights over a politics of the good,* and in the broadest of terms, the triumph of a *secular liberal-Protestant vision of selfhood* (the sort of Kantian self-actualized moral agent) together with a *secularized public space*. Furthermore, as the popular wisdom goes, if only those intractable, fundamentalist Jews, Christians, Muslims, or Sikhs could accept these eminently reasonable principles, we would solve the problem of intolerance. And the sooner the better.

My argument here is that this vision is no longer tenable, for at least two reasons: first, the progress of secularization—one of the central sociological hypotheses of the 1960s—has been seriously called into doubt (and more) by contemporary events. More than anyone else, David Martin's work has documented the spread of evangelical Protestantism, most markedly in Latin America but also in Southeast Asia, Korea, China, Africa, and, increasingly, in Eastern Europe (Martin 1991).

Peter Berger has tended to see this phenomenon in terms of processes of globalization and as a development sui generis—though there is some debate here, for instance on the spread of a new Confucianism among certain elites in China, of Islam in Africa, or the return to Orthodoxy among a new generation of affluent American Jews (Berger 1997; Weller 1998; Ming Tu 1991). So there may well be many comparative cases after all. The point is that we are witnessing a major reorientation of belief structures that puts the lie to any simple belief in the march of secularization.

It is also clear that the Islamic world has not secularized in ways that were long thought to be necessary to the development of modern economies and societies. And while the Western press tends to focus on instances of Islamic fundamentalism, there are, as we all know, significant phenomena of a very different nature—the movements of a "liberal" Islam in Indonesia, the Nahdlatual Ulama, counting some 22 million members, being a case in point (Hefner forthcoming). Indonesia, the largest Muslim country in the world, has a population of 210 million, of which some 80 percent are Muslims. The problem, then, is apparent on the empirical level. If the only source of tolerance is a secular, liberal, political, and social order, we may all be in for some difficult times, for secularism seems to be in retreat and liberal assumptions of self and society are under attack in many places.

With this we come to the second problematic aspect of the "Enlightenment as end of history" argument: that the very institutionalization of modernity calls forth its own antithesis. This old sociological insight into the paradox of institutionalization calls to mind the history of the Catholic Church, as well as of sectarian Protestantism. And it is just as relevant for the development of secular modernity.

The flip side of secularization is fundamentalism: both are inventions of modernity. The very institutionalization that brings more and more realms of social life under the rubric of an abstract and universal reason will sooner or later evoke a reaction, as modernity calls forth its own antithesis. This reaction can take many forms—the growth of primordial, racial politics being perhaps the most malevolent. But we see it as well in the blossoming of gender and sexual preference as modes of identity and as political statements. And of course we see it in the return to religious identities and commitments as an increasingly important affective aspect of individuals' lives in different parts of the world.

In this sense, these identities may well be a clear concomitant of globalization. I believe this is the case in the Middle East among both Jews and Muslims. If the Israeli political elite sees peace as necessary to the development of a liberal capitalist order, the darker side of this development takes the form of reemergent religious identities, among the disaffected not so connected or enthralled by such a "global village." There seems to be a widespread dynamic at work driving the production or even the reproduction of what some had come to think of as "pre"-modern forms of identity and commitment. There is, it seems, a need to express constitutive aspects of the self and of personality. Whereas the self predicated on autonomous reason cannot adequately meet this need, both primordiality and the idea of the heteronomous fill in the breach. So regardless of the reason, the return to religion that we are witnessing today is often a return to religion in its most primitive, unsophisticated, blind, and ignorant versions.

Moreover, it is more than possible that historians in another hundred or hundred and fifty years will look back on the period from roughly 1750 to 2050 as a brief, 300-year secular parenthesis in a history of humanity that was always religious. However, if indeed rationality gives way to a return to faith, it will be a faith of a different order from that of the faith of prerational times. It will be a faith that has passed through the crucible of the Enlightenment understanding of reason. While we cannot know the nature of such faith, at least two possibilities present themselves to our understanding. One would be an intensification, if not absolutization, of the modernist tensions between faith and reason. In such a scenario, a fundamentalist religiosity would prevail as a reaction to a fundamentalist reason. That is certainly the case among many in the Middle East. Intimations of this are unfortunately not too hard to perceive in many contemporary societies. Recent mass demonstrations in Israel for and against the Israeli court system (seen as *the* institutional realm of modern liberal-democratic assumptions) following the conviction of the leader of Israel's fastest growing religious party on bribery and corruption charges is a good case in point. Almost all the demonstrators in favor of the courts were secular Jews, almost all the demonstrators against the courts were religious. Other examples can of course be brought from other societies, whether of the religious right in the United States or similar situations in contemporary Turkey, Algeria, Egypt, and Indonesia.

The other possibility is, however, of a faith in perpetual dialogue with the dictates of reason and with its justificatory procedures. To be sure, a simple return to the Deism of the eighteenth century or of the beliefs of the Cambridge Platonists is no longer possible. Yet, the emergence of a self-reflective faith, where reason is no longer alien but is integrated into its very domain assumptions, is a real possibility. Certainly the recent papal encyclical letter *Fides et Ratio* bears witness to a perceived need within the hierarchy of the Roman Catholic Church to further this very integration, as do similar moves within the Jewish and Islamic worlds (*Encyclical Letter* 1998).[1]

If we wish to avoid a return to the worst excesses of the past, we need to chart a new course and bring to light possibilities only dimly realized at present. Take, for example, the meetings of Rabbi Menachem Frumin, chief rabbi of Tekoa, with Sufi shaykhs. Too often today religion is dismissed as "fundamentalist" with a sweeping condemnation. This reflects willful ignorance of other aspects of religion. It reflects that totalizing propensity of reason to absolutize the tensions of human existence, including the tensions of sacred and profane realms (as well as of pluralist normative injunctions), into irreconcilable contradictions between which no compromise or dialogue is possible. This then makes it very difficult to articulate a position of principled toleration or an acceptance of pluralist value commitments predicated on anything other than some form of indifference or (absolute) relativism. In contrast to this, it is precisely within a religious orientation that one can find the foundation of a very different sort of orientation, one of a real toleration. Indeed, one could claim that the bases of a principled toleration can be found only within a religious perspective (though the concrete venues of such are not always those most stressed in religious education). How so?

Tolerance of something, we must never forget, implies tolerance of practices and beliefs whose validity or normative status we reject as wrong, unreasonable, or undesirable. Otherwise we would not need to be tolerant of it. Tolerance does not, however, involve coming to accept these beliefs as correct or somehow less wrong. Rather, it involves the ability to abide beliefs we continue to think of as wrong or misguided.

Yet if one group of people simply hates another, we would demand not tolerance of them but rather the abandonment of the hatred. Moreover, we do not consider the bigot tolerant if, through a vast expenditure of psychological energy, he refrains from acting on his prejudice. The fact that, though he had the opportunity, he did not go down to a church in Alabama and burn it down does not make him a tolerant individual. This is not to say that toleration does not involve restraint, but it is a restraint of more than action.

It is a restraint of thought, a restraint quite possibly of judgment, as John Horton pointed out some time ago (Horton 1996).

Thus, toleration involves some tension between commitment to one's own set of values or principles or religious edicts and a willingness to put up with, to abide, those who adhere to beliefs one thinks are wrong. Moreover, the tolerance we would presumably be looking for is principled. Thus, we would not be advocating a tolerance simply of indifference (where one's tolerance of the other's belief was akin to a tolerance of his taste, say, in bathroom tiles); a sort of Hobbesian calculus of differential *power* (tolerant because we cannot impose our will); or toleration as a sort of second-best solution, though we often must settle for this. Thus, if we cannot get the racist to overcome her racism, at least we can get her to tolerate those others whom she despises.

As we well know, for the past two hundred years or so tolerance in the Western world has rested not on religious bases but on a decidedly secular foundation. The privatization of religion—which can be seen as one aspect of its secularization—is itself rooted in the institutionalization of Protestant religiosity. It has led to the circumscription of religious truth claims to the realm of the private rather than that of shared, public culture. The epistemological foundations of this orientation were laid in part by John Locke. He argued that since religion was a matter of belief, any coercion of the will would simply not work in enforcing religious conformity—for the structures of belief were not subject to the workings of the will (Waldron 1988). This argument is fine as far as it goes; yet it also betrays its own particular religious assumptions in its stress on belief at the center of religious consciousness, reflecting a certain type of Protestant religiosity. For while belief cannot indeed be coerced, practice—and most especially public practice—certainly can. And there are religions where the public practices are significantly more central than the structure of individual belief systems. If we look to Hinduism, Islam, or Judaism, we immediately recognize that this is so. Large numbers of believers continue to be engaged in violent, illegal, and often repressive behavior in many parts of the world precisely over issues of religious practice; whether coffeehouses can be open in Jerusalem on the Sabbath, whether women must go veiled in public, whether they can attend university, and so on.

Similarly, we should note that the tolerance advocated by Thomas Hobbes, the tolerance of a minimalist morality and of a skeptical consciousness (though a skepticism that is secular rather than religious), was predicated on a *pragmatic politics*. In given situations, such pragmatism could also deny tolerance for dissent in the name of the same principles of public order and civil peace in whose name it was promulgated.[2] With Hobbes, even more than Locke, religion is privatized: so while I may have every right to repel my neighbor's attempts on my person or property, I cannot take up arms against him to impose my own conception of his salvation. However, the State may well have the right to suppress the public statement of heretical beliefs for the same reason that it can act to suppress walking naked in the streets (the Quakers in mid-seventeenth-century England and New England, we may recall, did both and were duly suppressed). Such suppression is but a police matter: it has nothing to do with belief. Yet the result is the conception of a potentially intolerant State upon which social peace and order could rest.

It is on these positions that our contemporary Western and liberal assumptions on tolerance to a large extent are seen to rest. In fact, we should note that the liberal synthesis and the way toleration has developed in the West European and North Atlantic communities over the past two hundred years have embedded within them aspects of both intolerance and indifference. In the first instance, the liberal distinction between public and private realms is, among other things, a distinction in realms and types of toleration: certain beliefs and/or practices are deemed private and so almost by definition are to be tolerated. Here then we have a kind of principled indifference, not quite indifference *simpliciter*. For one has no *right* to intervene in private matters or even to judge them. In this reading, all conflicting views are reduced to matters of taste or aesthetics. But is this in fact tolerance? Principled indifference or neutrality toward different conceptions of the good is not the same as tolerance for alternative conceptions of the good.

Similarly, the politics of rights over the good, of individual autonomy over shared public conceptions of the good, often leads to tolerance not in principle but simply as a temporary expedient until such subgroups that value nonautonomy come to share the assumptions of liberalism. Liberalism's much-vaunted toleration may then well be more complicated and problematic than we often assume, as it tends in fact to be constantly in danger of slipping into either indifference or intolerance.

There is, however, one critical basis of toleration within the liberal tradition: individual autonomy. Toleration as a practice flows from autonomy as a virtue or a good. Yet if this is so, then the supposedly liberal indifference to the idea of the good is untenable. As Bernard Williams has stated: "Only a substantive view of goods such as autonomy can yield the value expressed by the practice of toleration" (Williams 1996: 25). The positing of a good always involves us in that familiar situation of a "conflict of goods," which liberalism does not address but nonetheless cannot really avoid.

A liberal foundation for tolerance seems then either to be no tolerance at all, but rather indifference—or to involve us in a contradiction. And that is precisely the contradiction between the practice of tolerance predicated on a politics of rights, rather than of the good, and the very principle of individual autonomy as a prime good upon which such toleration is to be based. This principle, however, is contradictory, for it involves a refusal to advance a politics of the good while at the same time resting on at least one very clearly defined principle of the good, that of individual autonomy. From this perspective, the very practice of toleration thus contradicts the basis of the practice itself. At the very least, it leads to a discussion of conflicting goods that we had best hoped to avoid. In that case, then, in such a debate over conflicting goods, a good other than individual autonomy may be considered of greater value, a good that in effect "trumps" autonomy—for example, the view that abortion is murder and the prevention of murder is the greater good and thus takes precedence over individual choice.

Our own concern at present, however, is not to rescue liberalism from its own contradictions. Further, we must acknowledge that liberalism as a philosophical program holds only in certain societies. Moreover, the very principle of individual autonomy is under attack in many venues and societies and at different levels of social praxis, from the so-called Southeast Asian model of development to evangelical Protestantism in Korea to the postmodern politics of English professors in Berkeley. If tolerance is to continue to exist as a virtue, it would thus seem to require a foundation independent of individual autonomy.

Historically there has been another foundation posited for toleration, one that for a period even shared the stage with what became the liberal argument for autonomy but then retreated to the background. This was the argument based on skepticism, explored most fully in the early work by Richard Popkin (1979). Very briefly, Popkin shows how the Reformation, in challenging the church's infallibility, challenged existing ideas of certitude as well. (We should recall here that what constituted probability reasoning in the seventeenth century was quite distant from what we consider probability today, involving only the veracity of received authorities.) Debate in the sixteenth and seventeenth centuries was also characterized by arguments over sufficient evidence. Ultimately, the failure to justify faith on the basis of knowledge led to pure fideism (that is, belief by faith alone) on one hand and a sort of mitigated skepticism on the other. This was the position of Sebastian Castellio in his condemnation of the burning of Miguel Servetus by John Calvin—that since we cannot be sure of truth, we cannot be sure of the nature of heresy, and hence cannot go to such extremes as burning heretics (Popkin 1979: 8–19).

This debate and others took place in an atmosphere characterized by the revival of classical Pyrrhonism—the doubting of all propositions, including those of doubt itself. This position was itself engendered by the search to justify an infallible truth via a self-evident criterion; thus while the Protestants contested papal authority, the Catholics made short shrift of inner conscience. Françoise Veron, one of the masters of the Counter-Reformation polemic, demonstrated how (1) the Protestant claim that Scripture was self-evidently clear was manifestly false and in need of interpretation, and (2) predicating interpretation on individual conscience opened the floodgates to sectarianism and antinomianism—that "search for heaven and their lusts as well," as one early-seventeenth-century Congregationalist described his more zealous neighbors (Weld 1644: 74).

The one side claimed that the Catholic demand for infallible knowledge led to the discovery that no such knowledge exists—and hence to complete doubt and Pyrrhonism. The other claimed that the very proliferation of opinions engendered by Protestantism ended in complete uncertainty in religious belief and consequently led to total doubt.

Certain positions emerged from this debate. One was fideism—faith justified by no structure of knowledge—that provided a way to toleration via a diffusion of those realms ruled by faith and those ruled by rational knowledge. This could offer a means to reconceptualize the public/private distinction without incorporating the liberal Western idea of self and society. Another position was the faith advocated by Montaigne: endowed with a highly modern sensibility, he conceived of tolerance as lived nature and custom, springing from Pyrrhonist principles—perhaps a kind of Christian *Sittlichkeit,* an interesting platform from which to develop tolerance.

Historically, the emergence in the West of the argument for a tolerance based on skepticism was overtaken by three developments: the liberal argument for autonomy, the process of secularization itself, which obviated the very need for religious tolerance, and the Cartesian revolution, which reoriented the whole issue of certitude as well as the position of the knowing subject.

The contingency of history aside, a principled tolerance is indeed a difficult position to maintain, as it would seem that people have a marked preference for some sort of certitude. To adhere to a position of belief while at the same time maintaining a position of skepticism as to its truth claims—indeed, a skepticism so great that one is tolerant of other such claims—is a truly stoic position. But it is one that must first and foremost rest on some belief; otherwise, the whole issue of tolerance becomes moot.

What becomes clear from the above is that the critical variable for tolerance is some sort of pluralism of value positions and orientations. Peter Berger has made us all aware of how the very fact of pluralism undermines the "taken-for-grantedness" of beliefs and values (Berger 1969). Yet most social scientists, all too uncritically, have identified this pluralism with modern secular reality and the taken-for-granted beliefs and values with traditional religious worldviews. But the truth of Berger's statement is that it works both ways: the pluralism of religions or even (and this is my point) of a single religion with its built-in tension between reason and revelation, between knowledge and faith, also tends to undermine the taken-for-grantedness of the beliefs and values of modernity. They are after all later identified with a rather totalizing Jacobian project; one that has all too often conflated a substantive rationality with an instrumental one and sought to promulgate an overarching, totalitarian, and all-encompassing ideology (whether of the right or the left). The very homogenizing tendencies of the modern worldview can themselves be brought into question by the pluralism inherent in religious doubt, that necessary concomitant of faith itself.

In this pluralism, what cannot be subsumed into the universalism of the modern worldview contains what may well be the necessary sources of tolerance in the twenty-first century. Some light can be shed on this, at least metaphorically, by recalling the reality of Sarajevo before the 1992–95 war and the nature of commensality there: the move between the particular *mahala*s or neighborhoods and the city center, the Charshiya. As explained in an evocative work by Dzevad Karahasan: "Upon leaving the Charshiya, all Sarajevans retreat from human universality into the particularity of their own cultures. Namely, every *mahala* continues the enclosed lifestyle of the culture that statistically prevails in it. Hence, Byelave, for example, is distinctly a Jewish *mahala,* whose everyday life completely realizes all the particularities of Jewish cultures; life in Latinluk goes on in accordance with the particularities of Catholic cultures; in Vratnik in accord with Islamic cultures; and in Tashlihan according to the particularities of Eastern Orthodox cultures (Karahasan 1993: 9).

In this move between cultures, with its almost enforced pluralism, a new form of tolerance may perhaps be found. It would be one that abjures the false universalism of Jacobian modernity. It would be one that must admit of the particular as well as of the universal and which, in the move between them, would bracket that certitude of knowledge upon which all tolerant attitudes must in the end founder.

My sense is that the very necessity imposed by a religious consciousness of the move between faith and reason can play a role in bracketing out this certitude in a way equivalent to the bracketing that I believe is imposed by the practical concerns of commensality. What may be involved in this process, how certitude is, as it were, bracketed out and people schooled in a praxis of uncertainty and modesty, is a question not only sociological and philosophical in nature, but one rooted in the internal orientations of different religious traditions.

In this context, we may recall a famous tale told in the Babylonian Talmud, in *Tractate of Erubim* (13:b), on a dispute between the two major schools of law, the school of Hillel and that of Shammai:

> For three years there was a dispute between Beth Shammai and Beth Hillel, the former asserting, "The *halakhah* [the corpus of Jewish law that regulates the minute details of daily life] is in agreement with our views." Then a *bath kol* [a heavenly voice] issued announcing, "[The utterances of] both are the words of the living God, but the *halakhah* is in agreement with the rulings of Beth Hillel." Since, however, "both are the words of the living God," what was it that entitled Beth Hillel to have the *halakhah* fixed in agreement with their rulings?—Because they were kindly and modest, they studied their own rulings and those of Beth Shammai, and were even so [humble] as to mention the actions of Beth Shammai before theirs.

Here then the very creation of *nomos*, of rule-giving order is tied to the act of listening, to the restraint involved in studying the rulings of one's adversaries.[3]

The idea of *anva*, humility, is central in all monotheistic traditions, and we have already noted the role of an epistemological modesty in the arguments posed by Castellio to John Calvin in the case of Miguel Servetus. In Islam, a similar concept provides an analogous repertoire. The concept of *hilm* combines qualities of moderation, forbearance, and leniency with self-mastery and dignity. In some ways it is surprisingly akin to the idea of civility among the eighteenth-century Scottish Moralists. According to the great Islamic scholar Ignaz Goldziher (1947, 201-8), "hilm" combined moral integrity with mildness of manners and is juxtaposed to *al-Jahiliyya*, that pre-Islamic period of Arab tribal warfare where emotions governed actions and where "haughtiness, arrogance and insolence" ruled, rather than the humble submission of Islam (Izutsu 1964, 148-229). Toshihiko Izutsu's study of Jahiliyya and of hilm provides us with a good sense of how central these terms are to appreciating the inner phenomenology of Islam, how the "haughtiness" of the Jahiliyya is contrasted with the forbearance of the *halim* in defining the idea of Islamic behavior. In the Prophet's transvaluation of values wrought on Arab society, the practice of forgiveness and leniency were considered halim—an attribute of the patriarch Abraham and, ultimately, of Allah. In this move, the Prophet replaced the values of tribal vengeance with that of forgiveness. Existential modesty and humility, no less than epistemic doubt, exist within religious traditions as principles of tolerance rooted in the very term within which we face the other—recalling Buber's dialogue of mutual relation.

Other religious traditions still await the type of history of their skepticism that Popkin brought to Western Christian thought. Yet some preliminary efforts are in evidence, for example, in the work of Menachem Fisch on the role of counterfactual evidence in Talmudic discourse and on the tension between reason and received authority in the redaction of the Babylonian Talmud. The paradigmatic case discussed by Fisch, and by others as well, is that of the excommunication of Rabbi Eliezer ben Hyrcanus described in the Babylonian Talmud as follows:

> We learned elsewhere: If he cut it into separate tiles, placing sand between each tile: R. Eliezer declared it clean, and the Sages declared it unclean and this is the oven of Aknai. . . . On that day R. Eliezer brought forward every imaginable argument but they did not accept them. Said he to them: If the *halakhah* agrees with me, let this carob tree prove it! Thereupon the carob tree was torn a hundred cubits out of its place—others affirm four hundred cubits. No proof can be brought from a carob tree, they retorted. Again he said to them: If the *halakhah* agrees with me, let the stream of water prove it! Whereupon the stream of water flowed backward. No proof can be brought from a stream of water, they rejoined. Again he urged: If the *halakhah* agrees with me, let the walls of the schoolhouse prove it, whereupon the walls inclined to fall. But R. Joshua rebuked them, saying: "When scholars are engaged in *halakhic* dispute, what have you to interfere?" Hence they did not fall, in honor of R. Joshua, nor did they resume the upright, in honor of R. Eliezer; and they are still standing thus inclined. Again he said to them: "If the *halakhah* agrees with me, let it be proved from Heaven!" Whereupon a Heavenly Voice cried out: "Why do you dispute with R. Eliezer, seeing that in all matters the *halakhah* agrees with him!" But R. Joshua arose and exclaimed: *"It is not in heaven."* What did he mean by this? Said R. Jeremiah: That the Torah had already been given at Mount Sinai; we pay no attention to a Heavenly Voice, because Thou hast long since written in the Torah at Mount Sinai, *After the majority must one incline.*
>
> R. Nathan met Elijah [the prophet] and asked him: What did the Holy One Blessed be He, do in that hour?—He laughed [with joy], he replied, saying, "My sons have defeated Me, My sons have defeated Me." (*Tractate Baba Mezia:* 59b)

To understand the full import of this story, one must realize (1) that Rabbi Eliezer was *the* expert on laws of purity and impurity, upon which this dispute turned; (2) that he was reputed to be an almost superhuman storehouse of received wisdom and would not utter a pronouncement on law that was of his own making: all his wisdom was received wisdom that could be traced to the revelation of Moses on Sinai; and (3) the quote from the Pentateuch noted at the end (in Exodus 23:2) is in fact taken out of context and used to make a point quite at odds with the obvious meaning of the text. Thus, the story has assumed its rather paradigmatic place in the Jewish corpus as a defense of the use of reason (through the debates and decisions of the majority) over against a simple appeal to received authority in the practicalities of moral reasoning (Goldin 1988; Fisch 1997).

A resource of reason is also always a resource of skepticism. This also holds, I believe, as regards the true toleration that can indeed be found in all religious traditions. The Islamic *kalam* no less than the Jewish halakhah presents a method of reasoning and legal interpretation based on what John Clayton has termed "localized reasoning," instances of what he terms "group-specific reasoning" (Clayton 1999). That is, they rely on processes of moral reasoning that in addition to recognizing sacred authority also recognize the limits of human reason—and hence the inherent abyss between general principles and their instantiation in the orders of the world. Again, then, the *phronesis* of casuistry or for that matter of Jewish halakhic thought may provide a basis for toleration from *within* a recognized authority rather than from a world defined solely by power, where tolerance can never be more than a contingent balance of forces.

Other responses to modernity have evolved in all religious communities in their respective encounter with modernity. We can, for example, look to Judaism to see how an idea of epistemological modesty has sustained not modern pluralism but rather a degree of tolerance—a position that can be culled from the writings of a number of ultra-Orthodox thinkers. One such scholar, the Chazon Ish (R. Avraham Yeshiya Karelitz, d. 1958)—the main ideologue of ultra-Orthodoxy in contemporary Israel—argued that since we live in a time when the sources of revelation are occluded, there is no authority for implementing divine commandments. As explained by Shlomo Fischer, since the epistemological condition of exile sustains unbelief, adherents thereof cannot be held culpable (Fischer 1999). While such a position perhaps does not support a positively privileged pluralism, it does maintain a position of principled tolerance and restraint. This is a critical component of religious traditions not inculcated with Christian and most especially Protestant notions of individual moral autonomy.

Similarly, Ayatollah Shariatmadari protested the reintroduction of drastic criminal penalties in postrevolutionary Iran (such as the cutting off of hands). Short of the construction of the perfect society and the coming of the Hidden Imam, no justification for such actions could be offered, he claimed, as there was always the possibility that "Satan could be held to have misled the criminal" (Mottahedeh 1985: 389). Shariatmadari's argument resonates with the claims of the medieval Jewish philosopher Maimonides on the tolerance one must hold toward Jews who have lost their knowledge of the laws and the codes of communal worship (*Hilchot Mamrim* 3:3; Fischer 1999). This was an argument used by many rabbis to understand the place of secular Jews in modern-day Israel. It was explicitly utilized by thinkers such as R. David Hoffman of Berlin to see modern public violation of the Sabbath in terms of the existence of a plurality of value positions that must abrogate the severity of halakhic norms, and the argument has since been developed by religious thinkers in Israel and abroad.

Maintaining the truth of the community, rather than the individual terms of truth-claims articulated in liberal modernity, these thinkers, Jewish and Muslim both, nevertheless provide principles for toleration culled from within traditional doxa. It is a language that continues to address the terms of Being, and yet, as we can see, from Shariatmadari to the Chazon Ish, it is a language that can in fact be translated.

This translation is the challenge facing us all. If the secularization thesis has indeed been proved incorrect and the further progress of modernity—and perhaps even postmodernity—will not be accompanied by the further spread of a secular consciousness but by some sort of return to religious orientations, then how can a principled position of toleration be maintained? For such a return, I maintain, is almost mandated by the human need for self-statement, by the need for at least a certain aspect of self to be seen as constituted by a heteronomous authority and not simply as autonomous. As people return to positions of principled belief, there is the possibility either of returning to some of the most horrendous authoritarian terrors of the past or, as I believe is preferable and possible, of *resurrecting a language of toleration based on skepticism toward one's own principled beliefs*. To do this we must enlist the help of precisely those beliefs—chief among them beliefs in revealed, transcendent truth—of the three revealed monotheistic religions. In discussing this once with Peter Berger, he elegantly glossed the problem as being not *what* one believes but *how* one believes. And we must seek that *how* in the nature of the belief itself, though no doubt a skeptical one as well.

Notes

1. Programs such as Yesodot in contemporary Israel, which seek to teach democratic norms to the heads of state religious schools, are a case in point.
2. On Hobbes's ideas of toleration, see Ryan 1988.
3. True, the dispute concerns disagreements *within* the halls of the academy. The degree that one can extrapolate from this to disputes outside of the academy, to disputes with strangers, pagans, or converts is a matter of some contention. Interestingly, a similar concern with the limits or boundaries of legitimate debate can be found among pagan philosophers as well.

References

Berger, Peter. "Four Faces of Globalization." *National Interest* 49 (fall 1997): 23–29.
———. *The Sacred Canopy: Elements of a Sociological Theory of Religion.* New York: Anchor Books, 1969.
Clayton, John. "Common Ground and Defensible Difference." In *Religion, Politics, and Peace,* ed. Leroy Robuner, 104–27. Notre Dame, Ind.: University of Notre Dame Press, 1999.
Encyclical Letter, Fides et Ratio, of the Supreme Pontiff John Paul II: To the Bishops of the Catholic Church on the Relation between Faith and Reason. Washington D.C.: U.S. Catholic Conference, 1998.
Fisch, Menachem. *Rational Rabbis.* Indianapolis: Indiana University Press, 1997.
Fischer, Shlomo. "Intolerance and Tolerance in the Jewish Tradition and Contemporary Israel." Unpublished paper presented April 1999 at ISEC Conference on Religious Toleration, Institute for the Human Sciences, Vienna.
Goldin, Judah. *Studies in Midrash and Related Literature.* Philadelphia: Jewish Publication Society, 1988.
Goldziher, Ignaz. *Muslim Studies,* vol. 1. London: George Allen, 1947.
Hefner, Robert. *Civil Islam: Muslim Democrats and the State of Indonesia.* Princeton, N.J.: Princeton University Press, forthcoming.
Horton, John. "Toleration as a Virtue." In *Toleration: An Elusive Virtue,* ed. David Heyd, 18–27. Princeton, N.J.: Princeton University Press, 1996.
Izutsu, Toshihiko. *God and Man in the Koran.* Tokyo: Keio Institute of Cultural and Linguistic Studies, 1964.
Karahasan, Dzevad. *Sarajevo, Exodus of a City.* New York: Kodansha International, 1993.
Maimonides, *Hilchot Mamrim.* Mishue Torah (Hebrew).
Martin, David. *Tongues of Fire.* Oxford: Basil Blackwell, 1991.
Ming Tu, Wei. "The Search for Roots in Industrial East Asia: The Case for Revival." In *Fundamentalisms Observed,* ed. Martin Marty and R. Scott Appleby, 740–81. Chicago: University of Chicago Press, 1991.
Mottahedeh, Roy. *The Mantle of the Prophet: Religion and Politics in Iran.* Harmondsworth: Penguin, 1985.

Popkin, Richard. *The History of Skepticism from Erasmus to Spinoza.* Berkeley: University of California Press, 1979.
Ryan, Alan. "A More Tolerant Hobbes." *Justifying Toleration: Conceptual and Historical Perspectives,* ed. Susan Menus, 37–60. Cambridge: Cambridge University Press, 1988.
Tractate Baba Mezia (Soncino Translation). London: The Soncino Press, 1934.
Tractate Erubim (Soncino Translation). London: The Soncino Press, 1934.
Waldron, Jeremy. "Locke: Toleration and the Rationality of Persecution." In *Justifying Toleration: Conceptual and Historical Perspectives,* ed. Susan Mendes, 61–86. Cambridge: Cambridge University Press, 1988.
Weld, Thomas. Preface to John Winthrop's *A Short History of the Rise, Reign and Ruine of the Antinomians, Familists and Libertines.* London, 1644.
Weller, Robert. "Divided Market Culture in China." *Market Culture: Society and Morality in the New Asian Capitalisms,* ed. Robert Hefner, 78–103. Boulder, Colo.: Westview Press, 1998.
Williams, Bernard. "Toleration: An Impossible Virtue?" In *Toleration: An Elusive Virtue,* ed. David Heyd. Princeton, N.J.: Princeton University Press, 1996.

IV

On the Use of Religion in Contemporary
Middle Eastern Politics

7

Imposed Normalization and Cultural Transgression

Cultural Politics in Egypt and Israel since the 1979 Peace Treaty

Joel Beinin

The 1979 Egyptian-Israeli peace treaty stipulates that there will be normal diplomatic, economic, and cultural relations between the two parties.[1] The *Middle East Contemporary Survey* published by Tel Aviv University's Dayan Center for Middle Eastern Studies, a source close to Israeli government circles, assesses the two states' views on normalization of relations in these arenas as follows: "For Israel, normalization was the first and only tangible gain it could show for returning the Sinai to Egypt.... The pace and quality of the development towards normalization was seen in Israel as a yardstick to measure Egypt's commitment to peace." In contrast, "Egypt saw normalization as a means to advance the settlement of the Palestinian problem by linking it to progress in the autonomy talks" (1979–80: 370).

The Egyptian-Israeli peace treaty did not and was not designed to lead to a settlement of the Palestine question or a comprehensive Arab-Israeli peace, and the Egyptian government was not anxious to press forward with cultural exchanges with Israel while these issues were unresolved. From time to time, often under pressure from Israel, and by and large with significant constraints, the Egyptian government did permit certain cultural exchanges, visits of intellectuals, and so on. The majority of Egyptian intellectuals—Islamists and those with a secular orientation alike—adopted a much harsher stance. They absolutely opposed even the smallest expressions of cultural normalization and refused all contacts with Israel or Israeli culture.

Egyptian Islamists and the Conflict with Zionism

It is not surprising that Egyptian Islamists have advocated total rejection of Israel and Israeli and even Jewish culture since 1979. This had been their position for decades before the peace treaty. Since the 1930s there has been a current of militant Islamist opinion in Egypt that has commingled anti-

Zionism with anti-Semitism, sometimes using themes and imagery imported from Europe, sometimes using a specifically Islamic discourse. The organizations most prominently associated with this current are the Society of Muslim Brothers, the Young Men's Muslim Association, and Young Egypt (which was not purely an Islamist organization, but shared aspects of the Islamist outlook). In the 1930s and 1940s, they directed verbal threats and physical violence at Egyptian Jews. Young Egypt and the Muslim Brothers called for an economic boycott of Egyptian Jews, accusing them of dominating the economy of Egypt and other such spurious historical and contemporary conspiracies. They considered the entire Egyptian Jewish community to be collaborators with Zionism, whereas the great majority certainly were not. In 1938–39, Islamists and members of Young Egypt attacked and attempted to bomb Jewish neighborhoods and businesses in Cairo and several provincial cities (Jankowski 1980, 1984). These forces were responsible for the degeneration of the demonstration against the Balfour Declaration on 2 November 1945 into anti-Jewish rioting in which six people were killed, several hundred injured, and dozens of stores owned by Jews, Copts, and Muslims were looted. This was the first occasion in modern Egyptian history when Jews were collectively threatened by physical violence on a large scale.

The majority of Egyptian political opinion did not resort to anti-Semitism in discussing the Palestinian-Zionist conflict. The largest political parties—the Wafd and the Liberal Constitutionalists—insisted that Egyptian Jews were distinct from the Zionist project in Palestine and that their rights should be protected. Elite Jews were prominent in finance, business, and entertainment and were favored by King Faruq. Islamically motivated anti-Zionism and anti-Semitism were on the margins of Egyptian political life until 1948.

The 1948–49 war with the emergent State of Israel, the monarchy's concessions to what it perceived as popular opinion, and its manipulation of Islam to enhance its legitimacy in its struggle with the Muslim Brothers made Islamic themes more prominent in Egyptian representations of the Arab-Zionist conflict after the creation of the State of Israel. The short-lived collaboration of the Muslim Brothers with the Free Officers who overthrew the monarchy on 23 July 1952 also gave the Brothers and their approach to the conflict greater legitimacy. The titular head of the new regime, General Muhammad Naguib, went to great lengths to establish good relations with the Jewish community in the months after the coup. But the close relations of some of the Free Officers—most prominently Anwar al-Sadat—with the Muslim Brothers created an additional opening for propagation of an Islamic discourse on the conflict with Israel and relations with Egyptian Jews. However, this was only a limited phenomenon, because of the secular orientation of some elements of the new regime as well as the dramatic end to the collaboration between the Muslim Brothers and the Free Officers following a Brothers-inspired attempt to assassinate Gamal 'Abd al-Nasir in October 1954. The Society of Muslim Brothers was banned for a second time, and thousands of members were jailed under harsh conditions for years.

A clash between the Muslim Brothers and the Jewish community of Egypt only months after the Free Officers came to power illustrates the coexistence and contention of different tendencies within the new regime. In February 1953, Shaykh Ahmad Hasan al-Baquri, the minister of pious endowments and formerly a Muslim Brothers student organizer, spoke on the state radio on "The Influence of Religion in the Formation of a Proper Citizen." The shaykh acknowledged that Judaism was a valid religion, but he went on to say that Judaism was no longer a religion and had become a racist ideology like Nazism and should be destroyed by the free peoples of the world. He referred to Jews as swine, an egregious insult in both Muslim and Jewish terms (*al-Ahram,* 9 February 1953). In response to Shaykh Baquri's insult, the Egyptian chief rabbi, Haim Nahum, wrote to General Naguib and pointed out that Baquri's words contradicted Naguib's own policy statements on the status of Jews in Egypt.[2] Naguib answered by demanding that Shaykh al-Baquri formally apologize to Rabbi Nahum. When al-Baquri proposed to express his regrets by telephone, Naguib insisted that he visit Nahum at his home and deliver a proper face-to-face apology (Mizrahi 1977: 57).

The sharp contention between the Egyptian state and the Muslim Brothers from 1954 until the early 1970s constrained the influence of Islamist understandings of the conflict with Israel. This began to change in the early 1970s when President Anwar al-Sadat released the Brothers from jail and granted the organization a semilegal status in order to use it in his efforts to roll back Nasirism.

The Muslim Brothers and their journals, *al-Da'wa* (The call) and *al-I'tisam* (Perseverance), and the newer student-based Islamic groups were among the most vociferous opponents of the 1979 peace treaty with Israel and of normalization of diplomatic, economic, and cultural relations. They were joined by the Socialist Labor Party, one of the three political parties legalized by the al-Sadat regime in 1976 ("socialist" was dropped from the name in the late 1980s). The organizational progenitor of the Labor Party is Young Egypt. The political affinity between the Labor Party and political Islam was consummated by an electoral alliance with the Muslim Brothers in 1987, which remained in effect despite the regime's increasingly undemocratic measures, including attempts to limit its parliamentary representation and ultimately a ban on the Labor Party.

Egypt's Secular Intelligentsia and the Post-1979 Boycott of Israel

The Islamists opposed peace with Israel on the basis of what they regarded as religious principle. In contrast, much of Egypt's secular intelligentsia would have been prepared to accept a peace with Israel that restored Egyptian national territory occupied in the 1967 Arab-Israeli war and achieved a just settlement of the Palestinian-Israeli conflict. However, it was precisely the institutional strongholds of secular nationalism—the Bar Association, the Journalists Union, the Medical Association, the Pharmacists Union, the Cinema Arts Union, the Actors Union, the Writers Union, and the General Federation of Egyptian Trade Unions—that led the opposition to the terms of the Egyptian-Israeli peace treaty and vociferously opposed any normalization of cultural relations with Israel.[3] These associations and many prominent secular intellectuals and artists endorsed the total boycott of Israel, including rejection of cultural exchanges of any sort initiated by the Committee to Defend the National Culture—a multitendency coalition sponsored by the legal-left National Progressive Unionist Party (Tagammu').[4] The committee collaborated with the Labor Party and others in organizing demonstrations against the participation of Israeli publishers in the annual Cairo Book Fair in 1984 and 1985 and other such cultural and economic presences that Israeli diplomatic representatives rather disingenuously claimed had no political content (Lajnat al-Difa' 'an al-Thaqafa al-Qawmiyya 1994: 53–63).

The 1993 Palestinian-Israeli Declaration of Principles and the ensuing negotiations made no difference in this regard. In 1994 the playwright 'Ali Salim visited Israel and published a book about his trip (Salim 1994). He was expelled from the Egyptian Writers Union. In response to his actions, a special issue of the avant-garde journal *al-Kitaba al-Ukhra* (Other writing) was devoted to strong antinormalization statements by twenty-one authors (*al-Kitaba al-Ukhra* 1994).

Israeli Intellectuals and Egypt

There is a tradition in Israel, and before that in the Jewish community of mandatory Palestine (the *yishuv*), of intellectual interest in Egypt. Some of the most prominent founding fathers of Israeli Middle East studies and their students at the Hebrew University of Jerusalem were motivated by a desire to promote peaceful coexistence between the yishuv and its Arab neighbors. The towering figure in this constellation is S. D. Goitein, author of a multi-volume study of the Cairo *Geniza* and many other works. One of the central arguments of Goitein's magnum opus on the Geniza (an archive of ancient

Jewish manuscripts) is that in terms of daily life, economic activities, and general culture, the Jews of medieval Cairo were not very different from their Muslim and Christian neighbors; the principal source of difference was religious faith and practice (Goitein 1967–93). Goitein's colleague, Gabriel Baer, is a pioneer in the field of the social history of modern Egypt. In the early years of his career, Yehoshua Porath also belonged to this tendency, although his areas of specialized interest did not include Egypt. This school of Hebrew University Orientalists supported binationalist or left-Zionist approaches to the Arab-Zionist conflict.

In part because of the "soft" approach of several of the Middle East scholars at the Hebrew University, the newly formed Israeli state apparatus had to turn elsewhere to develop professional sources of intelligence about the Arab world. The Shiloah Center of Tel Aviv University (appropriately named for a labor, Zionist, Arab affairs intelligence specialist) became the center of gravity of a different style of Israeli engagement with Egypt: "know your enemy" studies shaped largely by the requirements of the Israeli military and diplomatic service. The Shiloah Center was subsequently transmuted into the Dayan Center for Middle East Studies. The leading representative of this tendency is Shimon Shamir, an academic specialist in modern Egypt who became director of the Israeli Academic Center in Cairo and then Israel's ambassador to Egypt following the 1979 peace treaty.[5] Despite the preponderant influence of the Dayan Center and its orientation, the approach to Egypt at Tel Aviv University is not monolithic. Several scholars, including Israel Gershoni, Sasson Somekh, and the late Matti Peled, are much more empathic than the prevailing tendency.

A third Israeli approach to Egypt is represented by the Department of Middle East Studies at Ben-Gurion University. The department's approach to Egypt is reflected in Yoram Meital's revisionist diplomatic history of Egyptian-Israeli relations in the 1967–73 period. Meital deploys a traditional methodology to challenge prevailing Israeli assumptions about Egyptian willingness to consider peace with Israel during this important period (Meital 1997). The department takes its students on organized study trips to Egypt and other Arab countries. Its journal, *Jama'a,* is the only Hebrew language forum regularly featuring empathic intellectual engagement with Arab society, culture, and history. The impact of Ben-Gurion University's approach to Egypt and the Arab world on broader Israeli society has been limited, and there are indications that its maverick approach may not be sustainable. The university is constrained by its remote location, the lack of a doctoral program in Middle East studies, pressures to conform, and the exclusion of critical scholars from the corridors of power in Israel. Another significant factor is the inability of many Egyptians to make the necessary distinctions to embrace the scholars of Ben-Gurion University. They are subject to the boycott of cultural relations with Israel only to a slightly lesser degree than other Israeli scholars.

There have been efforts to promote knowledge of Egypt in Israel beyond those with a professional interest. Egyptian Jews were, in the first euphoric period after the peace treaty, especially prominent in such efforts. But particularly in light of the cold peace that has prevailed, there is little interest in Egyptian culture in the circles of Israeli high culture beyond professional Orientalists. Israel's secular cultural elite is overwhelmingly oriented toward Europe and the United States and aggressively promotes its vision of Israel as European and fundamentally different from the Arabs.

Many Israeli intellectuals, especially academic specialists in Middle East studies, have collaborated with their government's policy objective of normalizing Egyptian-Israeli cultural relations to the greatest extent possible, despite the boycott observed by a very large proportion of Egyptian intellectuals, artists, and public figures. Israelis have invited their Egyptian counterparts to attend conferences in Israel and to contribute to edited volumes, and they have sought invitations to appear in Egyptian venues. Many of Israel's cultural emissaries sincerely believe that spreading knowledge about Israeli culture in Egypt and promoting cultural dialogue with Egyptians will serve the cause of peace.

Nonetheless, as the case of Yossi Amitai indicates, they have been unable to extricate themselves from the logic of the boycott of cultural relations with Israel in Egypt. Amitai has a long record of principled criticism of Israel's policies in the Arab-Israeli conflict and support for the national rights of the Palestinian people in the form of a state in the West Bank and the Gaza Strip. He has met and formed close relations with like-minded Egyptians and representatives of the Palestine Liberation Organization since 1973. He was a founding member of the Israeli Council for Israeli-Palestinian Peace in 1975 and subsequently a close associate of Matti Peled in various political formations that advocated that Israel recognize and negotiate with the PLO, long before the conclusion of the 1993 Oslo Accords. Amitai's doctoral thesis was a study of the attitude of the Egyptian Left toward the Arab-Israeli conflict; he developed close relations with many of the subjects of his research (Amitai 1999). However, after Amitai accepted an appointment as director of the Israeli Academic Center in Cairo in the late 1990s, most of the same Egyptians who had warmly embraced him when they met in Europe refused to see him in Cairo. Yossi Amitai's experience demonstrates the utter failure of the cultural normalization anticipated by most Israelis as a consequence of peace with Egypt.

Inauspicious Political Circumstances Undermining Cultural Normalization

Contrary to the prevailing Israeli understanding, cultural normalization cannot be separated from the context of the political, military, and diplomatic relations between Israel and Egypt or Israel and its other Arab neighbors, especially the Palestinians. There was no movement toward resolution of the Palestinian-Israeli conflict for fifteen years after the 1978 U.S.-Egyptian-Israeli Camp David summit conference. During the same period, Israel repeatedly acted in ways that were widely understood in Egypt as indicating that it intended to continue pursuing aggressive polices in the Arab world and that the Arab-Israeli conflict was continuing despite the Egyptian-Israeli peace treaty. Israel reneged on its treaty commitment to return all of the Sinai Peninsula to Egypt by seeking to retain Taba, a stretch of coastline adjacent to Eilat. This issue dragged on through the 1980s until an arbitration procedure awarded Taba to Egypt on 15 March 1989. Israel invaded Lebanon in 1978 and 1982 and occupied some 10 percent of Lebanon's territory until May 2000. Israel bombed Iraq's nuclear reactor in July 1981, when Iraq enjoyed good relations with both Egypt and the United States because of its war against Iran. All of Israel's governments, Labor and Likud, aggressively expanded Israeli settlements in and around East Jerusalem and in the West Bank and the Gaza Strip and violated many UN resolutions condemning Israel's annexation of East Jerusalem and its actions in the Palestinian Occupied Territories as well as the provisions of the Fourth Geneva Convention relating to treatment of civilians in occupied territories. Israel suppressed the Palestinian Intifada that erupted in December 1987 with "force, power, and blows" as ordered by then defense minister Yitzhak Rabin, shocking world and Egyptian opinion (*Jerusalem Post*, 20 January 1988).

Despite the adverse political and military atmosphere created by these events, most Israelis expected that intellectual and cultural collaboration—conferences, joint publications, mutual visits, and the like—with Egyptians would continue. They understood "normalization" as an obligation incumbent on Egypt. However, Israel did not consider itself obliged to refrain from actions that the Egyptian government and political opinion regarded as incompatible with maintaining friendly cultural relations.

Spying as a Mode of Apprehending the Other

In Egypt, opposition to normalization of cultural relations is sustained by the common view that Israel's actions in the Arab world since 1978 confirm that it remains an enemy. As such, Israel is expected to be engaged in espionage against Egypt and to be seeking to undermine its national security, economic development, and culture. This expectation is amplified by constant reiteration in the Egyptian mass media, often with little distinction between fact and fantasy.

Early in 1992, four Israeli citizens—a Muslim man, his son and 17-year-old daughter, and a Jewish man—were arrested for spying against Egypt. Along with claims that the woman in the case, Fa'iqa al-Musrati, engaged in prostitution to further her espionage activities, there were reports in both the secular but increasingly lurid *Ruz al-Yusuf,* and the newspaper of the Islamist Labor Party, *al-Sha'b* (The people), that Israel was dispatching AIDS-infected prostitutes to seduce the flower of Egyptian manhood and undermine its fighting capacity. The usually more restrained progovernment dailies joined in: *al-Ahram* reported that Fa'iqa al-Musrati was HIV-positive; *al-Gumhuriyya* claimed that the entire Musrati family had AIDS (*Jerusalem Report,* 27 February 1992). The press, especially *Ruz al-Yusuf* and *al-Sha'b,* was full of dubious spy stories throughout 1992.

The Egyptian public was well prepared to believe that the Israelis arrested in this case were guilty as charged by the popular television serial *Ra'fat al-Haggan,* which premiered during Ramadan 1989 with a new series of episodes released each Ramadan for the next several years. It is based on the true story of Rif'at al-Gammal, an Egyptian who posed as a travel agent in Israel from 1954 to 1974 and engaged in heroic feats of espionage for Egypt against the Jewish state. The opening scene of *Ra'fat al-Haggan* invokes the infamous Operation Susannah (more commonly known in Israel as the Lavon affair) in which Egyptian Jews recruited by Israel military intelligence committed acts of terror and espionage in Cairo and Alexandria during 1954. Members of the amateurish conspiracy were tried and convicted. Several were imprisoned, and two were executed.

Another popular mass media treatment of the espionage theme is *Mission in Tel Aviv*—a low-brow film released in Cairo in 1992 starring Nadia al-Gindi, who cultivates a somewhat trashy sexy image.[6] The premise of the film is that despite the peace treaty between the two countries there is an ongoing conflict between Egypt and Israel that is expressed in mutual spying operations. The film suggests that Egyptian women who cavort in Parisian bars wearing miniskirts will do anything, even spy for Israel. But when they repent by spying against Israel for Egypt and wear proper skirts below their knees, they are welcomed back to their families and homeland.

The theme of Israeli spying is also common among intellectuals. The Israeli Academic Center in Cairo is the most visible institution in the Israeli effort to achieve cultural normalization. Entire books, as well as articles in the press, have been devoted to attacking it as a base for Israeli espionage against Egypt (Ahmad 1989; 'Arafa 1990). Muhammad Hasanayn Haykal resides in the same building as the Israeli Academic Center and unsuccessfully tried to have the center evicted, claiming that one of its objectives was to spy on him.

The capstone of the Egyptian preoccupation with Israeli espionage in the 1990s was the arrest and conviction of ʿAzzam ʿAzzam, a Druze citizen of Israel, on charges of spying for Israel. In August 1997 he was sentenced to fifteen years at hard labor. Two women, Palestinian citizens of Israel, his alleged accomplices, were convicted in absentia. An Egyptian accomplice was also convicted. Israel denied that the accused were its espionage agents and claims that the whole case is a frame-up. But it made similar vociferous denials and inflammatory charges of Nazi-like anti-Semitism in the Operation Susannah affair (Beinin 1998: 90–117). The complete falsehood of Israel's assertions in that case rendered its claims in this one questionable and enhanced the plausibility of the espionage theme.

Egyptian-Israeli spying and counterintelligence were also a theme in Israeli popular culture in the 1990s. In 1992 Haya Samir released an album of Hebrew songs with Arabic rhythms and intonation, *Kol Koreh* (A voice is calling). This has become a very popular style in Israeli music. Haya is the daughter of Yusuf Samir, a journalist for Radio Israel's Arabic Department. In a previous life, Yusuf Samir was an Egyptian journalist highly critical of the Nasir regime and very probably also a spy for Israel. He and his wife Lili fled Egypt and resettled in Israel after the 1967 war. Haya was born a month later and raised as a Jew. The family acknowledged their Egyptian identity only after Sadat's visit to Jerusalem in 1977. In the late 1980s Haya enlisted in the Israeli army and was publicly hailed as "the first Arab girl" in the Israel Defense Forces. She became a star in one of the army entertainment troupes. Her complex and unconventional biography was not an obstacle to her winning the prestigious Israeli pre-Eurovision (Kdam) song contest in 1995, producing a second album, and appearing as the Israeli representative on an album of world lullabies.[7]

Egyptian Representation of Jews and Israel

Another major theme of Egyptian opponents of cultural normalization is a very critical, indeed anti-Semitic, representation of the history of Egyptian Jews. In *The Dispersion of Egyptian Jewry* I argued that many Egyptian Jews were attached to Egypt and thought of themselves as Egyptians. This view is rejected by nearly all Egyptians who have written about the Jews of modern Egypt since 1979.[8] There is no substantial difference between Islamists and secular nationalists in this regard, although Islamists are generally more likely to think of Jews as belonging to an international conspiracy associated with Free Masonry or other such spurious conspiracies (e.g., Shalash 1986). In 1999, Qasim 'Abduh Qasim published a highly critical review of *The Dispersion of Egyptian Jewry* in a Cairo literary monthly elaborating at length the argument that Egyptian Jews were not really Egyptians (Qasim 1999). Another reviewer could not find a magazine that would agree to publish his more favorable assessment of the book. He had to suffice with mentioning it in *Bassatine News,* the web-based newsletter of the Cairo Jewish Community Council (Ra'fat 1999).

A high proportion of the Egyptians who write about Jews, Zionism, and Israeli affairs regularly employ well-known, crude, anti-Semitic motifs. History as a category of knowledge is often inextricably enmeshed in nationalist discourse. So this is perhaps not the best place to look for signs of dissent from the national consensus. Works of art directed toward a high-brow audience might be expected to have a more subtle and nuanced approach.

One such work is Youssef Chahine's 1978 film, *Alexandria Why?*—a nostalgic, autobiographical recollection of his youth in the Alexandria of 1942–45.[9] Edward Said describes well the cosmopolitan and elite colonial character of Victoria College where Yahya, Chahine's alter ego in the film, is a student (Said 1999). Many children of the Jewish haute bourgeoisie were students there. One is in the circle of Yahya's friends who are the central characters in the film. Chahine adopts a nationalist, but firmly anti-Nazi, viewpoint as he describes Yahya's formation as an artist, his infatuation with Hollywood, and his departure from Egypt to study acting at the Pasadena Playhouse in California. The film explores the complexities of Anglo-Egyptian relations, Italian-Egyptian relations, homosexuality, and Egyptian class relations with an uncommon sense of ambiguity.

Alexandria Why? is one of the first cultural artifacts of the era of Egyptian-Israeli peace to acknowledge that a Jewish community lived in modern Egypt, a fact many young Egyptians found difficult to imagine by the late 1970s. Nonetheless, the representation of the principal Jewish characters—Yahya's friend David and his sister Sarah—is flat and pedantic. Jews are sexually loose, associated with communism, and easily lured by the appeal of Zionism, though Sarah does not succumb and tries to remain faithful to her non-Jewish, communist lover. The Palestinian-Zionist conflict is represented briefly, with no effort to transcend the predictable (though certainly not false) imagery of Zionist cruelty toward Palestinians. The final scene with its stereotypical image of bearded ultra-Orthodox Jews on the deck of the ship as Yahya arrives in New York harbor is an ill-conceived attempt at absurdist humor that plays too loosely with anti-Semitic imagery to be acceptable by enlightened Western sensibilities.

Edwar al-Kharrat's autobiographical novel, *Girls of Alexandria,* takes up some of the same themes in the same setting as Chahine's film (al-Kharrat 1990). Al-Kharrat fondly evokes Alexandria of 1946–48, when as a youth he belonged to a Marxist circle that included several Jews. Like Chahine, al-Kharrat associates Jews primarily with communism and illicit female sexual allure. Al-Kharrat also acknowledges the anti-Zionism of his communist Jewish characters, though this does not redeem the rest of the community, even the noncommunist but also non-Zionist majority.

Both Chahine and al-Kharrat express some regret over the demise of cosmopolitan Alexandria. But their formulaic negative representations of Jews tend to undermine their suggestions that cosmopolitanism may have a positive cultural and social content. Perhaps their ambivalent and negative portrayals of Jews are attempts to defend the validity of cosmopolitanism from charges of Zionism. In any case, the experiences of the majority of the 35,000 Jews in Alexandria in the late 1940s are absent from both *Alexandria Why?* and *Girls of Alexandria*.

Unauthorized Crossings

Even if one argues, as I do, that Israel's aggressive actions in the Arab world bear a large share of responsibility for the picture I have painted here, the current situation is very grim. Public expressions of enmity and anti-Semitic portrayals of Israel and Jews in Egypt have increased considerably rather than diminished since 1979. But even in such inauspicious circumstances, cultural production and circulation breaks out of the boundaries established by states and institutions that seek to regulate it. Israel has not been able to impose cultural normalization on Egypt. Neither has the boycott of Israel sought by Egyptian intellectuals and artists succeeded. In both countries cultural elites have been unable to limit unauthorized cultural crossings. Youth, marginal, and opposition elements have appropriated elements of the culture of the other in ways that subvert the agendas of proponents of cultural normalization and their opponents.

Most Egyptian representations of the Israeli "other" are, on the surface, overwhelmingly negative. Nonetheless, some of these negative portrayals unintentionally undermine the stance of total hostility to which they appear to be committed. For example, *Mission in Tel Aviv* includes several snatches of untranslated Hebrew dialogue. This and the quick reference to several details about Israel suggest that the filmmakers expect the audience to have a degree of familiarity with Israel that is unimaginable anywhere else in the Arab world except Palestine. At the same time, the film promotes substantial misconceptions about Israeli society. Several scenes from the *Ra'fat al-Haggan* serial have a comparable character.

A much more substantial violation of cultural mores was the widespread circulation of black market copies of an audio cassette by Sa'ida Sultan in Egypt during 1994–95 (Swedenburg 2000). Sa'ida Sultan was born as Yaron Cohen to a Yemeni family that emigrated to Israel in the early 1950s. He grew up with the Arabic music of Yemen and the Persian Gulf as a part of his family heritage. After undergoing a sex-change operation, Yaron/Sa'ida achieved international recognition as Dana International, a singer of sexually provocative rock music in English, Arabic, and Hebrew. In 1998 she was Israel's entrant and the winner of the Eurovision song contest.[10] Singing in Hebrew and Arabic, Dana undermines the stability of the supremacy of Euro-Zionist culture in Israel (Ben-Zvi 1998). Her appeal in Egypt points to the existence of a shared Arab-Jewish Middle Eastern musical tradition as well as the willingness of some Egyptian youth to rebel by adopting what will commonly be perceived as the most outrageous thing available.

The pernicious influence of Sa'ida/Dana's music on Egyptian culture was denounced in a small Arabic book issued in 1995 from an anonymous press by an unheralded author: *A Scandal Named Sa'ida Sultan: Dana, the Israeli Sex Singer* (al-Ghayti 1995). The appearance of the book is evidence of Danna's popularity in Egypt. The author explains that Dana's music is an Israeli plot to undermine the moral fiber of Egyptian youth. He accuses her of being a Free Mason who advocates sensual delights and individuals' rights to happiness, principles invented by Zionist Jews to destroy society. This nonsense is so implausible that it probably enhanced Dana's popularity among Egyptian youth, especially given the book's pornographic (by Egyptian standards) cover.

The writing of Samir W. Raafat is full of Judeophilia. Like Youssef Chahine and Edward Said, Raafat is an old boy of Victoria College. His columns in Cairo's English press and his history of Ma'adi, a Cairo suburb developed largely by Jews, are full of nostalgia, celebrating the cultural cosmopolitanism of the monarchy era in contrast with the Arab nationalist monoculture of post-1952 Egypt (Raafat 1994). Raafat has also been the webmaster for the tiny remnant of Cairo's Jewish community.[11] Judeophilia, writing in English, and celebration of monarchy-era culture make Raafat suspect among nationalists. However, there is an audience for his topics and approach among Egyptian participants in the global corporate economy and others who enjoy outings to the upscale Le Pacha 1912 restaurant and similar spots.

Egyptian scholars of Hebrew have tried to remain aloof from the debate over cultural normalization with Israel. A few do violate the taboo by using the library of the Israeli Academic Center in Cairo. But to break ranks publicly would confirm widespread apprehensions that they are engaged in a suspect activity. A good example of the prevailing Egyptian view that Zionist/Israeli culture and society are inauthentic and transitory phenomena is the two-part article on contemporary Israeli literature and society by Abdel-Wahab el-Messiri, holder of a Ph.D. in English literature from Rutgers University and one of several former leftists who became Islamists in the 1980s (el-Messiri 1996, 1996–97). El-Messiri's Hebrew is either minimal or nonexistent. The range of literary production he examines consists almost entirely of works readily available in English. He is either unaware of or uninterested in more complex and critical texts. They certainly do not constitute the prevailing tendency, but their aesthetic and political qualities are nonetheless worthy of note, and they complicate el-Messiri's flat and predictable portrayal of Israel. El-Messiri may consider investing a significant time and energy to learn the language as a betrayal of his commitment to the boycott of cultural normalization with Israel. This does not prevent him from being presented as an authority on Zionism and Israel.

In early 1995, the prestigious literary journal *Ibda'* (Creativity) devoted three special issues to Israeli culture titled "The Propaganda of Normalization and the Dimensions of Confrontation." In her review of the three issues, Deborah Starr argues that this title anticipates that the contributions would be predictably belligerent reinforcements of the consensus opposing cultural normalization. Some authors, mainly those who are not actually specialists in Hebrew literature, conformed to this expectation. But many of the academic professionals engaged in serious examinations of Hebrew language and culture. The introduction to the third issue by the editor of *Ibda'*, the renowned poet Ahmad 'Abd al-Mu'ti Higazi, is equivocal: "What I know is that the Israelis say that their language is alive—perhaps this is a self-deception. We say that the Israeli language is dead—perhaps this is self-deception. This issue requires an objective study"(Starr 2000: 268). In other words, contrary to Arab nationalist suppositions, an Israeli Hebrew society and culture may exist.

A similar process of breaking taboos is apparent on the Israeli side of the line. Israeli cultural elites do not seek to boycott Egyptian culture. Rather, they engage with it to the extent necessary to promote cultural normalization while containing it within its designated boundaries as absolutely "other." Consequently, it is not simple enjoyment of Egyptian culture that constitutes transgression, but rather the validation of its perceptions and sensibilities.

Haya Samir left the Israeli army midway through her service. "It was the start of the Intifada; in one performance I broke down and started crying," she explained (*Jerusalem Report*, 14 January 1993: 43). Although she tried to minimize the political significance of her decision, clearly Israel's repression of Palestinian resistance to occupation posed too much of an identity crisis for her to remain in the army. Her actions affirmed the common Egyptian view that cultural normalization could proceed only if outstanding Arab-Israeli political issues were resolved.

Every year thousands of Israeli and French Jews of Moroccan origins flock to the Delta city of Damanhur to celebrate the *mawlid* (birthday) of the Moroccan rabbi Ya'akov Abu Hasira, who died there in 1880 on his way to Jerusalem. As Amitav Ghosh describes in a complex and beautifully written historical-ethnographic-literary text, Abu Hasira is revered by both Jews and Muslims (Ghosh 1994). Such religious syncretism and symbiosis is common in both Morocco and Egypt. But it is off the map of modern Israeli cultural possibilities, as Ronit Matalon, an Israeli Hebrew novelist from an Egyptian-Jewish family, explains regretfully:

> As an Israeli who was born and educated here, I was surprised by how preoccupied I was with cultural and political options that are not necessarily what Zionism proposes. Zionism and the cultural options it prefers are only one possibility, and not necessarily the most generous one. . . . As an Israeli, I was very, very attracted to the cultural and moral richness of the wandering Jew who does not have one nationality or one country, has many languages, is open to everything human, and does not always close himself off from [foreign] influences. In this sense, the Levantine option of live and let live, which in my opinion is the opposite of Zionism, very much attracted me. (Levtov 1995)

Matalon explored her attraction to Levantinism in a novel, *The One Facing Us,* that recounts her family's history in Egypt and their continuing of connections to Egyptian culture and social mores despite their dispersion in Cameroon, Israel, and New York (Matalon 1995). Matalon's novel is the aesthetic masterpiece of the wave of nostalgic positive recollections of Egypt by Egyptian Jews since the 1979 peace treaty.[12] The first expressions of this current—literature, cookbooks, return trips, and so on—were undertaken with the expectation that a warm peace open to cultural exchanges of all sorts was at hand. The transgressive significance of *The One Facing Us,* clearly articulated in Matalon's comment above, is all the more salient since it appeared after the grim terms of the cold Egyptian-Israeli peace were fully evident.

While popular music with Arabic or Turkish rhythms and intonations has been popular in Israel for some time, Zehava Ben went far beyond the transposition of regional musical culture into Hebrew. An Israeli Jew of Moroccan origins born in a poor neighborhood of Be'ersheba who grew up listening to Egyptian and Arabic popular music at home, Ben has made three albums singing the songs of the musical icons of Egyptian mass culture: Umm Kulthoum, Muhammad 'Abd al-Wahhab, 'Abd al-Halim Hafiz, and Farid al-Atrash, backed up by the Haifa Arab Orchestra conducted by Suhayl Radwan. She especially favors the songs of Egypt's premier diva, Umm Kulthoum.[13] Although her parents speak Arabic, Zehava was not raised as an Arabic speaker and took lessons to perform the music properly. She did well enough to be received with wild enthusiasm by Palestinian audiences in Jericho and Gaza during her 1996 tour.[14] Ben presents herself simply as a musician pursuing her career. It is consistent with the politico-cultural significance of a Jew performing Egyptian Arabic music for a Palestinian Arab audience that Ben produced a musical campaign ad for the Meretz Party in the 1996 Israeli elections. However, the import of her performances is far more radical by Israeli cultural norms than simply supporting a nominally dovish political party.

While Zehava Ben is committed both to living as a Jew in Israel and reproducing the sounds of Umm Kulthoum as precisely as she can, Natacha Atlas takes more liberties with her personal identity and with the Egyptian music she sings. Natacha is the daughter of an Egyptian-Jewish father whose family emigrated to Jerusalem and a British hippie mother.[15] She was born in Brussels and grew up in Moroccan and Jewish neighborhoods where she spoke French, Spanish, Arabic, and English, learned *raqs sharqi* (belly dancing), and absorbed Arabic popular culture. In her second album, *Halim,* she sings the songs of the Egyptian teen heart throb of the era of Gamal 'Abd al-Nasir, 'Abd al-Halim Hafiz, with an updated beat and instrumentation that is still recognizably close to the style of the original performances.[16] The album liner notes are decorated by paintings in the style of Egyptian murals by Natacha Atlas herself. Attracted by the spirituality of Islam, Natacha Atlas now lives half the year in London to promote her career and the other half in Cairo, which she prefers.

The final stop on this quick tour through subversive Israeli engagements with Egyptian culture is with the reflections of Immanuel Marx, professor of anthropology at Haifa University, upon his return to his regular academic post after serving as director of the Israeli Academic Center in Cairo. In an interview in the daily *Ha'aretz,* Marx argued that had it not been for Operation Susannah in 1954, a Jewish community would have remained in Egypt: "Those responsible for the dirty business (*'esek ha-bish,* i.e., Israeli military intelligence) exploited Jews in Egypt for unimportant purposes. This caused the rupture." Marx, like some of the elderly remnants of the Cairo Jewish community, believes that a Jewish community can and should be reestablished in Egypt. He is critical of the Israeli embassy in Cairo for opposing this project "because they are prisoners of Zionist ideas according to which all

Jews must immigrate *(la 'alot)* to Israel. We live in a post-Zionist era ... Israel has become quite a large state, and it's time we stopped the idiotic activity of encouraging the dissolution of Jewish communities throughout the world" (Elgazi 1996).

Complications and Conclusions

It is clear that the institutions and discourse of cultural regulation in both Egypt and Israel have been less effective than those who articulate the canonical norms in both camps would like to believe. Youth, Middle Eastern Jews, and dissident elements are prepared to look differently at the "other." The popularity of these unauthorized cultural crossings among the popular classes of both Egypt and Israel and also among certain cosmopolitan elites is possible because, despite generations of Arab-Israeli conflict, many cultural commonalities continue to be shared by Middle Eastern Jews and Arabs. I do not believe that cultural commonalities and unauthorized crossings can overcome unconducive political, diplomatic, and military conditions on their own. The phenomena I have surveyed in the last part of this essay may ultimately prove to be nothing but light human interest stories on the margin of an otherwise grim scene. Or they may become part of the mix of factors shaping a new politico-cultural future.

Notes

1. Egyptian Israeli Peace Treaty, Article III, 3.

The Parties agree that the normal relationship established between them will include full recognition, diplomatic, economic and cultural relations, termination of economic boycotts and discriminatory barriers to the free movement of people and goods, and will guarantee the mutual enjoyment by citizens of the due process of law. The process by which they undertake to achieve such a relationship parallel to the implementation of other provisions of this Treaty is set out in the annexed protocol Annex III Article 3. Cultural Relations. 1. The Parties agree to establish normal cultural relations following completion of the interim withdrawal. 2. They agree on the desirability of cultural exchanges in all fields, and shall, as soon as possible and not later than six months after completion of the interim withdrawal, enter into negotiations with a view to concluding a cultural agreement for this purpose.

2. Lettres Expediés, janvier–juin 1953, no. 55, Jamie Lehmann Memorial Collection: Records of the Jewish Community of Cairo, 1866–1961, Yeshiva University Archives, New York, Box 2, General Correspondence, 1926–57, Folder 7.

3. Several of these associations were taken over by Islamists in the late 1980s and early 1990s, see Wickham 1997.

4. The history of the committee's activities and lists of endorsers are presented in Lajnat al-Difa'a 'an al-Thaqafa al-Qawmiyya, 1994. Some of the professional associations listed here were taken over by the Islamic Current in the late 1980s or early 1990s, which only strengthened their opposition to normalizing cultural relations with Israel.

5. For examples of Shamir's work see his introduction and contributions to his edited volume, Shamir 1995.

6. *Muhimma fi Tal Abib* (1992), directed by Nadir Galal, produced by Aflam Muhammad Mukhtar, and starring Nadia al-Gindi, Kamal al-Shinnawi, and Sa'id 'Abd al-Ghani.

7. *The Planet Sleeps* (Sony, 1997).

8. The works of Siham Nassar, 'Awatif 'Abd al-Rahman, 'Arafa 'Abdu 'Ali, and Sa'ida Muhammad Husni are critically discussed in the final chapter of Beinin 1998.

9. *Iskandariyya Leh?* (Alexandria Why?, 1979), directed by Youssef Chahine, produced by Aflam Misr al-'Alamiyya and Radio et Television Algerien, starring Muhsin Muhyi al-Din, Farid Shawqi, 'Izzat al-'Alayli, and Yusuf Wahbi.

10. For more information on Dana, see her unofficial fan club website: http://d1o202.telia.com/~u222600821/Geir%20Site/GeirDana1.html

11. The URL is http://www.geocities.com/RainForest/Vines/5855/bassai.htm

12. For description and analysis of this wave, including a more detailed discussion of Matalon's novel, see Beinin 1998, especially 49–59, 207–40.

13. Ben's recording of Umm Kulthoum's classics, *Inta 'Umri* (You are my life) (Tel Aviv[?]: Helicon Records, 1995), is the only one of her albums I have been able to secure, thanks to the assistance of Ted Swedenburg.

14. Ben's career with Egyptian music and excerpts from several of her performances during the 1996 tour are presented in the film *Zehava Ben: Solitary Star/ Zehava ben: Kokhav ehad levad* (1996) directed by Erez Laufer.

15. Ted Swedenburg first introduced me to the music of Natacha Atlas. Biographical information is drawn from his forthcoming "Islamic Hip-Hop vs. Islamophobia: Aki Nawaz, Natacha Atlas, Akhenaton" and from http://www.worldmusicportal.com/Artists/European/Belgian/natachaatlas.htm

16. Natacha Atlas, *Halim*. London: Warner Chappell Music Ltd., 1997 (recorded at Sawt al-Qahira, Cairo; produced by Essam Rachid).

References

Ahmad, Rif'at Sayyid. *Wasf Misr bi'l-'Arabi: Tafasil al-Ihtiraq al-Isra'ili li'l-'Aql al-Misri* (The description of Egypt in Arabic: Details of the Israeli penetration of the Egyptian mind). Cairo: Dar Sina', 1989.

Amitai, Yossi. *Mitzrayim ve-yisra'el—mabat mi-semol: ha-semol ha-mitzri ve-ha-sikhsukh ha-'aravi-yisra'eli, 1947–1978* (Egypt and Israel—a view from the left: The Egyptian Left and the Arab-Israeli conflict, 1947–1978). Haifa and Tel Aviv: Hotsa'at ha-Sefarim shel Universitat Haifah and Zemorah-Bitan, 1999.

'Arafa 'Abduh 'Ali. *Gitu Isra'ili fi al-Qahira* (An Israeli ghetto in Cairo). Cairo: Maktabat Madbuli, 1990.

Beinin, Joel. *The Dispersion of Egyptian Jewry: Culture, Politics, and the Formation of a Modern Diaspora.* Berkeley: University of California Press, 1998.

Ben-Zvi, Yael. "Zionist Lesbianism and Transsexual Transgression." *Middle East Report,* no. 206 (winter 1998): 26–28.

Elgazi, Yosef. "Gam ha-gvul shelanu sagur" (Our border is closed too). *Ha'aretz,* 17 March 1996.

al-Ghayti, Muhammad. *Fadiha Ismaha Sa'ida Sultan: Dana, Mutribat al-Jins al-Isra'ili* (A scandal named Sa'ida Sultan: Dana, the Israeli sex singer). Cairo: al-Markaz al-'Arabi lil-Buhuth wa'l-Nashr, 1995.

Ghosh, Amitav. *In an Antique Land.* New York: Vintage Books, 1994.

Goitein, S. D. *A Mediterranean Society: The Jewish Communities of the Arab World as Portrayed in the Documents of the Cairo Geniza.* 6 vols. Berkeley: University of California Press, 1967–93.

Jankowski, James. "Egyptian Responses to the Palestine Problem in the Interwar Period." *International Journal of Middle East Studies* 12, no. 1 (1980): 1–38.

———. "Zionism and the Jews in Egyptian Nationalist Opinion, 1920–1939." In *Egypt and Palestine: A Millennium of Association (1868–1948),* ed. Amnon Cohen and Gabriel Baer, 314–31. Jerusalem: Ben-Tzvi Institute for the Study of the Jewish Communities in the East, 1984.

al-Kharrat, Edwar. *Ya Banat Iskandariyya.* Beirut: Dar al-Adab, 1990; English edition: *Girls of Alexandria,* trans. Frances Liardet. London: Quartet, 1993.

al-Kitaba al-Ukhra, no. 9 (October 1994).

Lajnat al-Difa' 'an al-Thaqafa al-Qawmiyya. *Min Muqawamat al-Tatbi' ila Muwajahat al-Haymana: Dirasat wa-Watha'iq, 1979–1994* (From opposing normalization to confronting hegemony: Studies and documents, 1979–1994). Cairo: Markaz al-Buhuth al-Arabiyya lil-Dirasat wa'l-Nashr, 1994.

Levtov, Yitzhak. "Kismah shel ha-optizia ha-levantinit" (Charm of the Levantine option). *Davar,* 28 April 1995.

Matalon, Ronit. *Zeh 'im ha-panim eleynu.* Tel Aviv: 'Am 'Oved, 1995; English translation: *The One Facing Us.* New York: Henry Holt, 1998.

Meital, Yoram. *Egypt's Struggle for Peace: Continuity and Change, 1967–1977.* Gainesville: University Press of Florida, 1997.

El-Messiri, Abdel-Wahab. "A Zionist Nightmare" and "Checking Out of Hotel Zion." *Al-Ahram Weekly,* 19–25 December 1996 and 26 December 1996–1 January 1997.

Middle East Contemporary Survey. New York: Holmes and Meier, 1979–80.

Mizrahi, Maurice. *L'Egypte et ses Juifs: Les temps révolu, xixe et xxe siècles.* Geneva: Imprimerie Avenir, 1977.

Qasim, 'Abduh Qasim. "Al-Yahud fi Misr: Safahat al-Tarikh al-Haqiqi!" (The Jews in Egypt: Pages of the true history). *Wujhat nazar* (Viewpoint) 6 (July 1999): 30–35.

Ra'fat, Samir W. Review in *Bassatine News* 1, no. 11 (July 1999). Website: http://www.geocities.com/RainForest/Vines/5855/basssa11.htm

———. *Ma'adi, 1902–1962: Society and History in a Cairo Suburb.* Cairo: Palm Press, 1994.

Said, Edward. *Out of Place*. New York: Vintage Books, 1999.
Salim, 'Ali. *Rihla ila Isra'il* (A trip to Israel). Cairo: Dar Akhbar al-Yawm, 1994.
Shalash, 'Ali. *Al-Yahud wa'l-Masun fi Misr: Dirasa Tarikhiyya* (The Jews and Masons in Egypt: A historical study). Cairo: al-Zahra' li'l-I'lam al-'Arabi, 1986.
Shamir, Shimon. *Egypt from Monarchy to Republic: A Reassessment of Revolution and Change*. Boulder, Colo.: Westview Press, 1995.
Starr, Deborah. "Egyptian Representation of Israeli Culture: Normalizing Propaganda or Propagandizing Normalization?" In *Review Essays in Israel Studies*, ed. Laura Zitrain Eisenberg and Neil Caplan. Albany: State University of New York Press, 2000.
Swedenburg, Ted. "Islamic Hip-Hop vs. Islamophobia: Aki Nawaz, Natacha Atlas, Akhenaton." In *Global Noise: Rap and Hip Hop Outside the USA*, ed. Tony Mitchell. Middletown, Conn.: Wesleyan University Press, forthcoming.
——. "Saida Sultan/Dana International: Transgender Pop and the Polysemiotics of Sex, Nation, and Ethnicity on the Israeli-Egyptian Border." In *Mass Mediations: New Approaches to Popular Culture in the Middle East and Beyond*, ed. Walter Armbrust, 88–119. Berkeley: University of California Press, 2000.
Wickham, Carrie Rosefsky. "Islamic Mobilization and Political Change: The Islamist Trend in Egypt's Professional Associations." In *Political Islam: Essays from "Middle East Report,"* ed. Joel Beinin and Joe Stork. Berkeley: University of California Press, 1997.

8

Islamic Themes in Palestinian Political Thought

Alexander Flores

Partly in light of the ongoing unrest—termed the al-Aqsa Intifada because it was sparked by events on the Temple Mount—but also more generally, many assume that religion is a key motivating and mobilizing factor behind the Palestinian struggle against Israel. I believe one should at least qualify this assumption. To the extent that religious convictions and prescriptions figure in the conflict, they do not do so as independent variables but in a context largely shaped by the given sociopolitical situation and the interests of the respective participants. In this century and for the Palestinians, the context largely determining their convictions and behavior has been the conflict over Palestine itself.

The Palestine Conflict

In substance, this conflict is nonreligious. The Zionist movement was the nationalist reaction to the oppression of Jews in Europe and hence a secular movement. Its project—the creation of a Jewish state in Palestine and large-scale Jewish migration to that country—was basically secular in orientation. When Zionists stressed Judaism it was to foster the appeal of the project for the largely religious Jews of Eastern Europe and because they needed the religious divide to clearly distinguish their own constituency from everybody else. The reaction of Palestinians to the realization of the Zionist project in turn was nationalist and hence secular. This was true for Palestinian Muslims as well as Christians. They shared a common fate insofar as they were all excluded from and threatened by Zionist settlement. Thus, a sharp cleavage emerged between two population groups in Palestine, a rending characterized more and more by mutual enmity as well. The ethnic and political division coincided in a way with a religious bisector: on one side, the Jews, however nominal, on the other, Muslims and Christians. This opened the possibility for supplementary mobilization of the respective masses along religious lines. On the Palestinian side, that was facilitated by the circumstance that the vast majority of Palestinians (more than 90%) are Muslims. Thus, although the fact that Palestinians belong to more than one religion pushes them to formulate their common defense against Zionism in secular terms, it is also possible to strike up the Islamic religious chord without losing too much popular appeal. Furthermore, the British mandatory authorities, while officially recognizing a Jewish community in Palestine, did not grant official status to the Palestinians as such, though they did with respect to the Muslim community.

By and large, the Zionists were the more active party to the conflict. This was logical since they were the factor that had still to be implanted in the country—a colonization accomplished with British support. The Palestinians were on the defensive; in many instances, basically they just reacted to Zionist initiatives. Hence they were strongly influenced by the thrust of Zionist actions, and when the Zionists had recourse to the religious theme, that was additional impetus for them to do the same.

Judaism from an Islamic Angle

If Palestinian Muslims (the vast majority of the Palestinians) wanted to mobilize people against the Zionist project with Islamic arguments, there were primarily two complexes they could use: the statements of Islamic tradition pertaining to Judaism and Jews, and the special place of Jerusalem in Islam. The attitude of Muslims toward Jews has been marked by ambiguity from the very birth of Islam. Muhammad saw his mission as a continuation of and at times even identical with earlier prophetic missions, and Jewish prophecy was by far the most important. The history of salvation as drawn by the Qur'an in the Meccan period is in its essential outlines the Jewish one; biblical tales and prophets figure prominently in the relevant passages. Already in the Meccan period, Jerusalem marked the first *qibla* (focus for prayer) of the Muslims, and other features of ritual such as prayer and fasting also reflected Jewish models. In his first stay in Medina, Muhammad envisaged an alliance with the Jews of that city, as is evident from the so-called Constitution of Medina. All in all, the Qur'an reflects a basically positive relationship with Jews and Judaism at this stage.

Yet when the Jews of Medina refused to recognize Muhammad as a prophet and to participate in the war against Mecca, the picture changed. Muhammad and the Muslims turned against the Jews and drove them out of Medina, tribe after tribe, with ever-increasing harshness, including a massacre. Yet contrary to the relationship between Judaism and Christianity, the conflict between Muslims and Jews was not primarily a theological opposition but a down-to-earth political struggle. Theologically, the sole accusation against the Jews was that for base motives, they had falsified the revelation given to them.

This turn against the Jews found expression in the basic texts—in the Qur'an only in a rudimentary form, but elaborated in the Prophet's biography and the *Hadith* (Vajda 1937). These later texts present a somewhat negative overall impression. This fact notwithstanding, the basic texts retain the possibility of both positive and negative attitudes regarding Jews. A whole range of attitudes and behaviors in that respect can thus be legitimized Islamically, as for instance with the help of the precedent established by the differential treatment accorded different Jewish tribes in Medina.

In general, in order to deal with Jews and other non-Muslim communities in Islamic states, Islamic law developed the institution of the *dhimma*, a contractual relation by which non-Muslims, after payment of a special tax, were guaranteed their lives, property, and the freedom to practice their religion. At the same time, the dhimma was a form of legal discrimination of non-Muslims. As a general rule, Jews in the premodern Islamic world fared better than in Christian Europe, but by no means as idyllically as some would like to suggest. Their treatment by the authorities and the majority population varied considerably, dependent not so much upon seemingly invariable religious attitudes and precepts as upon given specific politico-social circumstances.

The normally latent negative accent in the Islamic attitude toward Jews could be actualized in critical situations. Anti-Jewish feelings could be expressed in Islamic terms and with Islamic slogans. When the Arab world was modernized, the institution of dhimma, which had meant inferior status but also a certain protection for Jews, was called into question (Lewis 1984: 154–91). In the twentieth and early twenty-first centuries, the potentially anti-Jewish stance of Islam was often accentuated in connection with the Palestine conflict. In such cases, the harm done to the Palestinians in that conflict was ascribed not to Zionism as a distinct political movement or to the State of Israel, but to "the Jews" as allegedly "eternal enemies" of the Muslims. After major Arab defeats, such views were also disseminated or furthered by Arab governments. In the wake of the emergence of anti-Jewish animus, partly spontaneous and partly officially sponsored, several hundred thousand Jews left the Arab countries and migrated to Israel, Europe, or North America after 1948.

After the Arab defeat in the June 1967 war, there was a marked intensification of anti-Jewish statements by Arab intellectuals and politicians. Thus, the Academy of Islamic Studies of al-Azhar convened a conference in September 1968 at which scholars from many Islamic countries presented their views on the relationship between Islam and Judaism. In quite one-sided fashion, the negative characterizations of Jews in the Qur'an and Hadith were emphasized. Such a view could promote a notion of the conflict that conceptualizes it not as a result of a clash of interests but a manifestation of an eternal opposition between Jews and Muslims, with implications for final salvation (Green 1971: 13–39, 42–47).

Yet this openly anti-Jewish version of the anti-Israel stand did not meet with general approval by the Arab public, some perhaps because they saw too clearly the political nature of the conflict, others perhaps because they wanted to avoid the virtually ever-present accusation of racism and anti-Semitism. Many Arab nationalists and leftists strove for a clear distinction between a political enmity toward Israel, anti-Zionism, and a general enmity toward all Jews. This subject was debated with great intensity among the Palestinian resistance groups, which tried to clarify the distinction for the broader Arab public (Gresh 1983: 51–54; El Fath 1970).

Be that as it may, the accentuation of anti-Judaism in Islamic terms followed the junctures in the development of the conflict. This points up a nexus between political and social circumstances and the prevailing attitudes toward the Jews. Several studies of the situation of the Jews in Arab countries around the middle of the twentieth century arrive at the same conclusion (Krämer 1983; Bunzl 1989: 42–80). It follows that there was a certain anti-Judaism in Islamic tradition—normally latent but always ready to be actualized in situations of sharp conflict.

Jerusalem in Islam

The other theme from Islamic tradition that has been pivotal for the Palestine conflict is the notion of the sanctity of Jerusalem in Islam. Several facts and developments lie at the basis of this notion. Jerusalem or its environs are the scene and stage for a large segment of salvation history in the Qur'an; it is situated in the "Blessed Land" (Qur'an 7:137; 21:71; 21:81); many prophets lived there and left sites associated with them (Abraham, Moses, Samuel, Salomo, and others). It was the first direction of prayer (*qibla*) in Islam, and, according to the Qur'an (17:1), it was the destination of Muhammad's "nocturnal journey" *(isra')*. Only the Prophet's biography relates Muhammad's miraculous journey to heaven *(mi'raj)*. The Qur'an is silent on this. Yet subsequently both these events—isra' and mi'raj—are taken as proof of Jerusalem's Islamic importance. Early Islamic rulers tried to underline this importance by erecting magnificent monuments, first and foremost the Dome of the Rock (Le Strange 1890; Duri 1989).

Thus, since early times, Jerusalem enjoyed considerable esteem in Islamic eyes. The exact degree of the city's sanctity in Islam was subject to an inner-

Islamic controversy. It ended provisionally with its consecration as the third most holy place in Islam after the sanctuaries in Mecca and Medina. One should only go on pilgrimage to these three places; the rites in Jerusalem should clearly differ from those of the *hajj* (Kister 1969). The "Islamic" image of Jerusalem underwent further development and elaboration. In mystical and popular Islam, Jerusalem often was attributed an importance that went beyond its officially recognized status, a fact noted quite critically by the stern Hanbalite scholar Ibn Taymiyya (d. 1328). And this theme, normally of little political import, could be emphasized and used as, for instance, during the Crusades, when the sanctity of Jerusalem was instrumentalized to help prepare for its reconquest. The so-called Fada'il al-Quds literature (works praising Jerusalem) flourished at the time. And after Salah al-Din had indeed reconquered Jerusalem, the sacredness of the city remained quite vital in general Islamic consciousness: witness for instance the large number of buildings endowed by Ayyubid, Mamluk, and Ottoman rulers and notables in a city of rather limited political and economic importance at the time (Sivan 1985).

Two things should be noted: first, the important place Jerusalem was accorded in Muslim eyes early on, and second, the political instrumentalization of this space when the need arose. Consequently, the Jerusalem motive has been emphasized since the emergence of the Palestine conflict. Muslim sovereignty over Jerusalem was endangered especially after 1917; in 1917, the city fell under British, that is non-Muslim, control; in 1948, its western part was conquered and occupied by Israel, and, in 1967, Israel took control of its eastern part with the Old City and the holy places. The Jerusalem motive appears a convenient tool to address and mobilize for the Palestinian cause: not just the Palestinians and neighboring Arab populations who are more or less immediately concerned, but also Muslims throughout the world. In this context, it seems expedient to fuse the religious and national aspects of the Palestine question—or rather to portray this question, undoubtedly national in essence, in a religious light. To highlight Jerusalem is a convenient way to do so.

A master of such propaganda was the mufti of Jerusalem in mandatory times, the famous—and notorious—Hajj Amin al-Husaini. At the end of the 1920s, he made the Temple Mount/Haram al-Sharif the focus of a campaign against Zionist plans concerning the extension of Jewish rights at the Wailing Wall: "After the first stage of the major repair work of the mosques of al-Haram al-Sharif was completed in 1928, they became within a year a symbol of the struggle against Zionism in Palestine. This was the best way to bring home the danger threatening the Palestinian Arabs from Zionism. Instead of abstract nationalist slogans about self-determination, majority rights etc. they now had a concrete symbol which was clearly understood by the Muslim masses" (Porath 1974: 272).

It is interesting to note that these Zionist plans had exactly the same purpose on the other side: to address a Jewish audience beyond the Zionist rank and file and to mobilize them in the Zionist interest by highlighting religious issues. The contiguity of the holy places of both religions contributed to the ease with which the issue could be exploited. The tension exploded in the bloody unrest of August 1929: the background to these disturbances was clearly political, but they took the form of an intercommunal clash, thus contributing to the ethnicization of the conflict (Flores 1993: 106–9).

When the rest of eastern Jerusalem fell in 1967, the Jerusalem horn was sounded frequently—not only as a mobilizing factor in the fight for usurped rights but also as a means for expressing grief or providing consolation. Arab nationalism dominated the discourse at the time. Consequently, Islamic themes were stressed, but within a nationalist framework. Characteristically, these themes were invoked along with Christian motifs. The Jerusalem songs of the Lebanese singer Fairuz were a moving artistic expression of this mix of Christian and Islamic motifs and a means for its dissemination. Just take the song "Zahrat al-Mada'in": its lyrics mention Jesus ("the child in the grotto and Mary, his mother") and alluded to the Prophet's *isra'* and *mi'raj* ("Oh night of the journey, oh way of those who went to heaven").[1]

In the past few years, Jerusalem, and the Temple Mount in particular, has also played a role in accentuating the sharpness of the conflict. Let me but recall the events of October 1990, the so-called tunnel war of September 1996, and, of course, the eruption of rage in September 2000 that has still not subsided.

So there are two sets of Islamic themes that can be evoked in the context of the Palestine conflict: the motif of Islam contra Judaism and the Islamic meaning of Jerusalem. They have surfaced from time to time, the latter more frequently, and generally meshed with the perceived needs of the parties concerned and the junctures of a given situation. Since the overall dynamics of the conflict were national, nationalism saturated its ambience.

A close look at the Palestinian national movement indicates that most of its components have been nationalist and thus secular in character, even when some of the leading figures posed as devout Muslims. Under the mandate, that was apparent in the fact that the official body of the movement was the Muslim-Christian Association. Though there was often an Islamic tint to the movement's rhetoric, the content of its ideology was not specifically Islamic. It was only too obvious that the conflict was basically a political one over who was to possess and control Palestine. Even where religious

Islamic concepts such as martyrdom were intoned, they were wrapped in a secularized form. Take, for example, the poem by the Palestinian writer Abdarrahim Mahmud (1913–1948), who fell in the struggle for Palestine in 1948. In his poem "The Martyr," he evokes the spirit of a fighter who seeks martyrdom, yet nowhere in the poem is there any mention of God or the quest for Paradise. The martyr struggles for an earthly cause—the fatherland—and his paradise is the memory of his kinfolk (Mahmud 1985: 99–103).

The new Palestinian resistance movement that emerged in the 1950s was likewise secular in character—in spite of the fact that some of its leading figures were former members of the Muslim Brotherhood. Going through the literature of its heroic period, one finds very few references to Islam. For example, the special issue of *Filastin ath-Thaura*, the PLO's main periodical (then a weekly), that was produced for the tenth anniversary of the launching of the armed struggle in 1975, an issue almost 200 pages thick that covered many aspects of the Palestinian movement and its experience, does not contain a single article with any bearing on Islam. Even pictures of the Dome of the Rock figure only twice in the issue and are removed from any religious context (*Filastin ath-Thaura* 1975).

Palestine, Islam, and Islamic Activism

One might suppose that with heightened stress on religion and the emergence and spread of the Islamist movement over the last twenty years or so, an Islamic theme would have gained currency and thus influenced the perception of the conflict in broader circles. That should especially be true with respect to the Islamists themselves. To check the validity of this assumption, let us look briefly at the most important organization among the Palestinian Islamists, Hamas. Hamas is by far the biggest Islamist organization in Palestine. Here I want to look at both its features, as an *Islamist* organization *in Palestine*. As an Islamist organization, Hamas deplores any real or alleged deviation by Islamic societies from true Islam and demands that such deviation be rectified by a variety of means, including education, legal measures, and peaceful activities. But by no means does it exclude the possibility of violent forms of struggle. Hamas espouses the necessity of an Islamic state or Islamic system and the introduction of shari'a law. Like Islamists elsewhere, Hamas stresses Palestine as a central component in its ideology. In its view, the country is an inalienable part of the Dar al-Islam. Since Palestine has fallen under non-Muslim rule, the land should be liberated. Consequently, Hamas's position toward Israel is uncompromising: negotiations and compromises with Israel are explicitly rejected. It also comes as no surprise that as far as Jews in general are concerned, Hamas subscribes to the essentialist viewpoint alluded to earlier. It views the Jews as eternal enemies of the Muslims; they have to be fought against and can only be tolerated as dhimmis, that is, as subordinate subjects of an Islamic state. Until that goal is achieved, unrelenting and resolute struggle is the only conceivable stance vis-à-vis the Jews.

Their uncompromising ideological stand notwithstanding, Islamists nonetheless have to reckon with the political and social frame within which they operate—in general, a nation-state with all its associated problems. That holds true for Hamas as well, although there is as yet no Palestinian national state. The organization works in a Palestinian context characterized by an intense national conflict and the concomitant nationalist ambient and rhetoric. Any organization that does not want to be marginalized or virtually excluded from the realm of Palestinian politics must seek to adapt to this frame and atmosphere. And up to a certain degree, this adaptation has been underway: after a long period of abstinence from active resistance, many Palestinian Islamists took part in the early stages of the first intifada and founded Hamas or rather renamed the Muslim Brotherhood, turning it into Hamas. They simply could not stand idly by as the heightened nationalist mobilization exploded. Even their literature and discourse contain certain concessions to nationalism that seemingly contradict their overall rigidly Islamist and thus *anti-nationalist* ideology (Flores 2000: 270–77).

Recent Shifts

Oslo has brought about further modulations. Before the Intifada, the Palestinian factions affiliated with the PLO generally tried to resist the occupation; the Islamists hardly made themselves felt in this regard. With the founding of Hamas bearings began to shift, and the signing of the Oslo Accords signaled a fundamental change of roles: the PLO now became Israel's partner in the peace process, while Hamas emerged as the largest force in opposition to that process of rapprochement and compromise. As a result, it was subjected to severe Israeli (and Palestinian) suppression. Since Hamas is the largest, best organized, and most fundamental opposition force in the Palestinian camp, it gained credibility and support far beyond the nucleus of its sympathizers—especially at times when the peace process has brought additional burdens for Palestinians. Ironically, in such a situation, Hamas, despite all its antinationalist rhetoric, sometimes appears as more (and more sincerely) nationalist than the old nationalist avant-garde of the PLO.

Yet all this has to be seen in proper perspective. Whereas it is true that

Hamas has in some ways adapted to the national dynamics of the conflict and broadened its mass following in the process, it has not given up core elements of its ideology. It still propagates an essentialist view, it still portrays Jews as the eternal enemies of Muslims, and so on. Viewed through that prism, the conflict appears existential and unamenable to solution by human endeavor. If that perspective gains a broad following, it can be a genuine impediment to any viable solution or regulation of the conflict. A conflict that is eternal cannot be resolved; it can only be lived through, endured, and suffered.

In sum, there are two large camps in the Palestinian movement, one secular nationalist and the other Islamist. The nationalists see the conflict basically as political—a confrontation between the patently political movement of Zionism and the Palestinians, who have been victimized by the realization of the Zionist project. Although this conflict appears to be unrelenting, it is in this analysis not insoluble. Especially following the emergence of the two-state solution as a practicable alternative, there is hope that a workable compromise might be found.

By contrast, the Islamists see the conflict in terms of two adversarial groups irreconcilable by virtue of their religious affiliations and beliefs. From this vantage, the conflict appears everlasting and insoluble, at least on the stage of human action. One of Hamas's favorite slogans, often encountered as graffiti in Palestine, is *"Zawal Isra'il hatmiyya qur'aniyya"* (Israel's disappearance is a Qur'anically grounded historical necessity), a phrasing from the Qur'an. It is clear that such an essentialist mentality cannot imagine a solution on the plane of human action and negotiation. Should such views gain in popularity, they can of course further complicate a practical solution of the conflict. Yet that will hinge on the political fate of Hamas, which in turn depends on the jagged course of development the conflict itself will take. Even in its engaged form as Islamism, Islam is thus no independent variable in the complex equation: it remains dependent on the political and social context in which its zealots act.

Notes

1. A recording of this song is included on the CD *Jerusalem in My Heart/al-Quds fi-l-Bal* of the Lebanese firm Voix de l'Orient (A. Chahine and Fils), VDL CD 510.

References

Bunzl, John. *Juden Im Orient: Jüdische Gemeinschaften in der islamischen Welt und orientalische Juden in Israel.* Vienna: Junius 1989.

Duri, Abdul Aziz. "Jerusalem in the Early Islamic Period, Seventh to Eleventh Cen-

turies A.D.." In *Jerusalem in History*, ed. K. J. Asali, 105–25. Backhurst Hill, Essex, U.K.: Scorpion 1989.
El Fath. *La révolution palestinienne et les Juifs*. Paris: Minuit, 1970.
Filastin ath-Thaura. Adad Khass: Adh-Dhikra al-Ashira. Beirut, 1975.
Flores, Alexander. "Die Entwicklung der palästinensischen Nationalbewegung bis 1948." In *Die Palästina-Frage, 1917–1948*, ed. Helmut Mejcher. Paderborn, Germany: Schöningh, 1993.
———. "Islamismus in Palästina." In *Subjekte und Systeme. Soziologische und anthropologische Annäherungen. Festschrift für Christian Sigrist zum 65. Geburtstag*, ed. Günter Best and Reinhart Kößler. Frankfurt am Main: IKO-Verlag, 2000.
Green, D. F., ed. *Arab Theologians on Jews and Israel*. Geneva: Editions de l'Avenir, 1971.
Gresh, Alain. *OLP: Histoire et strategies vers l'État palestinien*. Paris: SPAG-Papyrus, 1983.
Kister, M. J. "'You shall only set out for three mosques.' A Study of an Early Tradition." *Le Muséon* 1969: 173–96.
Krämer, Gudrun. "Die Juden als Minderheit in Ägypten, 1914–1956: Islamische Toleranz in Zeichen des Antikolonialismus und des Antizionismus." *Saeculum* 34, no. 1 (1983): 36–69.
Le Strange, Guy. *Palestine under the Moslems: A Description of Syria and the Holy Land from A.D. 650 to 1500*. London: Alexander P. Watt, 1890.
Lewis, Bernard. *The Jews of Islam*. Princeton, N.J.: Princeton University Press, 1984.
Mahmud, Abdarrahim. *Ruhi ala rahati*, ed. Hanna Abu Hanna. Tayyiba, Israel: Markaz Ihya' at-Turath, 1985.
Porath, Y. *The Emergence of the Palestinian-Arab National Movement, 1918–1929*. London: Frank Cass, 1974.
Sivan, Emmanuel. "The Sanctity of Jerusalem in Islam." In *Interpretations of Islam, Past and Present*, E. Sivan. Princeton, N.J.: Darwin Press, 1985.
Vajda, Georges. "Juifs et musulmans selon le *Hadit*." *Journal Asiatique* 229 (1937): 57–127.

9

Israel, Religion, and Peace

Avishai Ehrlich

Introduction

I live in Tel Aviv near a small river. Over the river there is a bridge. Under the bridge someone (a left-wing youngster, I would guess) painted a graffito in black that reads: "After we finish making peace with the Arabs—then we'll finish with the religious!" That was several years ago, when the Oslo process was on the agenda, Rabin was alive, and peace seemed just around the corner. Much bloodied water has flowed under the bridge since then: Rabin was assassinated, Oslo has come and gone, and peace is as illusive as the Jewish Messiah.

What the youth wrote was and remains in a nutshell the common conception on the "liberal left" in Israel. Its three underpinning postulates are:

1. The two most important cleavages in Israeli society, the secular-religious and the Jewish-Palestinian, are separate, or at least autonomous, one from the other.
2. It follows that if the two schisms are separate, one conflict can be resolved before or without the other.
3. Inherent here is a belief about the order (sequence) of resolution: first things first, namely the resolution of the Israeli-Palestinian conflict.

My anonymous graffiti writer was not alone. Not long ago, Sammy Smooha, one of Israel's leading sociologists, expressed the same basic view:

> Although it appears that the religious enjoy uncontestable power, peace will deal a blow to them and even usher in an internal war. For most Israeli Orthodox Jews, who believe that no land should be given back to the Arabs, the return of the bulk of Judea and Samaria and the dismantling of some of the settlements are a defeat and also a clear infraction of Jewish religious law. For the religious nationalists, with-

drawal also means that messianic redemption is coming to an end. Another damaging consequence that the religious Jews will have to bear is the failure of their strategy to reach the highest levels of leadership in Israeli society by forming a new Zionism, settling as pioneers in Judea and Samaria, and spearheading the resistance to the peace process. As a result, religious Zionists may feel that their broader historical strategy to influence the nonreligious majority and the state has failed; hence some will retreat into ultra-Orthodoxy or join the moderate traditionalists.

Globalization and mass immigration will also lessen the power of the religious. The nonreligious will become more individualistic, competitive, materialistic, hedonistic, and secularized. They will feel further alienated from the religious and less willing to accept the religious restrictions and impingement of unequal status in orthodoxy between men and women and between Jews and Arabs. The Russian immigrants will also weaken the numerical and electoral power of the religious because of the extremely high proportion of secularists, mixed marriages, and non-Jews among them. These newcomers will play an auxiliary role in the fight. The mounting assaults on the religious status quo will be the opening of an internal war. The struggle of the nonreligious majority, reinforced by the changes triggered by peace, will bring about a greater separation between state and religion. (Smooha 1998:26)

Smooha, like other left-Zionist or even post-Zionist writers (such as G. Shafir and Y. Peled), does not qualify his predictions about the coming of peace, so sure is he when he avers: "Peace in the Israeli-Arab case is real and irreversible." Neither does Smooha take into consideration countervailing forces in Israel or among the Arabs that may hamper its progress.

Although Smooha's principal past claim to fame was his attack on the modernization thesis in Israeli sociology (Smooha 1978), in this passage he seems to concur with that same thesis of which secularization is a basic tenet. Why was he so certain that the conflict was about to end? Why was he confident that the Occupied Territories and the Jewish settlements built there were going to be handed back? The answer is that Smooha, like many other left-liberal Zionists (including Shafir and Peled), were avid believers in the ideology of globalization, which, they trusted, would herald universal peace and usher in a new era of global advance.

In the wake of Prime Minister Rabin's assassination and the vicious election campaign that preceded it, it has become clear that a broad section of the Israeli-Jewish population, not just the settlers, is willing to resist withdrawal from the territories by almost any means. Any move that would involve dismantling many of the Jewish settlements created after 1967 would destroy the delicate internal balance within Israeli society and lead to the collapse of the government, mass disobedience, and even widespread armed internal violence, perhaps spiraling into the nightmare scenario of a civil war.

Netanyahu used this section of the population as leverage on his road to power. He stood by this constituency so as to avoid implementing further stages of the Oslo agreements. However, Israel had also made a commitment to the United States, the European Union, and the international community to push ahead with the Oslo process, brokered with great effort by the international community. Netanyahu's government tried to maneuver its way between those two poles: he provoked the Palestinians by opening the underground tunnel from the Jewish Quarter to the Temple Mount, which resulted in scores of dead and wounded. He defaulted on the implementation of the third staged withdrawal stipulated in the Oslo agreement and further inflamed the situation in Jerusalem by founding a new Jewish suburban settlement ("Har Homa" or "Jabel Ranaim"), threatening to cut off Arab Jerusalem from Bethlehem. Under mounting international pressure and with the loss of external and internal credibility due to public pretense and prevarication, Netanyahu buckled under international pressure in the Wye Plantation negotiations, agreeing to the third stage of transfer of occupied territory to the Palestinian Authority. After this controversial accord, Netanyahu's coalition broke apart; eventually his government was voted out when a large section of the religious camp bolted.

Netanyahu was succeeded by Labor's Ehud Barak. In order to form a majority coalition, Barak was constrained to include much of the religious bloc in his government. Barak will be remembered in the annals of the Israeli-Arab conflict as the Israeli leader who succeeded in ending the Oslo peace process (the only game in town) and, in the event, condemned Israeli-Palestinian relations to the cataclysm of what threatens to become a prolonged low-intensity war.

The basic logic of Oslo was grounded in a gradual trust-building process between the protagonists before they would have to grapple with the more thorny issues awaiting final settlement. One may well doubt whether it could have succeeded, but any workable chance hinged on a gradual approach. Israel's ceaseless expansion of settlements in the Occupied Territories and Palestinian terrorist attacks on Israel did little to create an atmosphere of cooperation and trust. As usual, each side accused the other of breaching agreements.

Barak's strategy was to terminate the gradualist approach of the Oslo process. Against the advice of army intelligence and members of his party, he decided to speed headlong into the final settlement. Moreover, he did it without a majority in the Knesset and without any preparation of public opinion about the real on-the-ground concessions that Israel would have to make in a final settlement—involving territory, settlements, Jerusalem, and the Temple Mount as well as the 1948 refugee problem. One must bear in mind that many of Israel's voters are in the 18–30 age bracket or immigrants who have very little knowledge about the evolution of the conflict.

In addition, we still do not really know what Barak offered the Palestinians at Camp David—there is only hearsay; in any event, it was set within an impossibly short time frame, between his faltering efforts to hold onto the premiership after the breakup of his flimsy coalition and President Bill Clinton's final months in office. The failure of this plan was overdetermined. Barak's cavalier "take it or leave it, the sale ends tomorrow" approach resulted in the present conflagration—the al-Aqsa Intifada. Whatever was offered at the last-minute negotiations at Taba was too late; Barak was a lame-duck prime minister and, as the results have shown, had no mandate from the people. Was it sheer arrogance, or a premeditated decision? What was the role of Clinton and his advisory team in the derailing and burial of the Oslo process? Only history will tell.

Netanyahu and Barak shared a refusal to relinquish the bulk of Israeli settlements in the West Bank and Gaza and to cede full sovereignty to the Palestinians over Arab Jerusalem. These positions are not whimsical; rather, they are indeed the expression and reflection of what is currently deemed possible in Israel given the delicate political balance of power. At this juncture, it is hard to see how it is going to change in the foreseeable future. Let us turn to some underlying structural features that can shed more light on the train of events.

In my analysis, the two most important internal variables that led to this situation are the long-term decline of the two main parties, Likud and Labor, and the growing power of the religious bloc of parties.

The Long Decline of Likud and Labor since 1980

The trend shown in table 1 highlights the electoral changes in Israel over the last twenty years. Labor and Likud were, since the late seventies, the "hub" parties that formed alternate governments. Likud and Labor were always in coalition with other, smaller parties but in each coalition held the upper hand as strongest partner. Both parties adopted a "center" image in order to garner more votes, and they became, save on the peace issue, more and more alike. However, issues that characterized Israel's political agenda in the last two decades, that is, the future of the Occupied Territories, relations be-

Table 1. Decline in the number of Likud and Labor MKs in consecutive Knessets

	10th Knesset 1981–1984	11th Knesset 1984–1988	12th Knesset 1988–1992	13th Knesset 1992–1996	14th Knesset 1996–1999	15th Knesset 1999–
Labor	47	44	39	44	34	26
Likud	48	41	40	32	32	19
Total Labor and Likud	95	85	79	76	66	45
Other candidates	25	35	41	44	54	75

Source: Adapted from Neuberger, 1997: 244.

tween Arabs and Jews in Israel, relations between secular and religious Jews, and relations between Oriental and Occidental Jews, polarized the electorate. This polarization led to the strengthening of the smaller parties, which articulated more clearly than the big parties the interests of different sectors of the voters.

The fragmentation and sectorialization of voting patterns made it more difficult to manage coalitions. In order to resolve this problem, the majority decided on a technical panacea, namely, a major change in the electoral system.

First, they decided to strengthen the premiership in a more presidential manner by direct popular election of the prime minister (PM) (rather than electing the PM by Knesset representatives) and to separate the elections of the prime minister from the elections for members of the Knesset (MK).

Second, they decided to make it more difficult for parliament to topple a government by requiring a larger majority to bring down a PM and by linking the dismissal of a PM to new parliamentary elections.

The new election system did not solve the problems but only exacerbated them, as can be seen from the figures in table 1. By splitting the elections for PM from the elections for parliament, the voters tended to optimize their interests by a kind of ticket splitting: voting one way for a PM and another for MKs. Faced by the difficult decisions created by the Oslo peace process, the last two prime ministers, Netanyahu and Barak, could not even manage to complete a full four-year term in office. The power of Likud and Labor had diminished so dramatically (from 79% of the Knesset in 1981 to 37.5% in 1999) that the PMs had to include other diverse parties in the coalition, bolstering their power to block any major political initiative. This led to incoherent policy maneuvers and wheeling and dealing, necessitated by the need to appease contradictory forces in the coalition. This zig-zagging was often mistakenly attributed to the personalities of Netanyahu and Barak; it was alleged they had corroded Israel's international credibility, wasted money, increased corruption in politics and society, and eroded popular trust in the political system. Rabin could still muster a majority for a compromise agreement with the Syrians and/or the Palestinians, but Netanyahu and Barak were stymied; they apparently were too late in terms of their power to master a majority!

In one of its first moves, the unity government headed by Sharon in 2001 restored the pre-1996 election system in the hope that this would return more power to the two major parties. At the moment, all we can say for certain is that a major shift to the right has occurred in Israeli electoral politics. Whether Labor will manage to pull itself back together and stage a comeback remains an open question.

The Growing Power of the Orthodox Religious Bloc

The term *Orthodox* refers here to varieties of Jewish religious practice that claim to fully uphold halakhic (scriptural) tradition, "Torah-true" Judaism. Such Orthodoxy stands in contrast to secular Judaism and Reform and Conservative Judaism, which attempted to adapt Judaism in the Diaspora to modern conditions. The Orthodox religious parties in the Israeli Knesset include the National Religious Party (NRP; Mafdal in Hebrew), the ultra-Orthodox Ashkenazi Party (sometimes two parties, Hassidim and Mitnagdim), Agudat Israel, and the Oriental ultra-Orthodox party, Shas. Space does not permit me to expound here on the religious differences underlying and driving these diverse currents.

The NRP is a Zionist party, with no qualms about participating in secular governments; its male members serve in the Israeli military. It alone of all the religious parties sees religious value in the Jewish state, "the beginning of our redemption," the first sign portending the coming of the Messiah. NRP's ideology tries to synthesize Judaism and modernity without changing halakha; its adherents are fully integrated into all walks of Israeli society. Since the 1970s, the NRP has become associated with the settlement project of the Occupied Territories in the West Bank and Gaza, spawning the religious settlers' movement Gush Emunim.

Agudat Israel represents the Ashkenazi (Occidental) non- or anti-Zionist religious. It does not see a religious value in the state; its members participate in elections and hold governmental positions, although their attitude to the polity is only instrumental, that is, they do not identify with the secular state. They try to maintain a separate existence within Israeli society: Based on a longstanding agreement, their youth studying in Talmudic seminaries are not inducted into the army, and they try to live in separate residential quarters, maintain a separate education system, and live apart as much as is pragmatically possible, governed by the rules laid down by their sages.

Table 2. Ultra-Orthodox vote in the elections of 1988, 1992, 1996, and 1999

Elections	1988		1992		1996		1999
	Votes	%	Votes	%	Votes	%	Votes
Agudat Israel	102,714	4.5	86,167	3.3	98,655	3.2	125,741
Degel Hatorah	34,279	1.5	(ran under the combined banner of Torah Judaism)				
Shas	107,709	4.7	129,347	4.9	259,759	8.5	430,676
Torah Ultra-Orthodox	244,702	10.7	215,514	8.2	358,414	11.7	556,417
Total votes	2,283,123		2,616,831		3,015,594		3,331,838

Source: Adapted from *Israel Statistical Yearbook*.

Shas is the fastest-growing religious party; formed in 1984, it has become the third biggest party in the Knesset. It originated as a reaction against discrimination by Ashkenazi sages against Sephardi Oriental sages and religious scholars. As the movement burgeoned, it also sought to represent the social, economic, and cultural grievances of all Orientals against the way in which they have been absorbed into Israel, a long-smoldering dissatisfaction. The party is dominated by the all-powerful Rabbi Ovadiya Yossef. Shas's rhetoric is distinctive in that it articulates social grievances in religious terms and criticizes the secular establishment, positioning itself as a counterhegemonic force to the secular Zionist image: a Jewish alternative to Zionist identity. Shas's voters come from all social classes; however, Shas, following Ashkenazi orthodoxy, is forming its own separate education system as well as religious style and rabbinic code.[1] Table 2 shows the evolution of the electoral power of the ultra-Orthodox religious parties.

It can be clearly seen that the religious bloc's base of power has increased significantly, mainly due to the near-meteoric rise of Shas. To the above figures one must add the NRP, which has some 3 percent, so the Orthodox bloc now garners on average some 20 percent of the total vote.

Attitudes toward the Peace Process and Religiosity

There is in Israel a strong positive correlation between religiosity and political attitudes left and right. In a survey conducted in January 1998 (see table 3), the degree of religiosity was defined by behavioral variables such as frequency of visits to synagogues and adherence to dietary laws. The Jewish population was classified into four categories: ultra-Orthodox, religious, traditional, and secular. It was found that when asked to define themselves as being "left" or "right," the more religious the person, the more their self-definition was politically on the right of the spectrum. It must be understood that "left" and "right" in Israel are seen in terms of attitudes toward Arabs,

Table 3. Self-definition Left-Right according to degree of religiosity

	Ultra-Orthodox	Religious	Traditional	Secular
Right	100.0	81.3	55.3	22.0
Center	0	8.3	22.0	19.0
Left	0	10.4	22.7	59.0

Source: Harman and Yaar (1998).

the peace process, and the return of occupied territories to the Palestinians. Religiosity is associated with particularist values while secularism is associated with universalist values. Universalism sees all human beings as equal and, in principle, as entitled to the same rights. A particularist view differentiates between Jews and goyim, relating them to two different categories and thereby not equal members of a Jewish state. By traditional we mean praying on the Sabbath, kiddush, separate dishes, Passover dishes, blessing candles, koshering meat, and fasting on Yom Kippur (Kedem 1995: 35).

Other research reveals the same patterns.

Another indicator of the attitudes of the religious toward the peace process is manifest in the degree of honesty that different groups of Israeli Jews attribute to the Palestinian side in the peace negotiations (see table 4). This research was conducted in 1998, while Netanyahu was prime minister and in a period of relative quiet—not after the outbreak of the al-Aqsa Intifada. Here, too, a strong correlation existed: the more religious, the greater the distrust of the Palestinians. The ultra-Orthodox distrusted the Palestinians almost without exception. That lack of trust in the adversary's probity diminishes in direct proportion to increased secularity. The gap between secular and ultra-Orthodox is so vast as to indicate an almost completely different mind-set.

The research from which these tables are taken also gauged support for the Oslo process among respondents according to religiosity. We have data on consecutive years from 1994, when the Palestinian Authority was

Table 4. Israelis' perception of the honesty of Palestinians in wishing to conclude peace (according to religiosity)

	Ultra-Orthodox	Religious	Traditional	Secular
Palestinians honestly want peace	4.8	35.8	50.0	63.0
Palestinians don't honestly want peace	85.7	59.7	46.4	31.0
Do not know	9.5	4.5	3.6	6.0

Source: Harman and Yaar (1998).

founded, up to 1997. During this period, there was a strong correlation between degree of religiosity and objection to the process. The ultra-Orthodox were solidly united through this entire period against the peace process.

The Relation between the Secular-Religious Cleavage and the Peace Process

Sociologists and political scientists in Israel tend to talk about the principal special cleavages in Israeli society (i.e., cleavages that are not universal, such as class and gender, but unique to the Israeli social formation: the secular-religious, Jewish-Arab, Oriental-Occidental, and left-right divisions). While there is a vast amount of research on each of these conflicts, there is comparatively little investigation of the interrelations between cleavages and the causal determinations between them. I would argue that these are the key elements in understanding the process of structuration of Israeli society.

As pointed out, Smooha does not interlink the secular-religious conflict and the Israeli-Arab conflict. This is a serious error. The religious-secular divide does not relate only to keeping religious rules and maintaining a certain (private and public) lifestyle. It pertains to a whole dichotomous worldview. Sociologists have termed it a universalist versus particularist set of values. It represents a different moral standard for the in-group from that applied to "outside" groups; inter alia, a different attitude toward individualism, difference, and tolerance, authority and democracy; and a different perspective on the meaning attributed to the national state and citizenship. In Israel, this relates to the very meaning of "community." "Israeliness" and "Jewishness" are totally different conceptions of being and belonging. The first is inclusive: it could incorporate non-Jews, while the second is exclusive. Since the very inception of Zionism in the late nineteenth century, they have been a matter of controversy. A state where Jews are a majority, a "state of the Jews," as advocated by Herzl in *Der Judenstaat,* is entirely different from a Jewish state.

Table 5 shows that the majority of both secular and religious agree that the Oslo process brought about a distancing between secular and religious and that the polarization was felt more at the extremes, that is, more by the ultra-Orthodox and the secular than by the religious and traditional, or those in the middle of the broader band.

Looking at table 2 together with table 5, the explanation becomes clear. Left and right in Israel are not divided over issues such as welfare versus the market, that is, socioeconomic issues, as is the case in most of Europe. The left-right division in Israel is related to the way in which the resolution of the Israeli-Arab conflict is viewed, and it pivots especially around questions

Table 5. Influence of the Oslo process on relations between Israel's secular and religious (according to degree of religiosity)

	Ultra-Orthodox	Religious	Traditional	Secular
No influence	27.3	38.0	47.7	28.9
Caused distancing	59.1	42.0	38.6	47.5
Brought closeness	9.0	8.0	7.6	2.3

Source: Harman and Yaar (1998).

of ceding occupied territories for the sake of peace ("land for peace"). The left is willing to hand back most of the territories within a calculable security risk, while the right regards the land in religious terms as a sanctuary—and hence indivisible and nonnegotiable. This is most heatedly manifested in the question of Jerusalem.

All the religious parties oppose the uprooting of the settlers and are against the division of sovereignty over Jerusalem—calling for much less Muslim sovereignty on the Temple Mount/Haram al-Sharif—and against any dilution of the proportion of Jews in the total Israeli population by allowing Palestinian refugees to return. The religious voted, en masse, for Likud and brought it to power; they have not voted in significant numbers for Labor in the past, nor will they in the foreseeable future. The power of the religious bloc is not likely to decline. The best indicator for future trends is education. The key sphere of ideological reproduction, the Israeli education system, is split, divided into three ideological sectors, state-secular, state-religious, and ultra-Orthodox, autonomous in terms of content but state financed. Recent data show that the relative strength in numbers of the state-secular system is decreasing and the proportion of the religious sectors is on the rise. Within religious education, the ultra-Orthodox sector is growing fastest and has almost reached parity in numbers of students with the state-religious sector. All in all, the two religious sectors currently comprise some 40 percent of the entire Jewish school population.

Any Labor-headed coalition (if not a unity government of Likud and Labor) will depend on the support of the religious and thus will be hamstrung, prevented from offering the Palestinians a minimal program of a "reasonable and just peace" that could prove acceptable to moderate Palestinians. Hence, Israeli peace politics have been deadlocked over the last decade. This is also the interlinkage between the religious-secular cleavage and the peace process. The strength of the religious community within the electorate has been the major cause for the inability of Israel to offer the requisite conditions for a historic compromise. Projections for the future indicate that the power of the religious is bound to increase.

Barak's ostensible peace initiative at Camp David can be viewed as deriving directly from the internal dilemma faced by Rabin. The more we learn about his offers, the clearer it is that he made an offer that Arafat could only refuse. Barak took a decision to avoid the confrontation with the religious and the right, preferring an external confrontation with the Palestinians to an internal one with his own people. The present tragic situation in Palestine/Israel follows directly from this decision.

With Sharon's government, Israel and the Israeli-Arab conflict have entered a new dangerous phase, the death toll mounting daily. In some respects the conflict has reverted back to the period before Oslo, the era of the first intifada. This time, however, it is an armed intifada led by a quasi-state entity. It is thus of higher intensity and more deadly. The Palestinian alternative to negotiated agreement has been a revolt against the occupation, in part armed. There is virtual unanimity among Palestinians that there cannot be a continuation of Israeli occupation and settlement without resistance. In this respect, international law would appear on the side of the Palestinians.

Barak in effect succeeded in removing the step-wise Oslo process from Israel's national agenda. The alternative he conjured, the "final settlement"—if ever a viable alternative—is now dead as well. Both Israel and the United States have hastily announced its expiration. At present there are no workable peace plans on the horizon.

The unity government between Likud and Labor led by Sharon symbolizes the new turn. Since the late 1980s, the deep disagreements about the peace process and the future of the Occupied Territories prevented these two parties from uniting in such a sharing of state power. Now that the peace process has been abandoned, they can form a broader-based "coalition." How long they will be able to cooperate is uncertain, but as long as serious political negotiations appear impossible, some mode of bipartisan cooperation is likely.

The new government was ushered in after the eruption of the al-Aqsa Intifada. Barak had, with Clinton's help, managed to portray the situation in a manner that presented Israel as stretching itself to the limit in order to reach a compromise, while Arafat was pictured as unyielding. This seemingly brilliant maneuver did not save Barak; it has, however, compounded by the bloodshed of the Intifada, helped to convince a major segment of dovish Israelis that there is no real partner for negotiations and, as the right vociferously claims, peace now is a pipe dream. Half a year after the outbreak of the Intifada, public opinion polls showed that 80 percent of Israeli Jews supported Sharon's policy against the renewal of talks as long as there is violence (Yaar and Herman 2000). Public opinion polls on the Palestinian side (Rassan el-Hattib) showed a mirror image—exactly the same percentage of Palestinians supported the continuation of the armed struggle. Under the new circumstances, the polarization in Israel that peaked after Rabin's assassination has abated; settlers have been brought back into the national fold by the new consensus. The Labor Party, on the other hand, has fallen into internal disarray.

The situation that has emerged is very unstable and can easily escalate into a regional conflagration. Sharon has not offered any alternative to Oslo. All he has indicated is a willingness to negotiate "long-term interim agreements" that may increase the area under the Palestinian Authority to 43 percent of the Occupied Territories. However, Sharon refuses to negotiate as long as there is violence, and he has blamed Arafat and the Palestinian Authority as the real force behind the violence. The demand of no violence as a precondition to any negotiations constitutes a hardening of the Israeli position; it is seen as a demand for "unconditional surrender." The logic of Sharon's position, namely to hold Arafat directly responsible, is that if the Oslo process no longer exists, then its institutional outcome, the Palestinian Authority, is also redundant and thus in effect defunct. However, Israel cannot put an end to the Palestinian Authority. Using brutality and force to crush the Palestinians would leave Israel looking like Serbia in Kosovo and might provoke an international response. It would appear the two sides are locked in a prolonged war of attrition for some time to come. In the meantime, Israel continues to build new settlements and expand the existing ones.

Judaism, Judaisms, and Israeli Judaism

Since the nineteenth century, from Hegel to the Young Hegelians to Marx to Sombart, Weber, and Toynbee, it has become fashionable to search out the influence of religion on every aspect of modern life. This discourse served to bolster the claimed superiority of Christian civilization or the putative uniqueness of the West. In the last decade, it has become somewhat trendy to talk about world religions and their role in specific events in various parts of the globe. This has spawned a whole literature about fundamentalism and the clash of civilizations. Yet I remain somewhat dubious about the functions of this post–cold war discourse in the resurrection of an "antagonist" in a world that has lost its main adversary with the collapse of communism and the end of the cold war.

My main objection is not so much to examining the consequences of specific religious beliefs on social and political processes as it is to discussing the role of religion on a level of generalization and abstraction that renders the discussion ahistorical and unsociological. Judaism or Islam or rather "the idea of Judaism" and "the idea of Islam" are too broad and diverse to relate them directly to processes taking place in specific places at specific times. A lower-level abstraction might be more useful in the analysis of concrete political events and processes. Also worth underscoring is the mutuality of the determination: religion influences society, society influences religion.

This argument is nothing new, it has been long debated between Orientalists and anthropologists, Biblical scholars and social scientists. Ernest Gelner has pointed out the contributions of ethnographic research to revealing the religious diversity in many Islamic societies despite their scriptural unity, a view elaborated on by Clifford Geertz in his seminal study on two different Islamic societies, Morocco and Java.

This also applies to Judaism. Sociologist Arieh Tartakover, following in the footsteps of Arthur Rupin, coined the concept "the tribes of Israel" to describe the diversity of Jewish communities in the modern era. In his research, he distinguished six distinct types of Jewish communities: American, British Commonwealth, East European, Middle Eastern, Latin American, and Western European. The differentiation, claims Tartakover, is the result of the dispersion of Jews and the influence exerted by the surrounding environment on their way of thinking and internal development. Furthermore, Tartakover argues that there is "a chasm between the two parts of the nation, in exile and in Israel, whose origins are not only in differences of society and culture but—and this is the most important—in the fact that in the diaspora, the environment in which the Jewish people are immersed determines, in a major way, its modes of existence and reaction. This is not the case in Israel (and also in Eretz Israel before the foundation of the state), where the will of the nation is the determining factor, and under its influence there developed a fundamentally different life in several respects from life in the diaspora." Despite Tartakover's Zionist creed, he clearly distinguishes Israeli Jewry from Diaspora Jewry. Unfortunately, his Zionist blind spots cause him to overlook the crucial influence of the specific environment on the development of Judaism in Israel.

I would like to suggest the term *Israeli Judaism* as a more appropriate theoretical construct for conceptualizing the role of religion in the Israeli-Palestinian conflict and the peace process. Rather than subsume the specific way in which Judaism has evolved in Israel under the much wider field of "Judaism," I propose "Israeli Judaism" as an autonomous subject of study where the emphasis is not on its relatedness and similarity to the wider general category of Judaism but on its difference and uniqueness as a phenomenon sui generis.

The Five Major Contradictions of Israeli Judaism

"Israeli Judaism" can be briefly described as a specific amalgam of contradictions that can be traced back to modernity and its problems—a modernity that, in turn, created ideologies and movements to resolve the contradictions. Most of the contradictions represented in Israeli Judaism are the outcome of shifts—of people, communities, ideas, and systems of thought. These shifts transplanted old contradictions into a new context and created new encounters and contradictions. Israeli Judaism is an ongoing, unfolding, and transforming dynamic narrative and must be studied from a historical and comparative perspective. I will sketch briefly the five most important themes that infuse Israeli Judaism with its unique character. These componential themes also account for the political attitudes of the religious toward the Israeli-Palestinian conflict.

The Contradiction between "Patria/Home" and "Sanctum"

Judaism is a national religion or a religious nationalism. In the Jewish religion, God has created the whole universe but has chosen to dwell in a particular place. God has created all peoples but chose only one particular people. According to Jewish Scriptures, "The Place" belongs to God who, after a test of submission and faith (the sacrifice of Isaac), promised it to the Jews. God also singled out the Jews for his gift of the commandments (the law of the Torah). By submission they became his chosen people and God dwelt among them in a tent. Later on, after the conquest of The Place and its settlement, a permanent sanctuary was built in Jerusalem, *ha-bayit,* the Temple. This founding narrative contains three interconnected national components: faith, nation, and territory.

Jewish religion relates to Eretz Israel (the Land of Israel) as The Place *(Ha-makom).* This is The Place where God is closer to his chosen people and they are closer to Him, in this respect a "holy land," that is, God's Land, *Eretz ha-Kodesh.* This is why immigration from the Diaspora to The Place is described by the vertical term "ascension" *(aliya),* as if The Place is higher than other places. *Ha-makom* is also one of the many titles of God. There are 613 commandments *(mitzvot)* in traditional Judaism. An observant Jew strives to fulfill the maximum number of commandments. In Israeli Judaism, the commandment to live in The Place is paramount over all other commandments. Attached to The Place are also special commandments that observant Jews living in The Place must fulfill *("mitzvot ha-tluyot ba-makom").* An observant Jew in Eretz Israel can thus achieve a higher degree of fulfillment of worship then a Jew in the Diaspora and can consequently be a better, more pious Jew.

Through the centuries, before Zionism and unrelated to it, ultra-Orthodox Jews attempted to come and live in The Place in order to become more perfect and devout in the fulfillment of commandments. Those who come to dwell in God's Land see themselves as an elite, as fulfilling commandments that other Jews should but do not fulfill. To be in The Place yet neglect the commandments is tantamount to sacrilege, defilement of The Place. When economic conditions in Palestine in the nineteenth century did not permit a high standard of observance, many rabbis preferred to return to the Diaspora, rather than remain "impure" in the Land of Israel. From an ultra-Orthodox point of view, secular Jews in Israel are thus more sinful than secular Jews in the Diaspora.

Jewish eschatology is also bound up with The Place: it is in Jerusalem that the Messiah will appear and where the resurrection of the Jewish people and humankind will commence. Jewish messianic thinking ties together the Ingathering of the Exiles into The Place, the renewal of the Davidic kingdom in its capital Jerusalem, and the restoration of the Third Temple at its original site, the Temple Mount. Since the nineteenth century, messianic fervor has been a major cause for immigration to the Land of Israel by observant Jews. Many ultra-Orthodox, but not all, view the establishment of a Jewish state and its conquest of Jerusalem and the Temple Mount in 1967 as signs heralding the imminent coming of the Messiah. The intensity of these feelings is at the root of the religious settlers' movement in the Occupied Territories as well as the immigration to Israel by large numbers of religious Jews from North America and Europe. Jewish ultra-Orthodoxy in Israel, by dint of the religious definition of The Place, is thus more zealous and uncompromising toward itself and others, both Jews and non-Jews. These attitudes also influence other Jews in Israel. The Holy is an absolute and cannot be compromised (Gurevitch and Arran 1991, 1993; Kimmerling 1992; Ravitsky 1998).

The Contradiction between the Land of Israel *(Eretz Israel)*, the People of Israel *('Am Yisrael)*, and the People of the Land *('Am Ha'aretz)*

The encounter in the Land of Israel with the native population, the "People of the Land" *('Am ha'aretz, 'yelid, mkomi)*, and the struggle that ensued between them over the territory was problematic to religious and secular Jewish settlers alike. Among Zionist settlers, all the logical possibilities were voiced; some won a majority while others, such as removal and despair, were held only by a few.

Denial. They were not here: There is no problem or dilemma. "A people without land to a land without people" in accord with the ideology of the "unsettled void": "When we came the place was desolate, there were no Arabs here." A variant of this argument, claiming that most Palestinians came into Palestine after the Jews, was also mobilized in discourse in order to deny the right of return of the 1948 Palestinian refugees.

Removal. They should not be here: "They have many other places, all we have is this place." They do not belong here, they are a demographic problem. There can be no right of return for refugees—the only solution is transfer.

Compromise. We should both be here: Either the area should be partitioned because the ideal cannot be realized on the whole land, only on part of the land, or alternatively, we can live together in the whole land, but the resultant "unitary" state cannot be Jewish. The ideal cannot be realized without contradicting other universalist values (equality, democracy) that we hold higher (post-Zionist or anti-Zionist position).

Despair. We should not be here: The ideal cannot be carried out. We became colonialists, there is no solution, hence emigration is the proper path (anti-Zionist position).

Yet for observant Orthodox Jews, not all the above answers are available. The Rabbinic code (halakha) has a specific term, *gerim,* for non-Jews (Gentiles) who live in The Place. Although the term refers to those who dwell outside their country, it is not similar to the term *resident* as understood in modern democracies. The gerim cannot become full members of the national collective unless they convert to Judaism. According to religious law, non-Jews cannot become what secular Jews call "citizens." (The modern idea of citizenship was born in Europe, with no differentiation in civil terms between citizens according to their faith.) Although the halakha reminds Jews that in ancient times they were gerim in Egypt and hence should treat the gerim equally, this is equality within a different status. Other texts are less tolerant toward gerim, holding that they must be tolerated only if they accept the lordship and domination of the Jews in the land. If they resist or dissent, they must be expelled. For the vast majority of religious Jews, the conceptualization of Palestinians as gerim precludes a solution that also accepts their claims on The Place, for The Place is indivisibly Jewish by divine promise. Palestinians can be tolerated if they acquiesce in their inferior status. If they do not, they must be treated as Joshua dealt with the inhabitants of Canaan in the Bible (Joshua 9:21–25).

The Contradiction between Secular Judaism and Religious Judaism

Secular Jews were a product of European modernity. Before the advent of modernity, a Jew could leave religion only by conversion. Since modernity,

Jews have been able to leave the religious fold and stop practicing without adopting another religion, that is, they can become secular individuals of a Jewish background or extraction. Where racism was not rampant, most of these secularizing Jews assimilated. The Bund was the only rival movement to Zionism, which tried to build a secular Jewish *collective* identity. The Arbeter Bund strove to develop a cultural autonomy for the Yiddish-speaking nation in Eastern and Central Europe. It disappeared with the Nazi destruction of East European Jewry, Stalin's assimilatory policies, and the rapid linguistic assimilation of Yiddish speakers in America.

Religious Jews view secularization and the assimilation made possible by it as the greatest danger facing Judaism today. The religious definition of a Jew hinges on two criteria: an individual born of a Jewish mother who keeps the *mitzvot*. Secular Judaism is a contradiction in terms and anathema to religious Jews; a secular Jew fits one part of the definition but not the other—such a person is in effect a non-Jewish Jew. Zionism was viewed as the most alluring and dangerous form of secular Judaism, since it is easier to shed religious identity within a Jewish collectivity that offers an alternative nonreligious national semiotic of identity, with its associated symbols and practices. Zionism is seen as collective assimilation, and indeed some religious Jews deride secular fellow Jews in Israel as "Hebrew-speaking Gentiles." The antagonism between Zionism and the ultra-Orthodox did not first erupt after the foundation of the state but has existed since the very inception of Zionism in Europe. Yet only in Israel do religious Jews live among a majority of secular Jews, where the religious remain a minority under a secular Jewish hegemony. Until recently, the measures taken by the religious to protect themselves were a defensive bulwark: voluntary segregation and manifest hostility toward a Jewish secular way of life and culture.

This situation is now changing as a rapidly growing religious minority has begun to successfully challenge the cultural hegemony of the seculars. Among other domains, this culture war is expressed and contested in the political arena. The change is most obvious in the objection to the idea of partition of the Land of Israel. While in 1947 nearly all religious leaders concurred with the partition of Palestine, since the 1970s most of the religious leaders have struggled against any peace initiative and compromise with the Palestinians because it entails relinquishing parts of sacred territory within The Place to non-Jews. The name the Gush Emunim settler movement has chosen for itself, the Bloc of the Faithful, suggests that the others (propartition seculars) are regarded as unfaithful, that is, traitors to the Land of Israel.

The Oslo agreement was particularly associated with the secular initiative, hence the massive mobilization of the religious against it and the rabid militancy of the opposition, reaching its zenith in Rabin's assassination.

The Inherent Contradiction of a Jewish State without the Messiah

Judaism evolved differently in Israel as a result of the creation of a Jewish state and the political struggle over the Jewishness of the laws and the public sphere, leading to the development of Jewish politics in a Jewish state and the politicization of religion (Naor 1998; Friedman 1990; Leibovich 1979).

The Contradictions between Occidental Judaism and Oriental Judaism

The hegemonic religious conception of Judaism in Israel is Occidental and Orthodox, while a larger proportion of the nonsecular Jewish population in Israel is Oriental. The counterposing in Israel, as a result of the immigration process, of different, non-Western forms of Judaism creates a unique arena of discourse, interchange, fusion, diffusion, and adaptation as well as contestation and rivalry between communities within the context of a Jewish state and political religion.

Since the pre-state period, the hegemonic religious conception of religious Judaism in mandatory Palestine became Occidental and Orthodox. Most Sephardic and other Oriental rabbis tended to accept the authority, tradition, and rulings of the Ashkenazi rabbis. With the influx to Israel of much of the Jewish population of the Arab states, much of the nonsecular Jewish population in Israel has become Oriental. Oriental Judaism differs from Occidental Judaism, and not just as a result of the influence of Islam. The effects of the Enlightenment and secularization caused Occidental Judaism to become, in self-defense, exclusive, strict, intolerant, and militant. Ultra-Orthodoxy in Occidental Judaism is the reaction to modernity. Oriental Judaism, on the other hand, during its immigration to Israel, was still embedded in a traditional society where modernism affected Jews and non-Jews much less than in the West. Oriental Judaism was traditional and populist and is the larger proportion of the nonsecular Jewish population in Israel.

As a result of the immigration process of different, non-Western forms of Judaism, a unique meeting place is created—an arena for discourse, interchange, fusion, and adaptation as well as rivalry between communities; all taking place within the context of a Jewish state and political religion (Zohar 2001).

Conclusion

Our argument was developed in three stages: we began by challenging the widely held belief in Israel that peace will come first and then the secular camp in Israeli society will resume its hegemony and will continue to lead and shape the future of Israel. In a second stage, the evolution of the peace process since Rabin's assassination was traced. It was argued that the peace process could not have proceeded without creating a widening chasm among Jews, which could spiral out of control and threaten the very integrity of state and society. The third stage was reached when Israeli leaders balked at this possibility, choosing instead to back away from the price necessitated by a final and irreversible agreement with the Palestinians.

We then moved to a structural analysis of the long-term continuous weakening of the two main secular parties and the steady growth of the religious bloc of parties. It was argued that any government in Israel that is based on one major party requires the cooperation of the religious bloc. It was shown that the religious constituency does not trust the Palestinians and is strongly opposed to the peace process. We also argued that a unity government between Likud and Labor could not agree on a peace plan. Our conclusion is, therefore, that for the foreseeable future, a final agreement between Israel and the Palestinians will be blocked and thwarted by the religious camp and constituency in Israel. This conclusion is qualified: it can be altered by external factors such as a conflagration that engulfs the region and/or a fundamental change in U.S. policy.

The third tier of argument was that the attitudes of the religious in Israel against the peace process cannot be read from the constructed and abstract generalized idea of Judaism but must be understood in the context of the more specific concept of Israeli Judaism. We sketched five themes unique to Israeli Judaism: the attitude toward the land as holy, the attitude toward the People of the Land as gerim, the attitude toward secular Jews, the attitude toward the authority of the secular Jewish state, and the mixing and competition between different Jewish traditions. All these have interfused, resulting in a more militant, intolerant, and undemocratic form of Judaism than the liberal Judaism of Western Europe and North America or Middle Eastern traditional Judaism.

If the above analysis is valid, then the belief that a final agreement with the Palestinians can be achieved before or regardless of the resolution, in one way or another, of the cleavage between the religious and secular in Israeli society is mistaken. A lasting solution to the conflict with the Palestinians (and other Arab states) is not a process independent from resolving the debate on the identity and character of the state that the Jews established in Palestine in 1948. The Israeli-Palestinian conflict and the character of the Jewish state are two sides of the same volatile coin.

Postscript

This article was completed more than two years ago. Subsequently, I was asked by the editor to update it and comment on some of the major events that have occurred since its writing, reexamining the claims I made.

The decline of the two major parties' standing in parliament has been halted. This, I believe, was due to the return to the old election system whereby the prime minister is elected by the Knesset rather than by the people directly. As a consequence, the outcome of an election cannot result in a split vote. This has benefited both Likud and Labor.

The second intifada, which broke out as a result of the inability to broker an agreement between Palestinians and Israelis, removed the issues of relinquishing territories and dismantling settlements from the immediate agenda and left them for consideration after cessation of hostilities and the formulation of a new peace plan. In the face of hardships suffered by both Palestinians and Israelis, internal political schisms were temporarily put aside, and the fight against the external enemy led to a closing of ranks on both sides. In Israel, after many years of bitter polarization between Labor and Likud, the politicians were now able to join a coalition and reduce the influence of the smaller religious parties. As I demonstrated in the article, there is a strong correlation between level of religiosity and rejection of any peace settlement based on relinquishing territories. It is almost impossible to separate the secular-religious cleavage from the issue of the territories.

As long as Labor served as a partner in a government headed by Sharon, it was impossible to preserve Labor's distinctiveness, and the issue of coalition with Sharon remains critical to the crisis within Labor. After acrimonious, internal strife, Labor left the coalition on the pretext of an economic

Table 6. Comparison of the 15th and 16th Knessets in the number of MKs: The strength of the two major parties and of the religious bloc

Parties	15th Knesset (1999)	16th Knesset (2003)
Likud plus Labor	45	57
All other parties	75	63
3 religious parties	27	22

Source: www.Knesset.gov.il

Table 7. Comparison of the 15th and 16th Knessets in the number of MKs: Secular center and left Zionist parties

Party	15th Knesset (1999)	16th Knesset (2003)
Labor	26	19
Meretz	10	6
Shinui	6	15
Total	42	40

Source: www.Knesset.gov.il

Table 8. Comparison of the 15th and 16th Knessets in the number of MKs: Parties on the Right

Party	15th Knesset (1999)	16th Knesset (2003)
Likud	19	38
Religious	27	22
Right[a]	20	9
Total right	66	69

Source: www.Knesset.gov.il
a. Yisrael B'Aliya, Haichud Haleumi.

dispute, thus forcing early elections. The Labor Party was left split under new, inexperienced leadership and, like the Jewish left-wing Meretz, which also stood against a coalition with Sharon, it was decimated in the elections of January 2003.

The elections returned a decisive victory to Likud, which gained votes at the expense of Labor, the religious, and the extreme right. Many secular Jews shifted to Shinui, a center-right, Occidental, middle-class, secular party. Shinui captured the secular reaction against the religious as demonstrated in the article—especially the reaction against the Oriental religious party Shas. Shinui stands for a unity government with Sharon and is neoliberal in its economic approach.

The decline of the religious bloc is explained by the decline of Shas. The Oriental religious voters were traditionally supporters of Likud. However, since Shas's inception in the mid-1980s, it has attracted a large proportion of the more traditional Orientals. The decline of Shas is mainly attributed to a leadership split between the party's religious authority and its previous charismatic political leader. Many Shas votes went to the Likud and to parties further to the right.

The major surprise about Sharon's new government was that he opted for a coalition with Shinui, which is vociferously antireligious, leaving out both Labor and the two ultra-Orthodox religious parties. On the face of it,

Sharon's government looks secular, and this seems to fly in the face of my main argument. Indeed, the exclusion of the ultra-Orthodox from a coalition is a rare phenomenon in Israeli politics; Orthodox parties have been a permanent fixture in most coalitions led by Labor and Likud. How then can this be explained?

My answer is that this has to be seen against the background of the shift in the international arena, and as a result of the changed national agenda of the new government. The coalition anticipated the war in Iraq, and the war and its aftermath have reshuffled the architecture and timetables of the Middle East. Although the Intifada continues and security is still a major concern, ceding territories to the Palestinians as part of an agreement is not an immediate issue on the new government's table. On the other hand, continued world recession and severe effects of the Intifada on Israel's economy have become critical. The need to mobilize external investment and U.S. help compels Sharon to adjust even more to the ideological winds blowing from Washington and to implement a neoliberal economic restructuring in anticipation of a new Middle East. He will have to create more attractive conditions for foreign investment, break the remnants of organized labor, reduce public expenditure on welfare, and further reduce the public sector. The composition of the government reflects this revised priority.

At this phase of his term, Sharon's choice of partners is based on a "coalition of the willing": those parties that agree to reduce public expenditure, weaken labor, and further privatize. While labor is willing to accept cuts, it is still committed to Keynesian economics. Moreover, the religious sector is a major benefactor of welfare and state subsidies and would have resisted the new economic plan. Shinui, on the other hand, the party of the Occidental "white" educated middle class is at the forefront of a Darwinist zeal and lack of compassion for the poor.

The receding hope for settlement with a weakened Palestinian Authority, and decimation and disarray in the Labor camp leave Labor unable to challenge Sharon. The religious parties suffer most from their exclusion from the coalition: their ability to maintain the sectional institutions that underpin their way of life was dependent on special allocation of government money. Their inability to provide for their supporters may further weaken these parties. However, politically they support Sharon's steadfastness in the struggle against the Palestinians. Should the international conditions change, and should Sharon need them to resist international pressure, they will eagerly leap into his government.

What I describe here is a further move to the right in Israeli politics. Moreover, the political right is converting to an economic right, threatening to use its enlarged majority and the lack of electoral alternative to legislate for a curtailment of basic rights (such as joining a union and holding strikes) and to outlaw Palestinian-Israeli movements and parties in Israel. The core ideological right in Israel is still religious, but the majority of Israelis have shifted to the nationalist right.

The central thesis I started to develop in the article is not based just on electoral results. What mainly interest me are the hegemonic shifts of the Jewish project in Palestine and the rearticulation of this project by different hegemonic discourses: Labor, Liberal-Nationalist, and Religious. As these changes take place, different groups in Israeli society move to the core, and others are pushed to the periphery. Thus, I am primarily concerned with the changing justifications of the Israeli project and the ways in which the identity of the national community is being redefined.
(May 2003)

Notes

1. On the political stance of Shas, see Yaar and Herman 2000.

References

Friedman, M. "The State of Israel as a Jewish Dilemma." *Alpaim,* no. 3 (1990): 24–68 (Hebrew).
Gurevitch, Z., and G. Arran. "On the Place (Israeli Anthropology)." *Alpaim,* no. 4 (1991): 9–43 (Hebrew).
———. "The Hard Currency of the Place—a Concluding Answer to Many Response Articles to 'On the Place.'" *Alpaim,* no. 8 (1993): 173–77 (Hebrew).
Herman, T., and E. Yaar. "The Peace Process and the Secular-Religious Cleavage." *Peace in Short,* no. 1. Tami Steinmatz Institute for Peace Research and the Konrad Adenauer Foundation, 1998.
Kedem, P. "Dimensions of Jewish Religiosity." In *Israeli Judaism,* ed. S. Deshen, C. S. Liebman, and M. Shokeid. New Brunswick, N.J.: Transaction Publishers, 1995.
Kimmerling, B. "On Knowledge of the Place: Social History and the Self-Mobilizing Anthropology of Israel." *Alpaim,* no. 6 (1992): 57–68 (Hebrew).
Leibovich, Y. "Headings to Problems of Jewish Religion in the State of Israel." In Y. Leibovich, *Judaism, Jewish People, and the State of Israel,* 85–87. Jerusalem: Shocken, 1979 (Hebrew).
Naor, A. "The Sovereignty of the State of Israel in Orthodox Jewish Thought." *Politics,* no. 2 (December 1998): 71–96 (Hebrew).
Neuberger, B. *Political Parties in Israel.* Tel Aviv: Open University Press, 1997 (Hebrew).
Ravitsky, A. "The Coveted and Anxiety-Provoking Land: The Ambiguous Relationship to Eretz Yisrael in Jewish sources." In *The Land of Israel in Jewish Thinking*

in the Modern Era, ed. A. Ravitsky, 4–40. Jerusalem: Yad Ben-Zvi, 1998 (Hebrew).

Shafir, G., and Y. Peled, eds. *The New Israel: Peacemaking and Liberalisation.* Boulder, Colo.: Westview Press, 2000.

Smooha, S. *Israel: Pluralism and Conflict.* London: Routledge and Kegan Paul, 1978.

———. "The Implications of the Transition to Peace for Israeli Society." *Annals of the American Academy of Political and Social Science* 555 (January 1998).

Yaar, E., and T. Herman. "Shas: The Haredi-Dovish Image in a Changing Society." *Israel Studies* 5, no. 2 (2000): 32–77.

Zohar, Z. "The Vision of Ovadia." In *The Luminous Face of the East: Studies in the Legal and Religious Thought of Sephardic Rabbis of the Middle East,* 312–52. Tel Aviv: Hakibbutz Hameuchad, 2001 (Hebrew).

Contributors

Raja Bahlul teaches in the Department of Philosophy and Cultural Studies at Birzeit University in Palestine and has taught at Yarmouk University, Jordan, and Indiana University–Purdue University, Indianapolis. His research interests include metaphysics, classical Islamic philosophy and theology, and contemporary Islamic political thought. Among his recent publications are "People vs. God: The Logic of 'Divine Sovereignty' in Islamic Democratic Discourse," in *Journal of Islam and Muslim-Christian Relations*, 2000; "Perspectives on Islamic Constitutionalism," in *Lo Sato diritto: Storia, teoria, critica*, ed. Pietro Costa and Danilo Zolo (Milan: Feltrinelli, 2002); and "Toward an Islamic Conception of Democracy: Islam and the Notion of Public Reason," in *Critique: Critical Middle Eastern Studies*, ed. Eric Hoagland (Oxford: Oxford University Press, forthcoming). He also teaches in the master's program in democracy and human rights at Birzeit University, a program he helped establish and which he directed 1999–2001.

Helga Baumgarten has taught in the Department of History and Political Science at Birzeit University since 1993. She is presently engaged in a DFG-funded research project on transformation processes in the Arab region in cooperation with the University of Tübingen, Germany. Her research interests include the history and politics of the Palestinian National Movement, the Israeli-Palestinian conflict, migrations to the Arab Gulf, and state formation in the Middle East. She has published a study on the Palestinian National Movement entitled *Palästina: Befreiung in den Staat* (Frankfurt: Suhrkamp Verlag, 1991) as well as a political biography of Yasir Arafat, *Arafat zwischen Kampf und Diplomatie* (Munich: Ullstein, 2002). She also contributes regularly to the quarterly journal *Inamo* based in Berlin.

Joel Beinin has taught in the Department of History at Stanford University since 1983. His research interests include social and cultural history of the modern Middle East and Jewish communities of the Middle East. Among his publications are *Workers and Peasants in the Modern Middle East* (Cambridge: Cambridge University Press, 2001) and *The Dispersion of Egyptian Jewry: Culture, Politics, and the Formation of a Modern Diaspora* (Berkeley:

University of California Press, 1998). Prof. Beinin is a contributing editor of *Middle East Report* and was president of the Middle East Studies Association of North America in 2001–02.

John Bunzl has been the Middle East specialist at the Austrian Institute for International Affairs (ÖIIP) since 1980. He is also lecturer in political science at the Universities of Innsbruck, Salzburg, and Vienna. His research focus is on aspects of the Israeli/Palestinian conflict. Among his publications are *Between Vienna and Jerusalem: Reflections and Polemics on Austria, Israel, and Palestine* (New York: Peter Lang, 1997) and *Juden im Orient: jüdische Gemeinschaften in der islamischen Welt und orientalische Juden in Israel* (Hamburg: Junius, 1989); and *Psychoanalysis, Identity, and Ideology: Critical Essays on the Israeli/Palestinian Case* (coedited with Benjamin Beit-Hallahmi; New York: Kluwer Academic Publishers, 2002).

Avishai Ehrlich currently teaches sociology at Tel Aviv University and at the Academic College of Tel Aviv–Jaffa. He has previously taught at Middlesex University, London, and York University, Toronto. His research is mainly in the areas of the Israeli-Arab conflict, human rights, and ethnic relations in the Middle East. He is also a member of the board of the Research Committee on Ethnicity, Race, and Minority Relations of the International Sociological Association.

Alexander Flores teaches at the business school of Bremen University of Applied Sciences in Germany. He has also taught at the Universities of Essen, Erlangen, Hamburg, Berlin, and Würzburg as well as at Birzeit University, West Bank, Palestine. He has research interests in the modern history of the Middle East with a focus on the Palestine conflict, and the intellectual history of the Arab world, especially with regard to the accentuation of Islam. Among his publications are *Nationalismus und Sozialismus im Arabischen Osten* (Münster: Periferia Verlag, 1980), *Palästinenser in Israel* (ed. with Alexander Schoelch; Frankfurt and New York: Campus Verlag, 1983), and *Intifada* (Berlin: Rotbuch Verlag, 1988).

Herbert C. Kelman is Richard Clarke Cabot Research Professor of Social Ethics at Harvard University's Department of Psychology and director of PICAR (Program on International Conflict Analysis and Resolution). His major publications include *International Behavior: A Social-Psychological Analysis* (ed., New York: Holt, Rinhard and Winston, 1965), *A Time to Speak: On Human Values and Social Research* (San Francisco: Jossey-Bass, 1968) and *Crimes of Obedience: Toward a Social Psychology of Authority and Responsibility* (with Lee Hamilton; New Haven and London: Yale University Press, 1989). He has been engaged for many years in the development of interactive problem solving, an unofficial-third-party approach to the resolution of international and intercommunal conflicts, and in its application to the Israeli-Palestinian conflict.

Nissim Rejwan is a research fellow at the Harry S. Truman Research Institute for the Advancement of Peace, the Hebrew University, Jerusalem. He is the author of *Israel in Search of Identity: Reading the Formative Years* and *The Many Faces of Islam: Perspectives on a Resurgent Civilization* (Gainesville: University Press of Florida, 2000 and 2001). He is currently working on a book of memoirs entitled *Baghdad Exit: Memoirs*.

Adam B. Seligman is professor of religion at Boston University and research associate at Boston University's Institute for the Study of Economic Culture. His books include *The Idea of Civil Society* (New York: Free Press, 1992), *Inner-worldly Individualism* (New Brunswick, N.J.: Transaction Press, 1994), *The Problem of Trust* (Princeton, N.J.: Princeton University Press, 1997), *Modernity's Wager: Authority, the Self, and Transcendence* (Princeton, N.J.: Princeton University Press, 2000), and (with Mark Lichbach) *Market and Community* (University Park: Penn State University Press, 2000). At present he is working on the problem of religion and toleration, focusing in part on developing school curricula for teaching tolerance from a religious perspective, a joint project with colleagues in Berlin, Sarajevo, and Jerusalem. His latest book, *Modest Claims: Dialogues and Essays on Tolerance and Tradition* will be published soon by University of Notre Dame Press (Notre Dame, Ind.).

Index

Abayad, Aziz, 93
Abdel Rahman III, 48
Abduh, Muhammad, 5
Abu Hasira, Ya'akov, 150
Abu-Zaid, Nasr Hamid, 108, 110
Academy of Islamic Studies of al-Azhar, 158–59
Al-Afghani, Jamal al-Din, 5
Agudat Israel, 3, 4, 171
Ahmad, Eqbal, x, xi
Aida refugee camp, Palestine, 78
Ain Ebel, Lebanon, 75–76
Albo, Joseph, 47, 48, 51
Alexandria Why? (film), 146
Al-Amari refugee camp, Palestine, 79
Amir, Yigal, 1
Amitai, Yossi, 142
Anti-Semitism: in Arab history, 31–37; Christianity and, 8, 32, 33–37; in Egypt, 145–47; of Muslims, 6–7
Anva, 128
Al-Aqsa Intifada: Barak and, 169, 176; Christian-Muslim relations during, 75–81; effects on economy of Israel, 187; religion and, 1, 81–82; Temple Mount and, 156
Aquinas, Thomas, 54
Arabic language: translation of Jewish Bible into, 45. *See also* Judaeo-Arabic language
Arab nationalism, 87–88, 161
Arabs, historical record of relations between Jews and, 28–31
Arafat, Yasir, 68, 80, 90, 94
Aramaic, 45–46
Arbeter Bund, 182
Ashkenazic political party, 3, 171
'Ashoor, Abdul Fattah, 34
Ashtor, Eliyahu, *The Jews of Moslem Spain*, 38–39, 40

Assimilation: Judaism today and, 182; in Muslim Spain, 39–40
Atlas, Natacha, 151
Audi, Robert, 101
Austrian Institute for International Affairs, 9
Autonomy, individual, and toleration, 124–25
Avodah zarah, 22
Ayyubi, Nazih, 108
Al-Azmeh, Aziz, 101–2
'Azzam, 'Azzam, 145

Babylonia, 31
Baer, Gabriel, 141
Baghdad, 31, 33
Bahlul, Raja, 10–11
Balfour Declaration, demonstration against, 138
Balu, Joshua, 42–44
Al-Banna, Hassan, 5
Al-Baquri, Ahmad Hasan, 139
Barak, Ehud, 168, 170, 176
Al-Barghuti, Bashir, 88
Al-Barghuti, Mustafa, 88
Baron, Salo, 29–30
Bassantine News (newsletter), 146
Al-Battani, 38
Baumgarten, Helga, 10
Beinin, Joel, 11
Beit Jala, Palestine, 76–77, 78–79
Belief, 20, 123
Ben, Zehava, 150–51
Ben-Gurion University, Department of Middle East Studies, 141–42
Ben-Sasson, Haim Hillel, 34
Benvenisti, Meron, 92
Berger, Peter, 120, 126–27, 131
Berlusconi, Silvio, viii
Bethlehem, 80, 85, 93

Bhutto, Benazir, viii
Bible, translation of Jewish into Arabic, 45
Biblical criticism, 40–41
Bin Laden, Osama, viii
El-Bireh, Palestine, 79, 86
Bishara, Azmi, 87, 102, 108
Al-Bishri, Tariq, 108
Book of the Kuzari (Halevi), 24–26, 46, 50
Boundaries, traffic across, x–xi
Brahmin (Hindu), 20
British mandatory rule in Palestine, 82–83, 92, 157
Burckhardt, Jakob, 28
Burton, John, 69

Cahen, Claude, 33
Calvin, John, 125, 128
Camp David talks of 2000, 72
Castellio, Sebastian, 125, 128
Chahine, Youssef, 146, 147
Chazon Ish, 130
Checkpoint, Israeli, fracas at, 85–86
Christianity: anti-Semitism and, 8, 32, 33–37; biblical criticism and, 41; during Enlightenment, 20; evangelical Protestantism, spread of, 120; Judaism and, 6; in medieval times, 19–20; in Ottoman Empire, 8
Christians: Jerusalem and, 35; relations with Muslims in Palestine, 75–86, 92–94, 95
Church of the Nativity: Abayad and, 93; siege of, 78, 80, 85
"The Clash of Civilizations?" (Huntington), vii–ix, x–xi, xii
Clayton, John, 130
Cleavage, secular-religious, in Israel, 174–77
Cohen, Mark R., 36–37
Collective identity in Israeli-Palestinian conflict, 62–65
Commensality and toleration, 127–28
Communities, Jewish, types of, 178
Conduct (ethical) aspect of religion, 21
Conflict: dangers of "essentializing," 11; identity changes and, 65–67, 72–73; as zero-sum struggle, 62, 64–65. *See also* Israeli-Palestinian conflict
Confucianism, 120
Conrad, Joseph, x

Constitution, Islamic, 105–6, 107–11
Constitution of Medina, 157
Cordova, Spain, 40, 48
Covenant of Omar Ibn al-Khattab, 82, 83, 84
Croats, 66
Crusades, 32
Cultic-ritual aspect of religion, 21
Cultural assertions, inadequacy of, ix–x
Cultural crossings: Egypt to Israel, 147–49; Israel to Egypt, 149–52
Cultural interaction between Jews and Muslim Arabs, 37–41

Dana International, 148
Dante, xi
Dât, 26
Daud, Abraham ibn, 49
Dawn (weekly), x
Dayan Center for Middle East Studies, 141
Democracy: diversity, toleration, and, 111–14; Islamic approaches to, 99–100; Islamic view of, 103–6; popular sovereignty and, 107–11; secularism and received view of, 100–103
Dhimmi status: in Middle Ages, 33; modernization and, 158; People of the Book and, 8; political rights and, 114; poll tax and, 34–35
Diaspora and modes of existence and reaction, 178
Din: as comparative concept, 22, 23–24; as used by Halevi, 25
Al-Din, Salah, 35, 160
Distrust of Palestinians, 173
Diversity and democracy, 111–14
Divine sovereignty, 107–11
Dome of the Rock, 159

The Economist (journal), viii–ix
Education system in Israel, 175
Egypt: anti-Semitism in, 145–47; boycott of Israel by, 140, 142; breaking of taboos in, 147–49; Islamists in and Zionism, 137–39; Jewish intellectual interest in, 140–42; Jews in, 31; Muslim Brotherhood and, 88; political parties in, 138, 139; view of Israel in, 143–45

Egyptian-Israeli peace treaty, 137
Ehrlich, Avishai, 11
Elections: Islamic perspective on democracy and, 105; in Israel, 170–71, 185
Enlightenment, 20
Enoch, Moses ibn, 48
Epstein, Isidore, 31, 37
Eretz Israel, 179–80
Esposito, John, 105
Exclusivist character of identity, 63–64, 70–71
Ezra, Abraham ibn, 47
Ezra, Moses ibn, 53

Fada'il al-Quds literature, 160
Fairuz, 161
Faith: as aspect of religious concept, 20–21; rationality and, 121–22
Falaquera, Shem Tov, 48
Faruq (king), 138
Fatah, 88–91
Fatah/Tanzim fighters, 79
Feil, Ernst, 19
Fideism, 125, 126
Fides et Ratio, 122
Filastin ath-Thaura (periodical), 162
Fisch, Menachem, 129
Fischer, Shlomo, 130
Flores, Alexander, 11
Free Officers, 138–39
Frumin, Menachem, 122
Fukuyama, Francis, vii
Fundamentalism: Islam and, 5–6; in Israel, 4; in Middle East, 2; nature of, 94–95; secularization and, 120–21

Al-Gammal, Rif'at, 144
Gaon, Saadia, 43, 45
Geertz, Clifford, 178
Gelner, Ernest, 178
Geonic Period, 31
Gerim, 181
German Orient Institute, 9
Gershoni, Israel, 141
Al-Ghannouchi, Rachid, 103, 104, 105, 107, 112
Al-Ghazzali, Abu Hamid Muhammad, 49, 50, 55

Ghosh, Amitav, 150
Gilo settlement, Palestine, 76, 78–79
Al-Gindi, Nadia, 144
Girls of Alexandria (al-Kharrat), 146–47
Globalization, 121, 167
Goitein, S. D.: on Arabic, Hebrew, and Aramaic, 45–46; on Arabic as language of Jews, 44; on Geniza, 140–41; on *Guide for the Perplexed*, 55; on Hebrew poetry, 51–52, 54
Golden Age of Jewish literature or culture, 48
Goldstein, Baruch, 1
Goldziher, Ignaz, 128
Graetz, Heinrich, *History of the Jews*, 36
Guardian Council (Iran), 109, 110
Guide for the Perplexed (Maimonides), 50–51, 54, 55
Gush Emunim movement, 3, 118, 171, 182
Guttmann, Julius, 54

Habash, George, 87
Habibi, Emil, 88
Hadash party (Israel), 118
Haddad, Wadi', 87
Hadith: attitudes toward Jews in, 158; similarity of Talmud to, 30, 33
Hafiz, 'Abd al-Halim, 151
Hai of Iraq, 39
Halakha/shari'a, 5
Halevi, Judah: Arabic influence on, 53; *Book of the Kuzari*, 24–26, 46, 47, 50
Halim, 128
Halkin, Abraham, 52, 53–54
Hamas: fundamentalism and, 6; overview of, 162–64; position of on other Palestinian forces, 77–78; religion and, 1, 118
Hanagid, Samuel, 53
Haram al-Sharif. *See* Temple Mount/Haram al-Sharif
Haredim, political parties of, 3–4
Al-Hariri, 52
Al-Harizi, Judah, 46, 52
Harkabi, Yehoshafat, 67–68
Hasan, Hasan b. Mar, 38
Hass, Amira, 81
Haussig, Hans-Michael, 10
Haykal, Muhammad Hasanayn, 144–45

Hebrew language: Arabic language and, 44–47; Biblical version of, 43; Egyptian scholars of, 148–49; Judaeo-Arabic language and, 42; in Muslim Spain, 38, 39; poetry and, 39, 51–54
Hebrew University, 141
Hezbollah, 75–76
Higazi, Ahmad 'Abd al-Mu'ti, 149
Hilim, 128
Historical record of relations between Jews and Arabs, 28–31
History of religions, assumption of, 19
History of the Jews (Graetz), 36
Hobbes, Thomas, 123–24
Hoffman, R. David, 131
Horton, John, 123
Hovot Halevavot (Ibn Paquda), 49–50
Humility and toleration, 128–29
Huntington, Samuel, vii–ix, x–xi, xii
Hurgronje, Snouk, 33
Al-Husaini, Hajj Amin, 160
Hyrcanus, Eliezer ben, 129–30

Ibda' (journal), 149
Ibn al-Khattab, Omar, 82
Ibn Gabirol, Solomon: Arabic influence on, 53; *Mekor Hayyim* (*Fons Vitae*), 48–49; *Tikkun Middot Hanefesh*, 49; *The Treasury of Jewish Thought* and, 47
Ibn Hazm, 41
Ibn Paquda, Bahya, 47, 49–50
Ibn Taymiyya, 55, 160
Identity: changes in, 65–67, 72–73; national, struggle over, 62–65; negotiating, 67–69; problem-solving workshops on, 69–72; religious, reassertion of, 118–19; social construction of, 65–66
Indonesia, 120
Intertwined Worlds: Medieval Islam and Bible Criticism (Lazarus-Yafe), 41
Intifada, first, 78. *See also* al-Aqsa Intifada
Iran: constitution of, 108–9; Guardian Council, 109, 110
Iranian Revolution, 5–6
Iraq: Baghdad, 31, 33; transfer of center of Jewish learning from, 48
Islam: Ahmad on, x; concept of religion and, 22–24; as inside from start, xi; Islamism and, 5–6; Jerusalem in, 159–61; Jews conversion to, 33; Judaism and, 6–7, 157–59; in medieval times, 33; personification of, vii–ix; relations between Judaism and, 6–7. *See also* Islamic societies; Muslims; Qur'an; shari'a rule
Islam, as exclusive concept, 22–23
"Islam, Judaism, and the Political Role of Religions in the Middle East" conference, 9–10
Islamic Jihad, 1
Islamic societies: Jewish minorities in, 7–8; secularization and, 120; transformation of, 110–11
Islamism, 5–6, 162–63, 164. *See also* Hamas
Israel: breaking of taboos in, 149–52; checkpoint, fracas at, 85–86; court system in, 121; creation of State of, 8, 68, 83; economy of, 187; Egypt and, 137, 140, 142, 143–45; election system in, 170–71, 185; Hamas position toward, 162–63; Knesset, 4, 169–71; Left in, 166; move to right in, 187–88; Orthodox religious bloc in, 171–72, 184–85; religiosity and political attitudes in, 172–74; secular cultural elite of, 142; secular-religious cleavage in, 174–77; understanding of normalization in, 143. *See also* Israeli Judaism; Zionism; *specific cities*
"Israel Attempts to Provoke a Religious Discrimination between Palestinian Christians and Muslims" (press release), 77
Israeli Academic Center, 144–45, 148, 151
Israeli Judaism: characteristics of, 184; contradictions of, 179–83; description of, 178
Israeli-Palestinian conflict: national identity, struggle over, 62–65; as nonreligious, 156–57; problem-solving workshops on, 66–67, 69–72; as religious, 61, 118
Al-Istiqlal Intifada. *See* al-Aqsa Intifada
Izutsu, Toshihiko, 128

Jahiliyya, 5
Al-Jahiliyya, 128–29
Jama'a (journal), 141
Jerusalem: Christians and, 35; Islam and, 159–61; Muslims and, 157; secular-religious cleavage in Israel and, 175; view of, 64
Jerusalem Post, 77
Jews: conversion to Islam, 33; historical record of relations between Arabs and,

28–31; intellectual interest in Egypt of, 140–42. *See also* Israeli Judaism; Judaism
The Jews of Moslem Spain (Ashtor), 38–39, 40
Joint Working Group on Israeli-Palestinian Relations, 69, 71–72
Judaeo-Arabic culture, 47–48
Judaeo-Arabic language: adoption of, 44–45; as enriching Hebrew language, 44–47; origins of, 42–44
Judaism: Biblical, concept of religion and, 21; Islam and, 6–7, 157–59; in medieval times, 24–26; rabbinical, concept of religion and, 22; Zionism and, 2–6. *See also* Israeli Judaism; Jews; Zionism
June 1967 (Six Day War), 5

Karahasan, Dzevad, 127
Kedourie, Elie, 102
Kelman, Herbert, 10
Khadduri, Majid, 35
Al-Kharrat, Edwar, 146–47
Khatami, Muhammad, 103, 104, 105
Khazars, 24–25
Khomeini, Ayatollah, 5–6
Al-Kitaba al-Ukhra (journal), 140
Knesset, 4, 169–71
Kook, Abraham Isaac, 3
Kook, Zvi Yehuda, 3
Kulsthoum, Umm, 151

Labor Party (Egypt), 139, 140
Labor Party (Israel): Barak and, 168–69; decline of, 169–71; Sharon and, 176, 185–86, 187
Labrat, Nunash ben, 48
Land, relationship to, and identity, 63–64
Lazarus-Yafe, Hava: *Intertwined Worlds: Medieval Islam and Bible Criticism*, 41; *Studies in Al-Ghazzali*, 55
Lebanon: Ain Ebel, 75–76; French mandatory rule of, 89, 92; identity in, 95; Palestine compared to, 92–93; relations between Christians and Muslims in, 83–85
Left: in Israel, common conception of, 166; in Palestine, roots of, 88
Lewis, Bernard, "The Roots of Muslim Rage," vii–viii
Liberalism: political, 104, 111; toleration and, 124

Likud Party (Israel): decline of, 169–71; imagery of, 4; Sharon and, 176, 185–86
Locke, John, 123

Al-Maghribi, Samau'al, 41
Magnus, Albertus, 54
Mahmud, Abdarrahim, 162
Maimon, Moses ibn, 47. *See also* Maimonides
Maimonides: on Arabic, 46; *Guide for the Perplexed*, 50–51, 54, 55; Judaeo-Arabic and, 42, 43; legacy of, 54–55; position of, 36; theological works of, 42; on tolerance, 131
Makdisi, Ussama, 94–95
Maqama, 52
Martin, David, 120
Marx, Immanuel, 151–52
Massignon, Louis, xi
Matalon, Ronit, 150
Mawdudi, Abu al-A'la, 106
Mayer, Ann Elizabeth, 109
The Meaning of the Disaster (Zurayk), 87
Medieval times: Islam in, 23–24, 33; Judaism in, 24–26; religion as concept in, 19–20
Meital, Yoram, 141
Mekor Hayyim (*Fons Vitae*, Ibn Gabirol), 48–49
Meretz Party (Israel), 186
Mesopotamia, 32, 33
El-Messiri, Abdel-Wahab, 149
Middle Ages, relations between Jews and Muslim Arabs in, 37–41
Midrash Bereshit Rabbah, 22
MIFTAH, 77
Millet system, 8, 84
Minorities: Christian, in Orient, 8; Christian, in Palestine, 82–85; Jewish, in Islamic societies, 7–8, 158; in Muslim democracies, 113–14
Mishnah, 45
Mission in Tel Aviv (film), 144, 147
Modernity: institutionalization of, 120–21; intolerance and, 119–20; responses to, 130; secularization and, 131, 181–82. *See also* Israeli Judaism
Modernization, nationalism and, 87
Monolithic character of identity, 64, 71
Monotheism, persisting legacy of, xi
Montaigne, 126

Movement of Arab Nationalists, 87, 88
Muhammad: appearance of, 30; forgiveness and, 128–29; Jewish tribes and, 6, 30, 31, 157–58; mission of, 157; Treaty of Medina and, 35
Muslim Brotherhood, 88–91, 162, 163
Muslim Christian Association, 89, 161
Muslims: biblical criticism by, 40–41; in Europe and United States, xi; in Palestine, 75–82, 92–94, 95, 157
Al-Musrati, Fa'iqa, 144
Mu'tazilism, 112

Nagrela, Samuel ibn, 36
Naguib, Muhammad, 138, 139
Nahdlatual Ulama, 120
Nahum, Haim, 139
An-Na'im, Abdullahi, 112–13
Najjab, Suleiman, 88
Al-Nasir, Gamal 'Abd, 139
National identity: construction and reconstruction of, 66; Fatah and, 88–91; negotiating, 67–72; Palestinian Authority and, 86; as part of solution, 72–73; religious violence and, 94–95; struggle over, 62–65
Nationalism, Arab, 87–88, 161
National Progressive Unionist Party (Egypt), 140
National Religious Party (Israel), 171
Nazareth, 84–85, 93
Netanyahu, Benjamin, 168, 170
Normalization: Egyptian-Israeli peace treaty and, 137; political and military atmosphere and, 143
North Africa, 32

Occidental Judaism, 183
Occupied Territories: Christians and, 76; Harkabi and, 67–68; Palestinian resistance in, 176; Peace Now movement and, 67; proactive settlement of, 3; resistance to withdrawal from, 167–68. *See also* Gush Emunim movement
Omar, 35
The One Facing Us (Matalon), 150
Operation Susannah, 144, 145, 151
Oriental Judaism, 183
Orthodox religious bloc in Israel, 171–72, 184–85
Oslo Accords: Arafat, Rabin, and, 68; Barak and, 168–69; national-religious camp and, 3; Netanyahu and, 168; PLO, Hamas, and, 163; as secular, 183; secular-religious cleavage and influence of, 174–77; support for and religiosity, 173–74
Other: accommodation of, 71–72; demonization of, 64–65; Egyptian representations of Israeli, 147–48; generalizations in constructions of, 9; identity of, 62; negation of in conflict, 62–64; removal of negation of, 70
Ottoman Empire, 7–8, 84

Palaestina Tertia, province of, 29
Palestine: Beit Jala, 76–77, 78–79; el-Bireh, 79, 86; British mandatory rule in, 82–83, 92, 157; Christians in, 82–86, 92–94, 95; clash over, 9; issue of united front in, 79–82; Jews in, 31; Left in, 88; Muslim rulers and right of Jews to return to, 35; Muslims in, 75–82, 92–94, 95, 157; refugee camps, 78, 79; settlements, 76, 78–79. *See also* al-Aqsa Intifada
Palestine Liberation Organization (PLO), 68, 162, 163
Palestinian Declaration of Independence, 91–92
Palestinian-Israeli Declaration of Principles, 140
Palestinian National Authority, 80, 86
Palestinian National Movement, 87–92, 161–62, 164
The Palestinian Refugee Problem and the Right of Return (Alpher, Shikaki, et al.), 71–72
Particularist view, 173
Peace Now movement, 67
Peled, Matti, 141, 142
Peled, Y., 167
People of the Book (*Ahl al-Kitab*): Muslim view of, 34; in Ottoman Empire, 8
Pirenne, Henri, xi
The Place, 179–80
Pluralism and toleration, 126–27, 130–31
Poetry, Hebrew, 39, 51–54
Poliakov, Leon, 31–33
Political attitudes and religiosity in Israel, 172–74
Political parties: Ashkenazic, 3, 171; in Egypt, 138, 139; Hadash (Israel), 118;

of *haredim*, 3–4; Labor (Egypt), 139, 140; Labor (Israel), 168–71, 176, 185–86, 187; Likud (Israel), 4, 169–71, 176, 185–86; Meretz (Israel), 186; National Progressive Unionist (Egypt), 140; National Religious (Israel), 171; Sephardic, 3; Shas (Israel), 3, 4, 171, 172, 186; Shinui (Israel), 119, 186–87
Politicized religion, phenomenon of, 2
Popkin, Richard, 125, 129
Popular sovereignty, 102, 106–11
Porath, Yehoshua, 141
Pragmatism and tolerance, 123–24
Procedural conception of democracy, 103
Psagot settlement, Palestine, 79
Pyrrhonism, 125–26

Qasim, Qasim 'Abduh, 146
Quietists in Israel, 4
Qur'an: influence of, 43; *Israiliyyat*, 33; Jews of Arabia and, 30, 157; *jihad* injunction in, 32–33
Qutb, Sayyid, 5, 107

Raafat, Samir W., 148
Rabin, Yitzhak: Arafat and, 68; assassination of, 1, 3, 167, 183; compromise agreements of, 171; Palestinian Intifada and, 143
Ra'fat al'Haggan (television series), 144, 147
Ramallah, 79, 81
Rawls, John, 101, 103–4, 111–12
Reason and toleration, 129–30
Rejwan, Nissim, 10
Religio, 19
Religion: generalization and abstraction of, 177–78; global resurgence in, 2; origins of concept of, 19–20; sociopolitical perception of, 1. *See also* Religious concepts; *specific religions*
Religious, the, Smooha on, 166–67
Religious concepts: aspects of, 20–21; "exclusive" and "comparative," 20; Halevi and, 25–26; Islam and, 22–24; Judaism and, 21–22
Religious Parties and Schools of Philosophy (Shahrastani), 24
Rida, Rashid Muhammad, 5
Right, move to in Israel, 187–88

Rights, politics of, over politics of good, 124–25
"The Roots of Muslim Rage" (Lewis), vii–viii
Rosenthal, Erwin, 37, 40, 45
Rouhana, Nadim, 69
Rupin, Arthur, 178
Ruz al-Yusuf, 144

Sabah, Michel, 80–81, 85
Sabella, Bernard, 84–85
Al-Sadat, Anwar, 138, 139
Said, Edward, 146
Salim, 'Ali, 140
Samir, Haya, 145, 149–50
Samir, Yusuf, 145
Samuel the Nagid, 39
Schumpeter, Joseph, 103, 105
The Secret Agent (Conrad), x
Secularism: democracy, Islam, and, 104–5, 106, 113; received view of democracy and, 100–103; toleration and, 123
Secularization: fundamentalism and, 120–21; modernity and, 181–82; progress of, 120, 131
Sefer Ha 'Ikkarim (Albo), 51
Seligman, Adam, 11
Sephardic political party, 3
September 11, 2001, viii, 1, 6
Serbs, 66
Servetus, Miguel, 125, 128
Al-Sha'b (newspaper), 144
Shafir, G., 167
Al-Shahrastani, Abu al-Fath Muhammad ibn 'Abd al-Karim, 24, 26
Shamir, Shimon, 141
Shammas, Anton, 91
Shaprut, Hasdai ibn, 48
Shari'a rule, 105–6, 107–8, 112–13
Shariatmadari, Ayatollah, 131
Sharon, Ariel: election system and, 171; Israeli-Arab conflict and, 176; unity government of, 176–77, 185–88; visit to Temple Mount/Haram al-Sharif, 1
Sharpe, Eric, 24
Shas (Israel), 3, 4, 171, 172, 186
Shehab al-Din Mosque, 93
Shi'ite societies, Jewish minorities in, 7
Shiloah Center, Tel Aviv University, 141
Shinui Party (Israel), 119, 186–87

Singer, Charles, 47–48
Skepticism and toleration, 125–26, 131
Smith, Wilfred Cantwell, 23
Smooha, Sammy, 166–67, 174
Society of Muslim Brothers, 138, 139
Sociological aspect of religion, 21
Somekh, Sasson, 141
South Africa, identity in, 65
Spain: expulsion of Jews from, 36; Jews in, 32, 37–40; transfer of center of Jewish learning to, 48
Spying, theme of Israeli, 144–45
Starr, Deborah, 149
"Statement by Christians from amongst the People of Palestine" (editorial), 76–77
Studies in Al-Ghazzali (Lazarus-Yafe), 55
Sultan, Sa'ida, 148
Sunni societies, Jewish minorities in, 7
Symbolism of religion, political explosiveness of, 1

Tahkemoni (al-Harizi), 52
Talmud: Babylonian, 129–30; similarity to Hadith, 30, 33
Tartakover, Arieh, 178
Temple Mount/Haram al-Sharif: al-Aqsa Intifada and, 156; campaign against Zionism and, 160–61; secular-religious cleavage in Israel and, 175; Sharon's visit to, 1; Zionism and, 180
Territory, partition and redivision of, 114
Terrorists: Conrad on, x; as cult, viii
Themes, 9–11
Thought and expression, freedom of, 102–3
Tibbon, Jehuda ibn, 25, 26
Tibbon, Judah ibn, 42, 46
Tibbon, Samuel ibn, 46
Tikkun Middot Hanefesh (Ibn Gabirol), 49
Toleration: commensality and, 127–28; democracy and, 111–14; humility and, 128–29; individual autonomy and, 124–25; modernity and, 119–20; pluralism and, 126–27, 130–31; pragmatism and, 123–24; reason and, 129–30; religion and, 122; restraint and, 122–23; secularism and, 123; skepticism and, 125–26, 131
Tractate Erubim, 128
Transcendent identity, 64, 71, 72–73
Translation of Jewish Bible into Arabic, 45
The Treasury of Jewish Thought, 47–51
Treaty of Medina, 35
Tuma, Emil, 88
Turabi, Hasan, 103, 106

Universalism, 173

Veron, Françoise, 126
Voll, John, 105

Walzer, Michael, 114
West: discussions of democracy in, 101; indignant passion of, viii–ix; interreligious studies in, 1; personification of, vii–ix
Williams, Bernard, 111, 124
Wolfowitz, Paul, ix

Yahadût, 21
Yossef, Ovadiya, 4, 172
Young Egypt, 138, 139
Young Men's Muslim Association, 138

Zakat, 34–35
Zayyad, Taufiq, 88
Zero-sum struggle, conflict as, 62, 64–65
Zionism: Egyptian Islamists and, 137–39; Fatah and, 90; Israeli-Palestinian conflict and, 157; Judaism and, 2–6; National Religious Party and, 171; Palestinian view of, 63; as secular movement, 156, 182; struggle against in Palestine, 160–61; Temple Mount and, 180
Zurayk, Constantine, 87